From a Subordinate Clause to an Independent Clause

Hituzi Linguistics in English

No. 1 Lexical Borrowing and its Impact on English   Makimi Kimura-Kano
No. 2 From a Subordinate Clause to an Independent Clause
                                                       Yuko Higashiizumi
No. 3 ModalP and Subjunctive Present   Tadao Nomura

Hituzi Linguistics in English No. 2

From a Subordinate Clause to an Independent Clause
A History of English *because*-clause and Japanese *kara*-clause

Yuko Higashiizumi

Hituzi Syobo Publishing

Copyright © Yuko Higashiizumi 2006
First published 2006

Author: Yuko Higashiizumi

All rights reserved. Except for the quotation of short passages for the purposes of criticism and review, no part of this publication may be reduced, stored in a retrieval system, or transmitted in any form or by any means, electronic, mechanical, photocopying, recording or otherwise, without the written prior permission of the publisher.
In case of photocopying and electronic copying and retrieval from network personally, permission will be given on receipts of payment and making inquiries. For details please contact us through e-mail. Our e-mail address is given below.

Book Design © Hirokazu Mukai (glyph)

Hituzi Syobo Publishing
5-21-5 Koishikawa Bunkyo-ku Tokyo, Japan 112-0002

phone +81-3-5684-6871 fax +81-3-5684-6872
e-mail: toiawase@hituzi.co.jp
http://www.hituzi.co.jp/
postal transfer 00120-8-142852

ISBN4-89476-269-2
Printed in Japan

In Memory of
Akio Kamio
1942–2002
and
Atsuo Iguchi
1958–2002

He has given us a desire to know the future, but never gives us the satisfaction of fully understanding what he does. (Ecclesiastes 3.11, Good News Bible)

| kami | wa | mata, | hito | no | kokoro | ni | eien | e |
| God | TOP | also | men | of | heart | DAT | eternity | to |

| no | omoi | o | ataerareta. | sikasi, | hito | wa, | | |
| of | desire | ACC | has.given | but | men | TOP | | |

| kami | ga | okonawareru | miwaza | o, | hazime | kara |
| God | NOM | do | deed | ACC | beginning | from |

| owari | made | mikiwameru | koto | ga | dekinai. |
| end | to | fathom | NOMI | NOM | cannot |

(Ecclesiastes 3.11, Seisyo, Sinkaiyaku)

'He has also set eternity in the hearts of men; yet they cannot fathom what God has done from beginning to end (Ecclesiastes 3.11, Holy Bible, New International Version).'

Contents

List of tables	v
Acknowledgements	vii
Conventions	ix
Abbreviations	ix

Chapter 1 Introduction — 1

1.1 Aim of the present study	1
1.2 Functional diversity and grammaticalization	2
1.3 Organization of the present study	4

Chapter 2 Foundations — 7

2.1 Introduction	7
2.2 Grammaticalization	7
2.2.1 Definition of grammaticalization	7
2.2.2 History of research in grammaticalization	9
2.2.3 Characteristics of grammaticalization	10
2.2.4 The hypothesis of unidirectionality	13
2.2.5 The cline of clause-combining constructions in grammaticalization	16
2.2.6 Subjectification in grammaticalization	20
2.2.7 Summary	22
2.3 Some relevant studies	22
2.3.1 The range of meaning expressed in causal clauses	23
2.3.1.1 Causal clauses in English	23

2.3.1.2 Causal clauses in Japanese	29
2.3.2 Pragmatic markers	33
2.3.2.1 Pragmatic markers in English	33
2.3.2.2 Pragmatic markers in Japanese	36
2.3.3 Summary	38
2.4 A note on the methodology and sources of the present study	39
2.4.1 The methodology of collecting data	39
2.4.2 The sources of the present study	40
2.4.2.1 Data for English	40
2.4.2.2 Data for Japanese	41

Chapter 3 Development of English *because*-clauses   51

3.1 Introduction	51
3.2 *Because*-clauses in present-day English	52
3.2.1 Syntactic aspects of *because*-clauses in present-day English	53
3.2.1.1 *Because*-clauses as subordinate and paratactic clauses	53
3.2.1.2 *Because*-clauses as independent clauses	56
3.2.2 Semantic/pragmatic aspects of *because*-clauses in present-day English	60
3.2.3 Prosodic aspects of *because*-clauses in present-day English	65
3.2.4 Summary	68
3.3 History of *because*-clauses	69
3.3.1 A note on the history of causal clauses in English	69
3.3.2 A note on the history of *because*	72
3.3.3 Summary	75
3.4 Developmental path of *because*-clauses	75
3.4.1 A note on the English data for this section	77
3.4.2 From subordinate to independent clauses	80
3.4.3 From content to epistemic/speech-act conjunction interpretation	83
3.4.4 Summary	94

3.5 Discussion 97
   3.5.1 Multiple functions of *because*-clauses in present-day English 97
   3.5.2 Development of *because*-clauses as an instance of grammaticalization 99
   3.5.3 Development of *because*-clauses and the hypothesis of unidirectionality 101
   3.5.4 Other analogous cases in English 103

Chapter 4 Development of Japanese *kara*-clauses 117
4.1 Introduction 117
4.2 *Kara*-clauses in present-day Japanese 119
   4.2.1 A note on *kara* as a case marker 119
   4.2.2 *Kara*-clauses as subordinate and paratactic clauses 121
   4.2.3 *Kara*-clauses as independent clauses 124
   4.2.4 Summary 126
4.3 History of *kara*-clauses 127
   4.3.1 A note on the history of causal clauses in Japanese 128
   4.3.2 A note on the history of *kara* 132
      4.3.2.1 From a nominal to an ablative case marker 132
      4.3.2.2 From ablative case marker to causal clause marker 139
      4.3.2.3 Development of *kara* functioning as a causal clause marker 141
   4.3.3 Summary 147
4.4 Developmental path of *kara*-clauses 147
   4.4.1 A note on the Japanese data for this section 148
   4.4.2 From subordinate to independent clauses 151
   4.4.3 From content to epistemic/speech-act conjunction interpretation 159
   4.4.4 Summary 176
4.5 Discussion 179
   4.5.1 Multiple functions of *kara*-clauses in present-day Japanese 179
   4.5.2 Development of *kara*-clauses as an instance of grammaticalization 182
   4.5.3 Development of *kara*-clauses and the hypothesis of unidirectionality 184

4.5.4 Other analogous cases in Japanese 186

Chapter 5 Comparison of English *because*-clauses and Japanese *kara*-clauses 199
    5.1 Introduction 199
    5.2 Comparison 199
    5.3 Implications 209

Chapter 6 Conclusion 219

References 225
List of data (English) 253
List of data (Japanese) 259

Author index 267
Subject index 270

List of tables

3.1: The transition of the distribution of *because*-clauses by position	82
3.2: The distribution of (54) in "main" clauses in the synchronic data	86
3.3: The distribution of (54) in *because*-clauses in the synchronic data	87
3.4: The comparison of the distribution of (54) in "main" clauses between the diachronic and synchronic data	89
3.5: The comparison of the distribution of (54) in *because*-clauses between the diachronic and synchronic data	90
3.6: The comparison of the distribution of (54) in (51c) [*Because* CL] between the diachronic and synchronic data	93
4.1: The transition of the distribution of *kara*-clauses by position	152
4.2: The transition of the distribution of (49b) in the written colloquial data	154
4.3: The transition of the distribution of a *kara*-clause + FP	155
4.4: The transition of the distribution of the *kara*-clause + FP after the 1850s	157
4.5: The transition of the distribution of (49a) [CL1 *kara* CL2] in "main" clauses	166
4.6: The transition of the distribution of (49a) [CL1 *kara* CL2] in *kara*-clauses	167
4.7: The transition of the distribution of (49b) [CL1, CL2 *kara*] in "main" clauses	171
4.8: The transition of the distribution of (49b) [CL1, CL2 *kara*] in *kara*-clauses	172
4.9: The transition of the distribution of (49c) [CL *kara*]	175

Acknowledgements

This book is a revision of my doctoral dissertation submitted to Dokkyo University, Saitama, Japan, in 2003 under the same title. While I was writing the dissertation and this book, a number of people gave me moral and technical support. I would like to express my sincere gratitude to all of them, although it is not possible to mention them all here by name.

My first and special gratitude goes to my dissertation committee, Kinsuke Hasegawa, Yutaka Shimokawa, and Toshio Ohori. I am deeply grateful to them as well as the late Akio Kamio for their teaching, continual encouragement, insightful comments, and constructive criticisms. The dissertation could have never been written without them. I would like to take this opportunity to thank Hitoshi Kodama, Masatake Muraki, Minoru Shimozaki, and the late Toshio Gunshi for their guidance in linguistics at Dokkyo University. They have influenced me through their dedication to linguistics. I am also indebted to Dokkyo University Library and Dokkyo University Administration Office staff for their assistance in my study.

I wish to express my greatest gratitude to the following people for sharing their thoughts and insights in various ways: Miharu Akimoto, Tomoko Arakaki, Akira Honda, Paul J. Hopper, Kaoru Horie, Takeshi Ito, Wesley M. Jacobsen, Chie Kanamori, Momoko Kido, Chisato and Mary Kitagawa, Hiroaki Kitano, Yuka Kumagai, Yo Matsumoto, Susumu Nagara, Toshihide and Kumiko Nakayama, Noriko O. Onodera, Mariko Otsuka, Misa Otsuka, Masayoshi Shibatani, Ryoko Suzuki, Yukinori Takubo, and Ryoko Uno. My special thanks are due to Minoji Akimoto and Eric Long who gave me thoughtful and helpful comments at the manuscript revision stage of this book.

I thank my fellow teachers of Japanese at Tokyo University of Marine Science and Technology for their encouragement and moral support while I was writing the dissertation: Ryoko Iseda, Maki Nemoto, Yayoi Oshima, and Yukiko Yatabe. I am also indebted to the following for their moral support and friendship: Hajime and Emiko Inozuka, Naoko Kamio, Masahiko Komatsu, Kazuko Kuwabara, Haruko Miyakoda, Naoki Ogawa, Naoe and Fukuko Shusse, Asako Terauchi, and Ryuko Yokosuka.

Shortly after the doctoral dissertation examination, I had the wonderful chance to attend the 2004 Advanced Analysis Course at the European Training Programme (ETP), UK Campus in association with Summer Institute of Linguistics (SIL). My gratitude goes to all those who shared their time at Horsleys Green. They are too numerous to mention by name. However, I would like to mention Sukie Chie, David Crozier, Ivan Lowe, David Morgan, and Grace Tan for sharing their insights into language and giving me a new understanding of language for future research. I am also grateful to John Roberts for reading the earlier manuscript and providing me with insightful suggestions and comments. All the remaining faults are my own.

I would like to express my gratitude to Jane Boughton for her kind assistance in preparing the manuscript for publication. I wish to thank Isao Matsumoto and Hiroko Miyajima of Hituzi Syobo for their advice and support in editing. The publication of this book was made possible largely through Grant-in-Aid for Scientific Research (Grant-in-Aid for Publication of Scientific Research Results) from the Japanese Society for the Promotion of Science (No. 175163).

My final thanks are due to a number of friends in Christ and my family for their love, support, and encouragement. In particular, I am grateful to the Reverends Chuichi and Makiba Saoshiro for continuously remembering my family and me in their prayers. All the glory be to God.

NOMI	nominalizer
P	particle
PM	pragmatic marker
Q	question (particle)
QUO	quotative (particle)
SCM	subordinate clause marker
TOP	topic
VOL	volitional (verbal form)

Symbols

a. (before year)	ante, before
c. (before year, age)	circa, about
>	becomes, changes to
ø	no linguistic item
*	ungrammatical
??	infelicitous in the given context

Symbols for LLC

*Greenbaum and Svartvik, 1990, p. 7

#	tone unit boundary
{ }	subordinate tone unit
^	onset of the tone unit
**	simultaneous talk
++	simultaneous talk
.	brief pause (of one light syllable)
-	unit pause (of one stress unit or 'foot')
\	falling intonation

Conventions

Examples without the identification of sources are those that I constructed o translated. For Modern and present-day Japanese examples, the present study uses th Kunrei system of romanization, i.e., phonemic transcription. To express long vowels double vowels are used (e.g., aa, ee, ii, oo, uu). For proper nouns such as authors an place names, the Hepburn system is used. For Old and Middle Japanese examples, th present study uses an approximate literal representation of *rekisiteki kanazuka* 'traditional orthography'. For further details of romanization of Japanese, se Shibatani (1990:128–129), for example.

Abbreviations

Linguistic terms

ACC	accusative
ADN	adnominal (verbal form)
CL	clause
COMP	complementizer
COP	copula
DAT	dative
FP	final particle
GEN	genitive
GER	gerundive (verbal form)
IMP	imperative (verbal form)
INT	intensifier
N	noun
NOM	nominative

English and Japanese historical periods

*Note: the dates in (i)–(iii) are approximate.

(i) Stages of English (*CHEL*; LLC; Rissanen et al., 1993)

OE	Old English	450–1150
ME	Middle English	1150–1500
EME	Early Middle English	1150–1350
LME	Late Middle English	1350–1500
EModE	Early Modern English	1500–1710
LModE	Late Modern English	1710–1950
PDE	Present-Day English	1950–2000

Most historians of the English language employ a set of language stages comparable to those in (i). However, there are some disagreements regarding the defining dates among English historical linguists (Görlach (1991:9–11) for Early Modern English).

(ii) Stages of Japanese (Miller, 1967; Shibatani, 1990; Traugott and Dasher, 2002)

[Language Stage]			[Historical Period]	
OJ	Old Japanese	– 800	Nara	710–794
LOJ	Late Old Japanese	800–1100	Heian	794–1185
EMJ	Early Middle Japanese	1100–1330	Kamakura	1185–1333
LMJ	Late Middle Japanese	1330–1600	Muromachi	1336–1573
EModJ	Early Modern Japanese	1600–1870	Edo	1603–1867
LModJ	Modern Japanese	1870–1950	Meiji/Taisho/Showa	1868–1950
PDJ	Present-Day Japanese	1950–2000	Showa/Heisei	1950–2000

Different ways of dividing the Japanese language, such as from the viewpoint of phonological or structural change, have been proposed by Japanese historical linguists. For discussions of these different sets of language stages as proposed by various scholars, see, for example, Kokugogakkai (1980:400–401) and Tsujimura (1971:7–11).

(iii) A comparison of language stages of English and Japanese

[English]		[Japanese]	
OE	–1150	OJ	–800
		LOJ	800–1100
EME	1150–1350	EMJ	1100–1330
LME	1350–1500	LMJ	1330–1600
EModE	1500–1710	EModJ	1600–1870
LModE	1710–1950	LModJ	1870–1950
PDE	1950–2000	PDJ	1950–2000

Chapter 1

Introduction

1.1 Aim of the present study

The present study is concerned with an ongoing process of reanalysis of a subordinate clause as an independent clause with a pragmatic marker in the clause periphery in present-day English and Japanese (henceforth PDE and PDJ respectively). More specifically, it investigates the process of functional extensions undergone by English *because*-clauses and Japanese *kara*-clauses, so-called causal subordinate clauses in PDE and PDJ, from the perspective of grammaticalization.

Grammaticalization is defined here as the process whereby lexical items and phrases develop grammatical functions (Heine et al., 1991a; Hopper and Traugott, 1993, 2003; Bybee et al., 1994). The phenomena of grammaticalization have been studied from both diachronic and synchronic perspectives. The present study observes both diachronic and synchronic phenomena of *because*-clauses and *kara*-clauses and shows that they are counted as, if not textbook cases, examples of grammaticalization. Further, it illustrates that both clauses have been developing in the same direction in terms of structural and semantic/pragmatic functions although English and Japanese are typologically unrelated languages. From the diachronic perspective, both become more paratactic clause-combining constructions and come to be used to express more subjective meanings, i.e., subjectification (Traugott, 1989, 1995a, 1997, etc.; and Traugott and Dasher, 2002). From the synchronic perspective, both appear to be in the process of being reanalyzed as an independent clause with a pragmatic marker at the clause edge (Ohori, 1995a, 1997a). The purpose of the present study is to inquire into mechanisms and motivations behind the diachronic and synchronic phenomena of these clauses.

1.2 Functional diversity and grammaticalization

The present study focuses on the diachronic and synchronic phenomena of English *because*-clauses and Japanese *kara*-clauses, both of which are generally characterized as subordinate clauses with causal meaning in PDE and PDJ as in (1).

(1) a. John came back *because* he loved her.
 'John's reason for coming back was that he loved her.'

(Sweetser, 1990:77)

    b. Taroo wa Hanako o aisite-iru *kara* modotte-kita.
       Taro TOP Hanako ACC love KARA came.back
       'Taro came back *because* he loved Hanako.' =
       'Taro's reason for coming back was that he loved Hanako.'

In spoken or written colloquial discourse, however, it is pointed out that *because*-clauses and *kara*-clauses have some other functions. For example, there are cases where they can neither be regarded as subordinate clauses nor expressing causal meaning such as (2) and (3).

(2) a. John loved her, *because* he came back.
 'I believe/draw a conclusion that John loved her on my knowledge of John's coming back.'

(Sweetser, 1990:77)

    b. Taroo wa modotte-kita *kara* Hanako o aisite-iru no daroo.
       Taro TOP came.back KARA Hanako ACC love NOMI guess
       'Taro loved Hanako, *because* he came back.' =
       'I believe/draw a conclusion that Taro loved Hanako based on my knowledge of Taro's coming back.'

(3) a. What are you doing tonight, *because* there's a good movie on.

'I ask what you are doing tonight because I want to suggest that we go to see this good movie.'

(Sweetser, 1990:77)

b. soko ni soosu ga arimasu *kara* ziyuu-ni totte-kudasai.
there at sauce NOM exist KARA freely take-please

'(Lit.) *Because* the sauce is there, please help yourself.' =

'I recommend you to help yourself because I tell you that the sauce is there.'

(Alfonso, 1980:545)

Moreover, there are cases where *because*-clauses and *kara*-clauses appear without an accompanying grammatically associated "main" clause and express non-causal meaning as shown in (4).

(4) a. Irene: (describing a series of deeds) That's asinine, Henry.
Henry: *Because* you don't understand, see, because ith– it was done that way– =
Irene: I don't understand WHAT?

(Schiffrin, 1987:200)

b. sumimasen ga, moo owari desu *kara*.
excuse.me but now end COP KARA

'(Lit.) Excuse me, but *because* we close now.'

(Alfonso, 1980:1203)

It seems as if so-called subordinate clauses act as independent clauses and so-called subordinate clause markers act as pragmatic markers at the clause edge, i.e., a clause-initial pragmatic marker in English and a clause-final pragmatic marker (generally called *syuuzyosi* 'final particle') in Japanese.

The empirical goal of the present study is to explore synchronic diversity of *because*-clauses and *kara*-clauses as exemplified above and their diachronic processes from the perspective of grammaticalization. It demonstrates that there are significant similarities between these clauses in their developmental processes. The framework of grammaticalization comprehensively accounts for the synchronic and diachronic phenomena of these clauses.

The theoretical goal of the present study is to examine the hypothesis of unidirectionality broadly discussed in the literature of grammaticalization. One kind of unidirectional hypothesis taken up in this study is a unidirectional cline of clause-combining constructions in grammaticalization (parataxis > hypotaxis > subordination). The other is the increase in subjective meanings, i.e., subjectification, in the process of grammaticalization. A survey of the developmental processes of *because*-clauses and *kara*-clauses shows that the direction of structural extension is toward paratactic clause-combining constructions whereas that of semantic/pragmatic extension is toward increase in subjective meanings. It also points out that such extensions are motivated by conventionalization of pragmatic meanings.

1.3 Organization of the present study

The present study is organized as follows. Chapter 2 constitutes the foundations for the present study. First, it introduces the theoretical background, i.e., the framework of grammaticalization and major claims advanced in the literature. Next, it reviews some other studies relevant to the survey of causal clause constructions in English and Japanese. Lastly, it presents the methodology and the sources to be used.

Chapters 3 and 4 inquire into the processes of functional extension of English *because*-clauses and Japanese *kara*-clauses respectively. Chapter 3 first observes a variety of functions of *because*-clauses in PDE and reviews the history of *because*-clauses. Then, it traces the developmental path of *because*-clauses from the perspective of grammaticalization. In a similar way, Chapter 4 makes a survey of *kara*-clauses.

Chapter 5 compares their developmental paths and summarizes similarities and differences between them. It then discusses some implications of the findings for the study of grammaticalization and of language in general. Finally, Chapter 6 gives a conclusion.

Chapter 2

Foundations

2.1 Introduction

This chapter sets out the foundations for the surveys and discussions to be made in the remainder of this study. Section 2.2 introduces a major theoretical background to this study, i.e., the study of grammaticalization. Section 2.3 reviews some other studies relevant to the survey of causal clause constructions in English and Japanese. Section 2.4 presents the diachronic and synchronic sources as well as the method that will be used in Chapters 3 and 4.

2.2 Grammaticalization

This section reviews some major concepts underlying the study of grammaticalization. Section 2.2.1 defines the term grammaticalization. Section 2.2.2 outlines the history of research in grammaticalization. Section 2.2.3 takes up some characteristics typical of grammaticalization. Section 2.2.4 presents the hypothesis of unidirectionality. Section 2.2.5 focuses on the cline of clause-combining constructions from the perspective of grammaticalization. Section 2.2.6 introduces subjectification in grammaticalization.

2.2.1 Definition of grammaticalization

The French linguist Meillet is said to have invented the term grammaticalization.[1] He defines it as follows:

> l'attribution du caractère grammatical à un mot jadis autonome
>
> (Meillet, 1912:131)

> the attribution of grammatical character to an erstwhile autonomous word
>
> (English translation from Hopper and Traugott, 2003:19)

It appears to researchers in recent years that he places emphasis on the role of words although he discusses that of phrases in grammaticalization (Krug, 2000:13). Kuryłowicz (1965) employs the term "morpheme" instead of the term "words" in his definition of grammaticalization.[2]

> Grammaticalization consists in the increase of the range of a morpheme advancing from a lexical to a grammatical or from a less grammatical to a more grammatical state, e.g. from a derivative format to an inflectional one.
>
> (Kuryłowicz, 1965:52)

Incorporating the definition given by Kuryłowicz, Lehmann (1995 [1982]) defines grammaticalization as follows:

> a process which may not only change a lexical into a grammatical item, but may also shift an item "from a less grammatical to a more grammatical status", in Kuryłowicz's words. (Lehmann, 1995 [1982]:11)

It seems that most scholars in the literature have used more or less similar definitions, if not completely agreed on them.[3] The present study will use the definition by Hopper and Traugott (2003), one of the most cited definitions in more recent studies of grammaticalization.[4]

> the change whereby lexical items and constructions come in certain linguistic contexts to serve grammatical functions and, once grammaticalized, continue to develop new grammatical functions (Hopper and Traugott, 2003:xv)

It can be schematized in the following way:

(1) lexical item used in specific linguistic contexts > syntax > morphology

(Hopper and Traugott, 2003:100)

The diachronic and synchronic phenomena of English *because*-clauses and Japanese *kara*-clauses to be taken up in the following chapters are not necessarily identical to the above-mentioned schematization.[5] However, they do share characteristics associated with grammaticalization and draw our attention to the development of new grammatical functions.

2.2.2 History of research in grammaticalization

Let us turn to a brief history of research in grammaticalization.[6] Meillet not only first coined the term grammaticalization but also laid the ground for modern grammaticalization studies. He proposed two processes through which new grammatical forms emerge, that is, analogy and grammaticalization. The work of Meillet was succeeded mainly by Indo-Europeanists, and "grammaticalization was viewed mainly as being part of diachronic linguistics" up to 1970s (Heine et al., 1991a:10).[7] In the 1970s, with the growing interest in typology and pragmatics (e.g., the work by Givón, Greenberg, and Haiman), the study of grammaticalization gradually came to the attention of many linguists as an approach to synchronic language structures.

In the 1980s, interest in grammaticalization was renewed and significant work was carried out in the literature. For instance, Lehmann (1995 [1982]) directed our attention to the importance of the study of grammaticalization, which had continued roughly from the time of Humboldt to the present and introduced significant studies in grammaticalization up to that time. A group of researchers headed by Bybee conducted a cross-linguistic survey of morphology (mainly tense, aspect, and modality) and provided a set of hypotheses for the theory of grammaticalization (e.g., Bybee, 1985; Bybee and Dahl, 1989; Bybee, 1994; Bybee et al., 1991, 1994). Mainly based on the research on synchronic African languages, Heine and other linguists discussed cognitive factors of grammaticalization (e.g., Heine and Reh, 1984; Heine et al., 1991a, 1991b). Traugott and others studied principles of meaning change in the process of grammaticalization (e.g., Traugott, 1982, 1986, 1988, 1989, 1990, 1992, 1995a, 1997, 1999a, 1999b; Traugott and König, 1991; Traugott and Dasher, 2002, etc.). As interest in grammaticalization increased and examples of grammaticalization from a wide variety of languages accumulated, there arose a question of how the study of grammaticalization is integrated with theoretical work in descriptive and historical linguistics, and a question as to which phenomena we should appropriately speak of grammaticalization (Ramat and Hopper, 1998:1–2).[8]

It is noteworthy that grammaticalization has been studied from both diachronic and synchronic perspectives, typically with greater emphasis on the former.[9] The survey of *because*-clauses and *kara*-clauses in the present study will be carried out from both perspectives.

2.2.3 Characteristics of grammaticalization

As the study of grammaticalization progressed, a number of salient characteristics of grammaticalization came to be recognized in the literature. Heine et al. (1991a), for example, summarize them as follows:

(2) Some common linguistic effects of grammaticalization (Heine et al., 1991:213)

Semantic	Concrete meaning	> Abstract meaning
	Lexical content	> Grammatical content
Pragmatic	Pragmatic function	> Syntactic function
	Low text frequency	> High text frequency
Morphological	Free form	> Clitic
	Clitic	> Bound form
	Compounding	> Derivation
	Derivation	> Inflection
Phonological	Full form	> Reduced form
	Reduced form	> Loss in segmental status

It follows from (2) above as well as the definition itself that researchers generally agree on a tendency toward unidirectionality in the history of individual items. We will return to this point in the next subsection (2.2.4 below).

As mentioned above, the study of grammaticalization also has implications for synchronic aspect of languages. For the purpose of ordering linguistic units along a synchronic scale of grammaticalization (Heine et al., 1991a:18–20), Lehmann (1985, 1986, 1995 [1982]) proposes six parameters, namely, attrition, paradigmatization, obligatorification, condensation, coalescence, and fixation.[10] However, it is pointed out that these parameters are characteristics of grammaticalization at more advanced stages, that is to say, more easily identifiable stages of the process (Heine et al., 1991a:20, Hopper, 1991:21). As a supplement to Lehmann's parameters, Hopper (1991) proposes the following five principles in order to identify potential instances of grammaticalization, which are applicable to incipient, less easily recognizable, stages, as well as those at later stages.[11]

(3) Principles of grammaticalization proposed by Hopper (1991:22)
   a. Layering. "Within a broad functional domain, new layers are continually emerging. As this happens, the older layers are not necessarily discarded, but may remain to coexist with and interact with the newer layers."
   b. Divergence. "When a lexical form undergoes grammaticization to a clitic or affix, the original lexical form may remain as an autonomous element and undergo the same changes as ordinary lexical items."
   c. Specialization. "Within a functional domain, at one stage a variety of forms with different semantic nuances may be possible; as grammaticization takes place, this variety of formal choices narrows and the smaller number of forms selected assume more general grammatical meanings."
   d. Persistence. "When a form undergoes grammaticization from a lexical to a grammatical function, so long as it is grammatically viable some traces of its original lexical meanings tend to adhere to it, and details of its lexical history may be reflected in constraints on its grammatical distribution."

e. De-categorialization. "Forms undergoing grammaticization tend to lose or neutralize the morphological markers and syntactic privileges characteristic of the full categories Noun and Verb, and to assume attributes characteristic of secondary categories such as Adjective, Participle, Preposition, etc."

Let us take a few examples of grammaticalization and Hopper's (1991) principles. The English periphrastic auxiliary construction *be going to/be gonna*, which is extended from purposive to future, is a good example of (a), (b), and (d).[12]

(3') Examples of Hopper's (1991) principles (a), (b), and (d):
  a. Layering
  Within the functional domain "future tense", there are such constructions as *will, be about to, be going to/be gonna, be + ing,* and *be + to*. They "may exemplify quite vividly the different degrees of grammaticization attained by the different layers (Hopper, 1991:23)".
  b. Divergence
  The original lexical form *go* undergoes grammaticalization to auxiliary phrase in the context of purposive directional constructions with non-finite complements (i.e., *I am going to marry Bill*.) whereas it remains as an autonomous element in the context of directional constructions with the locative adverb (i.e., *I am going to London, I am going to London to marry Bill*). Such divergence "results in pairs or multiples of forms having a common etymology, but diverging functionally (Hopper, 1991:24)".
  d. Persistence
  The original aspectual meaning of *be going to* is reflected in the constraint on the use of the auxiliary of future. *Be going to* can occur as an aspectual meaning in the context where the future auxiliary verb *will* cannot (i.e., *If interest rates are going to climb/*will climb, we'll have to change our plans*.).

Examples of (c) and (e) are provided by the Modern French negative construction [*ne*

+ verb + *pas*] '[negator + verb + supportive negator]' (roughly translated as [*not* + verb + *step/pace*]).[13] In Old French, the original negator was *ne*, and a variety of adverbially used nouns, such as *pas* 'step, pace', *point* 'dot, point', *mie* 'crumb', *gote* 'drop', etc., were placed after the verb to reinforce the negation. In the course of time, these nouns fell into disuse and by the modern period, *pas* and *point* were the only two still in use. In Modern French, only *pas* became a general negator. In spoken present-day French, the original negator *ne* is usually dropped, leaving *pas* as the only mark of negation.

(3") Examples of Hopper's (1991) principles (c) and (e):
    c. Specialization
        Within the functional domain "negation", a variety of nouns were used in Old French. As grammaticalization progresses, a narrowing of choices takes place and only *pas* assumes negative meaning in Modern French.
    e. De-categorialization
        Pas in the negative construction becomes de-categorized in the sense that it does not function as a noun but as a general negator.

Hopper (1991) emphasizes that grammaticalization is a question of degree and that these principles are not criteria that distinguish processes of grammaticalization from those of change in general. Reference is made to these principles when we examine the development of *because*-clauses and *kara*-clauses in the following chapters.

2.2.4 The hypothesis of unidirectionality

In many studies of grammaticalization, it is implicitly or explicitly hypothesized that grammaticalization is a unidirectional phenomenon. The hypothesis of unidirectionality can be summarized as in (4).

(4) The hypothesis of unidirectionality in grammaticalization:
      there is a relationship between two states A and B, such that A occurs before

> B, but not vice versa. (Hopper and Traugott, 2003:100)

Note that the hypothesis is based on the view that language is in a state of flux as represented by the following statement.

> older and newer forms coexist for individual speakers as well as for communities over time. Indeed, A probably never "becomes" B without an intermediary stage in which A and B coexist: A > A/B > B. Such coexistence, which Hopper (1991) has called "layering", may last several hundred or more years. ... Alternatively, it may be quite short ... (Hopper and Traugott, 2003:49)

From the perspective of grammaticalization, the synchronic functional diversity of *because*-clauses and *kara*-clauses to be taken up in the present study illustrates an intermediary stage in which subordinate, non-subordinate, and independent clauses coexist.

With regard to the mechanisms that lead to grammaticalization, reanalysis primarily, and analogy secondarily, both of which have been broadly recognized as significant for change in general, have been widely discussed in the literature.[14] They are explained as follows:

> In reanalysis, the grammatical – syntactic and morphological – and semantic properties of forms are modified. These modifications comprise changes in interpretation, such as syntactic bracketing and meaning, but not at first change in form. Reanalysis is the most important mechanism for grammaticalization, as for all change, because it is a prerequisite for the implementation of the change through analogy. Analogy, strictly speaking, modifies surface manifestations and in itself does not effect rule change, although it does effect rule spread either within the linguistic system itself or within the community.
> (Hopper and Traugott, 2003:39)

Among motivations that operate these mechanisms, attention has been paid to "the role of speakers and hearers negotiating meaning in communicative situations (Hopper and Traugott, 2003:71)" in the study of grammaticalization.[15] In line with the discourse-pragmatic view, the present study examines the diachronic and synchronic functional diversity of *because*-clauses and *kara*-clauses from the perspective of grammaticalization.

Let us now turn to the hypothesis of unidirectionality in grammaticalization. There has been a lively discussion on the question of what kinds of unidirectionality in processes of language change are characteristic of grammaticalization. Tabor and Traugott (1998) summarize several kinds of unidirectionality that have been previously proposed in the literature in the following way:[16]

(5) Several kinds of unidirectionality summarized in Tabor and Traugott (1998:229–230)

    a. Grammatical change persistently involves a shift from more referential to less referential meanings (semantics/pragmatics).

    b. The meanings of grammatically metamorphosing elements tend to become more, rather than less, abstract (semantics).

    c. Their phonetic substance tends to be reduced (phonetic form).

    d. Their frequencies tend to increase (statistical form).

    e. Grammatical change proceeds across a cline of structural types (phrasal/ morphemic form), which Givón (1979:209) formulated as "discourse > syntax > morphology > morphophonemics > zero" and Lehmann (1995 [1982]:13–14) has described in the following terms:

> [W]e assume that grammaticalization starts from a free collocation of potentially uninflected lexical words in discourse. This is converted into a syntactic construction by syntacticization, whereby some of the lexemes assume grammatical functions so that the construction may be called analytic. Morphologization, which here means the same as agglutination,

reduces the analytic construction to a synthetic one ... In the next phase, the unity of the word is tightened, as the morphological technique changes from agglutinative to flexional.

It has been pointed out that there are instances of change in languages that cast doubts on the hypothesis of unidirectionality. Some can be dealt with as cases of lexicalization (Hopper and Traugott, 2003:133–135, 235 Note 2 in Ch. 4; Traugott, 1996; Cabrera, 1998, for example). However, others may pose a serious challenge to the unidirectional hypothesis (Ramat and Hopper, 1998; Tabor and Traugott, 1998, for example).[17] In the following subsections, we will focus on previous studies concerning the hypothesis of unidirectionality in terms of structure (i.e., (5e) above) in 2.2.5 and in terms of semantics/pragmatics (i.e., (5a) and (5b) above) in 2.2.6, both of which are relevant to the observation of *because*-clauses and *kara*-clauses.

2.2.5 The cline of clause-combining constructions in grammaticalization

This subsection will take up one kind of structural unidirectionality in the process of grammaticalization, i.e., a cline of clause-combining constructions from a less to a more integrated structural relationship. Recent studies of complex clause constructions have suggested that a traditional two-way distinction between coordinate and subordinate clause structure calls for further investigation (e.g., Haiman and Thompson, 1984).[18] In the framework of grammaticalization, Hopper and Traugott (2003) propose a three-way distinction in complex clause constructions based on more recent studies such as Matthiessen and Thompson (1988), Lehmann (1988, 1989), and Langacker (1991). Note that it is not built upon a clear categorization of complex clause constructions into three distinctive categories but on a continuum or spectrum that ranges in type "from multiple nuclei that are juxtaposed under one intonation contour but have no segmental (overt morphological or syntactic) indication of a grammatical relationship between them, to combinations of nucleus and margin in which this relationship is highly compressed (Hopper and Traugott, 2003:177)". Accordingly, they notice three "cluster points" of the continuum of complex clause constructions such as (6) and posit a cline of clause-combining constructions with them such as (7).

(6) Cluster points of complex clause structures
   a. "Parataxis," or relative independence, except as constrained by the pragmatics of "making sense" and relevance.
   b. "Hypotaxis" or interdependency, in which there is a nucleus, and one or more clauses which cannot stand by themselves, and are therefore relatively dependent. However, they are typically not wholly included within any constituent of the nucleus.
   c. "Subordination," or, in its extreme form, "embedding," in other words, complete dependency, in which a margin is wholly included within a constituent of the nucleus.

(Hopper and Traugott, 2003:177)

(7) A cline of clause-combining constructions in grammaticalization:[19]

parataxis	>	hypotaxis	>	subordination
– dependent		+ dependent		+ dependent
– embedded		– embedded		+ embedded

(Hopper and Traugott, 2003:178)

Appositional relative clauses (e.g., (11) below) and adverbial clauses, including temporal, causal, conditional, and concessive clauses, (e.g., (12) below) are usually classified as subordinate or embedded clauses in traditional grammars. Note that they are treated as hypotaxis in Hopper and Traugott (2003) on the basis of Matthiessen and Thompson (1988) who show that the relationship of dependency is different from that of the prototypical cases of subordinating or embedding (Hopper and Traugott, 2003:183). The present study agrees with them since there are cases where *because*-clauses and *kara*-clauses cannot be treated as subordinate in the sense of traditional grammars. However, the term "subordination" is used in the traditional sense in the remainder of this study in order to avoid confusion. I will specify in which sense I use the term if necessary.

The following are examples of parataxis, hypotaxis, and subordination respectively.

(8) [Parataxis: without overt clause-linkage markers (juxtapositon)]
    a. Veni, vidi, vici.
       'I came, I saw, I conquered.'
                (c.146, Suetonius, Jul. 37 [Hopper and Traugott, 2003:180])
    b. kita,   mita,   katta.
       came   saw   conquered
       '(I) came, (I) saw, (I) conquered.'

(9) [Parataxis: with overt clause-linkage markers (coordination)][20]
    a. I came and I saw and I conquered.   (Hopper and Traugott, 2003:181)
    b. kita.   sosite,   mita.   sosite,   katta.
       came   and   saw   and   conquered
       '(I) came. And (I) saw. And (I) conquered.'

(10) [Hypotaxis: clause chaining in Japanese]
    tosyokan   e   it-te   hon   o   karita.
    library   to   go-GER   book   ACC   borrowed
      '(I) went to the library and borrowed a book.'

(11) [Hypotaxis: appositional relative in English]
    Bill Smith, who is our president, would like to meet with you.
                                         (Hopper and Traugott, 2003:182)

(12) [Hypotaxis: adverbial clauses]

a. If you keep smoking those cigarettes, you're going to start coughing again.

(Hopper and Traugott, 2003:183)

b. sono tabako o sui-tuzukeru-to, mata seki ga deru yo.
that cigarette ACC smoke-keep-if again cough NOM start FP

'If (you) keep smoking those cigarettes, (you) are going to start coughing again.'

(13) [Subordination: restrictive relative]

a. I think the guy who just walked out of the store resembles the photo in the post-office window. (Hopper and Traugott, 2003:183)

b. ima mise kara dete-kita hito wa yuubinkyoku
now store from went.out guy TOP post-office
no madoguti no syasin no hito to/ni nite-iru
of window of photo of person with resemble
to omou.
QUO think

'(I) think the guy who just walked out of the store resembles the person in the photo in the post-office window.'

In this subsection, we have seen the cline of clause-combining constructions generally assumed in the study of grammaticalization. Notice that the cline (7) predicts that the direction of change is from more to less paratactic clause-combining constructions in the process of grammaticalization. In other words, it amounts to the hypothesis of unidirectionality toward structural bondedness (Givón, 1979; Lehmann, 1995 [1982]). While many studies of complex sentence constructions have supported the hypothesis, there are some instances of grammaticalization that call into question the claims of structural unidirectionality.[21] For example, Tabor and Traugott (1998) examine the claims that have previously been offered in the literature of grammaticalization and conclude that structural unidirectionality is not an appropriate criterion for judging which processes of language change are identified as instances of grammaticalization. The present study will show that the developmental process of *because*-clauses and *kara*-clauses can be counted as an instance of grammaticalization but does not conform to the unidirectional cline of clause-combining constructions.

In light of sources of clause-linkage markers, both English *because* and Japanese *kara* conform to the general tendency in the processes of language change. According to Hopper and Traugott (2003:184), "clause linkage markers have their sources in nouns, verbs, adverbs, pronouns, case morphemes (including prepositions and postpositions), derivational affixes, and in phrasal combinations of these." It is documented that English *because* has its source in phrasal combinations of a preposition and a noun such as *by (the) cause that, for the cause that,* etc. and Japanese *kara* in a formal noun.[22]

2.2.6 Subjectification in grammaticalization

This subsection will concentrate on the hypothesis of unidirectionality in terms of semantics/pragmatics in the process of grammaticalization. With regard to semantic/pragmatic change in the process of grammaticalization, it has been suggested that grammaticalization results in the development of new uses and meanings which often involve loss of older ones. On the one hand, the direction of semantic change is described as toward "fading" or "bleaching" when attention is paid to outcomes of grammaticalization (e.g., Heine and Reh, 1984; Sweetser, 1988; 1990; Heine et al., 1991a). On the other hand, it is characterized as "pragmatic enrichment" or "pragmatic strengthening" when emphasis is placed upon the beginnings of grammaticalization and the motivations that permit the process to begin (e.g., Traugott and König, 1991; Hopper and Traugott, 2003:94–98). We will focus on the latter in this subsection since it offers the key to understanding the diachronic process and synchronic diversity of *because*-clauses and *kara*-clauses.

On the basis of the functional-semantic model proposed in Halliday and Hassan (1976), Traugott (1982) proposed that semantic/pragmatic change in the early stages of grammaticalization is unidirectional and may proceed in the direction shown in

(14) and not vice versa.

(14) propositional > ((textual) > (expressive))   (Traugott, 1989:31)

She pointed out that "meanings with largely propositional (ideational) content can gain either textual (cohesion-marking) and expressive (presuppositional, and other pragmatic) meanings, or both" (Traugott, 1989:31). The terms in (14), which are based on three functional domains of language identified by Halliday and Hassan (1976), are explained as follows:

> The propositional component ("ideational" for Halliday and Hassan) involves the resources of the language for making it possible to talk about something. ... The textual component has to do with the resources available for creating a cohesive discourse. ... The expressive component (for Halliday and Hassan "interpersonal") bears on the resources a language has for expressing personal attitudes to what is being talked about, to the text itself, and to others in the speech situation.
> (Traugott, 1982:247–248)

She revised (14) as a set of semantic-pragmatic tendencies as in (15) below (König and Traugott, 1988; Traugott, 1989; Traugott and König, 1991, etc.).[23]

(15) Semantic-pragmatic tendencies in Traugott (1989:34–35)
Tendency I:
Meanings based in the external described situation > meanings based in the internal (evaluative/perceptual/cognitive) described situation.
Tendency II:
Meanings based in the external or internal described situation > meanings based in the textual and metalinguistic situation.
Tendency III:
Meanings tend to become increasingly based in the speaker's subjective belief

state/attitude toward the proposition.

In more recent studies, she focuses on the importance of "subjectification" in the process of grammaticalization (e.g., Traugott, 1995a, 1999b; Schwenter and Traugott, 1997; Traugott and Dasher, 2002). It is defined as follows:[24]

> the historical pragmatic-semantic process whereby meanings become increasingly based in the speaker's subjective belief state, or attitude toward what is said
> (Traugott, 1997:185)

The present study will illustrate that the developmental process of *because*-clauses and *kara*-clauses serves as an instance of subjectification, i.e., of unidirectional change in semantic/pragmatic meanings.[25]

2.2.7 Summary

In 2.2, we have given a brief introduction to the study of grammaticalization. Setion 2.2.1 defined the term grammaticalization and Section 2.2.2 sketched the research history of grammaticalization. Section 2.2.3 presented characteristics typical of grammaticalization. After introducing the hypothesis of unidirectionality in 2.2.4, the unidirectionality in structure and in semantic/pragmatic meanings was reviewed in 2.2.5 and 2.2.6 respectively. The present study will document the developmental processes of *because*-clauses and *kara*-clauses from the perspective of grammaticalization in Chapters 3 and 4.

2.3 Some relevant studies

Besides the study of grammaticalization, this section reviews some current studies that are relevant to the study of causal clauses in English and Japanese and provides a definition of key terms for later chapters.[26] Section 2.3.1 reviews the previous research on the range of meaning expressed in causal clauses. Section 2.3.2 introduces the notion of pragmatic markers.

2.3.1 The range of meaning expressed in causal clauses
2.3.1.1 Causal clauses in English

What meanings do "causal" clauses express? How can they be differentiated from each other? It has been recognized in English linguistics literature that they range over various semantic/pragmatic categories.[27] For example, Jespersen (1909–1949, Part V:387) notices that causal clauses do not necessarily indicate a single meaning. He not only describes causal clauses as expressing "necessary cause" or "necessary motive" as in (16), but also notes that there are sentences in which no real cause is indicated as in (17).

(16) John was scolded *because* he told a lie.
(17) I'm not saying that I ever liked Odell very much, *because* I didn't.

(Jespersen, 1909–1949, Part V:391)

Halliday and Hassan (1976) present a two-way distinction in causal meaning. They differentiate "external" meaning from "internal" meaning. "External" meaning is "inherent in the phenomena that language is used to talk about", whereas "internal" meaning is "inherent in the communication process" (1976:241). Other terms that have been used among linguists for "external" and "internal" meaning are "referential" and "non-referential" meaning respectively.[28] When we refer to a two-way distinction in causal meaning, we will from here on use the set of terms referential and non-referential in this study. Halliday and Hassan (1976) show that causal relations can be divided into two (1976:256–261). The following example gives an "internal", i.e., non-referential, use of a *because*-clause.[29]

(18) You aren't leaving, are you? *Because* I've got something to say to you.

(Halliday and Hassan, 1976:258)

In (18), *because* is used in a non-referential sense, meaning 'this is why I'm asking.'

What is meant by causal clauses can be differentiated into more than two types. For example, Dakin (1970) classifies "explanation" sentences, i.e., sentences including a *because*-clause, into three types. He argues that all of them can be put into the form "X explains Y" where X and Y are sentences describing events or states of affairs. Morreal (1977) further proposes that there are some other kinds of explanatory sentences that do not fit into Dakin's classification. In Morreal (1979), *because*-clauses are classified into physical causation as in (19a), a non-causal general law as in (19b), one's reason for doing that action or being in that state as in (19c), and evidential use as in (19d).[30]

(19) a. The ice is melting *because* the temperature is rising.
  b. The hypotenuse of this triangle is 5 inches long *because*, according to the Pythagorean theorem, any right triangle has an [sic] hypotenuse whose length is the square root of the sum of the squares of its other two sides.
  c. I'm hiding these chocolates *because* the kids have had too much candy already today.
  d. Ablma is probably sick, *because* she didn't show up for work.

(Morreal, 1979:231–232)

Although it has been noted that causal clauses embrace a few semantic/pragmatic distinctions, there seems to be no final agreement among linguists upon how many distinctions are necessary for the study of causal clauses.

Recently, however, a three-way distinction in causal meaning seems to be widely accepted in the literature. Van Dijk (1977:68–76), for example, discusses three distinguishable types of *because*-clause: one in which causality is involved, one which expresses implication, and the other which serves as an explanation.

(20) [Causality]
  a. *Because* it did not rain this summer, the soil has dried out.

b. The soil has dried out, *because* it did not rain this summer.

   (van Dijk, 1977:68)

(21) [Implication]
   John is at home *because* his lights are burning. (van Dijk, 1977:73)

(22) [Explanation]
   a. *Because* it did not rain this summer, we irrigated our fields.
   b. We irrigated our fields, *because* it did not rain this summer.

   (van Dijk, 1977:72)

Example (20) means that the event 'the soil has dried out' is caused by the event 'it did not rain this summer' in the actual world and that the drying out of the soil was inevitable. In (21), 'John is at home' is a conclusion inferred by the speaker on the basis of the state that 'his lights are burning.' *Because* in this example indicates inferential relationships between propositions. In (22), the absence of rain is a reason for the action of irrigating the fields. As this example shows, *because*-clause serves as an explanation.

In a similar vein, in the area of discourse analysis, Schiffrin (1987) classifies causal relations marked by *because* and *so* into three relations: fact-based causal relation, knowledge-based causal relation, and action-based causal relation. She argues that they are associated with three planes of discourse: ideational structure, information state, and action structure, respectively.[31] The following statement gives her explanation for each causal relation.

> A fact-based causal relation between cause and result holds between idea units, more precisely, between the events, states, and so on, which they encode. A knowledge-based causal relation holds when a speaker uses some piece(s) of information as a warrant for an inference (a speaker-inference), or when a speaker intends a hearer to do so (a hearer-inference). An action-based causal

relation holds when a speaker presents a motive for an action being performed through talk – either his/her own action or an interlocutor's action.

(Schiffrin, 1987:202)

The following examples, which are similar to the ones in van Dijk (1977), show the three types of causal clause differentiated by Shiffrin (1987).

(23) [Fact-based causal relation]
John is home *because* he is sick. (Schiffrin, 1987:202)

(24) [Knowledge-based causal relation]
John is home *because* the lights are burning. (Schiffrin, 1987:202)

(25) [Action-based causal relation]
Is John home? *Because* the lights are burning. (Schiffrin, 1987:202)

In (23), a fact-based causal relation holds between the event 'John is home' and the event 'John is sick.' The former is a result of the latter. In (24), the event 'John is home' is not a result of the burning lights. Based on this piece of information, the speaker draws a conclusion that 'John is home.' Information given in the *because*-clause is used as a warrant for an inference. In (25), the speaker is requesting a piece of information on the truth of 'John is home' and the *because*-clause presents the motive for the request.[32]

A more systematic formulation of the three-way distinction is developed in Sweetser (1990).[33] She points out that such multiple meanings are observable in English perception verbs, modality, and conjunctions in their diachronic and synchronic semantic structures. She shows that they fall into three domains of meaning, namely, content, epistemic, and speech-act domain; and diachronic change of meaning and synchronic polysemy can be analyzed and accounted for in a unified fashion in terms of metaphor. Note that these domains are not discrete categories but "cluster points" on the continuum of meaning where many features cluster, as we mentioned in 2.2.5.

Returning now to the three-way distinction in causal meaning, Sweetser (1990:76–86) characterizes causal conjunctions in each domain in the following way. A causal conjunction in the content domain indicates real-world cause of an event or a situation described in the main clause. In the epistemic domain, it marks the cause of a belief or a conclusion. Given sufficient context, however, "we can almost always force either a content-conjunction reading or an epistemic-conjunction reading on any pair of clauses conjoined with *because* (pp. 77–78)".[34] In the speech-act domain, a causal conjunction indicates causal explanation of the speech act being performed in the main clause.

(26) [Content conjunction]
John came back *because* he loved her.   (Sweetser, 1990:77)

(27) [Epistemic conjunction]
John loved her, *because* he came back.   (Sweetser, 1990:77)

(28) [Speech-act conjunction]
What are you doing tonight, *because* there's a good movie on.
(Sweetser, 1990:77)

The example (26) is understood as meaning that John's love for her was the real-world cause of his return. In (27), however, 'John loved her' is a belief or a conclusion made by the speaker based on his/her knowledge of John's coming back. The *because*-clause in (28) gives a causal explanation of the speech act of asking being performed in the main clause. Sweetser paraphrases (28) as 'I ask what you are doing tonight *because* I want to suggest that we go to see this good movie (p. 77)'.

The present study adopts the three-way distinction in causal clauses and a set of terms given by Sweetser (1990) on the grounds that it agrees with the view that "[n]o historical shift of meaning can take place without an intervening stage of polysemy (p. 9)".

A similar way of distinguishing causal clauses is adopted in recent historical studies of English. For example, in *The Cambridge History of the English Language (CHEL)*, Traugott (1992:252) calls the three types external, internal, and rhetorical respectively.

(29) [External]
    He came *because* he wanted to see you.   (Traugott, 1992:252)

(30) [Internal]
    He must be here *because* his bicycle is outside.   (Traugott, 1992:252)

(31) [Rhetorical]
    Since you are so smart, what is 234 times 468?   (Traugott, 1992:252)

These examples are interpreted as meaning (29'), (30'), and (31') respectively.

(29') 'His reason for coming was that he wanted to see you'
(30') 'The reason I think he is here is that his bicycle is outside'
(31') 'My reason for asking "what is 234 times 468" is that you claim you are so smart'

(Traugott, 1992:252)

The present study is also built upon the viewpoint that is taken in Traugott (1992).

While the studies reviewed so far approach causal clauses from different perspectives and describe each type in different terms, they agree on a three-way distinction in causal clauses on the basis of their semantic/pragmatic meanings (see also 3.2.2 below). The following summarizes the studies taken up in this subsection:[35]

(32) A three-way distinction in causal clauses reviewed in this subsection

van Dijk (1977)	Causality	Implication	Explanation
Schiffrin (1987)	Fact-based causal relation	Knowledge-based causal relation	Action-based causal relation
Sweetser (1990)	Content conjunction	Epistemic conjunction	Speech-act conjunction
Traugott (1992)	External	Internal	Rhetorical

2.3.1.2 Causal clauses in Japanese

We will go on to review some previous studies on the meaning expressed in causal clauses in Japanese (see also 4.2 below). In contrast to the large amount of studies on this topic in English, it appears that little attention has been paid to this question until recently in the area of Japanese linguistics.

Some linguists point out that *kara*-clauses do not necessarily express cause or reason. Before and independently of Sweetser's (1990) systematic analysis of conjunctions, Takubo (1987) differentiates *kara*-clauses giving "reason for actions (*koodoo no riyuu*)" from those expressing "evidence for speaker's judgement (*handan no konkyo*)".[36]

(33) [Reason for actions = content conjunction]
    [kare ga   itta   *kara*   kanozyo mo   itta]   no   desyoo.
    he   NOM went KARA she   also   went NOMI guess
    '(Lit.) I guess [because he went (there) she also did].' =
    'I guess [she also went (there) because he did].'

(34) [Evidence for speaker's judgement = epistemic conjunction]

kare	ga	itta	*kara*	[kanozyo	mo	itta]	desyoo.
he	NOM	went	KARA	she	also	went	guess

'(Lit.) Because he went (there), I guess [she also did].' =

'I guess she also went (there), [because (I know) he did].'

(Takubo, 1987:43)

According to his explanation, (33) is interpreted in such a way that the event 'he went somewhere' is the cause or reason for the action 'she also went to the same place' in the actual world. In (34), 'he went somewhere' is understood as evidence for the speaker's judging that she also went to the same place. The *kara*-clause in (33) modifies the proposition 'she also went there' in the consequent clause (restrictive) whereas the one in (34) modifies the modal expression *desyoo* 'guess' in the consequent clause (unrestrictive). Iwasaki (1995) agrees to Takubo's (1987) but claims that his terms should be replaced with "cause or reason for an event (*zitai no genin/riyuu*)" and "evidence for using a modal expression (modality-*teki taido no konkyo*)" respectively.[37] Whichever sets of terms are more appropriate, (33) and (34) can be regarded as corresponding to the content and epistemic conjunction interpretation in Sweetser's sense.

Some linguists pay more attention to speech-act conjunction. Alfonso (1980:545) notes that *kara*-clauses are not always interpreted as expressing cause or reason. According to his explanation, such clauses signal "mild reason", i.e., reason for invitations, requests, and suggestions that are expressed in their consequent clauses.

(35) [Mild reason = speech-act conjunction][38]

a.
soko	ni	soosu	ga	arimasu	*kara*	ziyuu-ni	totte-kudasai.
there	at	sauce	NOM	be	KARA	freely	take-please

'(Lit.) Because the sauce is there, please help yourself.'

b. watasi   wa   tyotto yoozi   ga   aru   *kara*
   I   TOP   some   business   NOM   have   KARA
   saki-ni kaette-kudasai.
   early   go.home-please

   '(Lit.) Because (I) have some business, please go home early.'

c. gohan   o   tabeta   *kara*   sanpo   ni   iki-masyoo.
   meal   ACC   ate   KARA   walk   to   go-VOL

   '(Lit.) Because (we) have eaten, let's go for a walk.'

(Alfonso, 1980:545)

The *kara*-clause in (35) can be interpreted as giving a causal explanation of the speech act of invitation in (35a), of request in (35b), and of suggestion in (35c) respectively.

More recently, Shirakawa (1995) worked on cases where a *kara*-clause cannot be regarded as a clause of cause or reason in the strict sense. When *kara* introduces what he calls a non-reason clause, its consequent clause expresses a speech act of order, prohibition, request, invitation, etc. The non-reason clause presents a piece of information on the basis of which the speaker expects the addressee to carry out what is expressed in the consequent clause.

(36) [Non-reason = speech-act conjunction]

sumanai   kedo,   syosai   no   tukue   no   ue   ni
excuse.me   but   study   in   desk   of   top   on
zisyo   ga   aru   *kara*, totte-kite-kure.
dictionary   NOM   exist   KARA   fetch-IMP

'(Lit.) Excuse me, but because there is a dictionary on the desk in the study, please (go and) fetch (it for me).'

(Shirakawa, 1995:189)

Shirakawa explains that in (36) the speaker conveys a piece of information about where the dictionary is in the *kara*-clause and gives an order in the consequent clause.[39] Here, the *kara*-clause can be understood as presenting a motive for the order speech act.

The type of *kara*-clauses which Alfonso (1980) and Shirakawa (1995) discuss can be regarded as corresponding to what Sweetser (1990) calls speech-act conjunction in that they can be interpreted as expressing a causal explanation or motive for a non-declarative speech act being performed in their consequent clause.

Building explicitly on Sweetser's (1990) framework, Uno (1996) examines some causal clause constructions in Japanese and demonstrates that *kara*-clauses range over the three types of causal meaning that Sweetser distinguishes.[40]

(37) [Content conjunction]
kare wa ii koto ga atta *kara*,
he TOP good incident NOM happened KARA
ukiuki-siteiru.
happy-be
'(Lit.) Because something good happened (to him), he (looks) happy.'

(38) [Epistemic conjunction]
kare wa ukiuki-siteiru *kara*,
he TOP happy-be KARA
ii koto ga atta n da.
good incident NOM happened NOMI COP
'(Lit.) Because he (looks) happy, something good happened (to him).'

(39) [Speech-act conjunction]
nani o it-temo muda daroo *kara*, sukini-si-nasai.
whatever ACC say-if useless guess KARA like-do-IMP
'(Lit.) Because whatever (I) say (it) seems useless, do (what you) like.'

(Uno, 1996:17)

The example (37) is interpreted as expressing that a real-world causal relation holds between 'he is happy' and 'something good happened.' In (38), from the piece of information that he is happy, the speaker draws the conclusion that something good happened to him. The *kara*-clause in (39) is read as presenting the speaker's motive or explanation for saying 'do what you like.'

Uno (1996) is the first inquiry into the applicability of the three-way distinction in semantic/pragmatic domain proposed by Sweetser (1990) to the distinctions in Japanese causal-clause constructions. Following Uno (1996), we will use the three-way distinction in causal clause constructions when we examine the developmental process of Japanese *kara*-clauses in 4.4 in order to compare it with that of English *because*-clauses examined in 3.4. We will compare them in Chapter 5.

2.3.2 Pragmatic markers
2.3.2.1 Pragmatic markers in English

In recent years, a considerable number of studies have been made on "pragmatic markers" or "discourse markers" such as *you know, well, so,* etc. However, there is little agreement as to the name itself, its definition, and which items are to be included in the category of pragmatic markers. For instance, Östman (1981) is known as one of the earliest studies on such expressions in English. He examines the expression *you know* and calls it "pragmatic particle". He claims that pragmatic particles "IMPLICITLY anchor an utterance to a situation. They implicitly convey the speaker's attitudes and emotions (Östman, 1981:6)". Schourup (1985) is yet another early study on such items. Through the observation of *well, oh, like,* and *y'know*, which are named "common discourse particles", he regards them as expressing a certain relationship between the speaker's mental processes prior to and during producing utterance. Schiffrin (1987) analyzed some functions of *oh, well, and, but, or, so, because, now, then, y'know,* and *I mean,* but again she proposes a different term "discourse markers". They are defined as "sequentially dependent elements which bracket units of talk (Schiffrin, 1987:31)". Although many studies on such expressions build later on her study, they are not in agreement on the name, the definition, and which items are to be included in the category. It is beyond the scope of this study to go into details about these problems.[41]

Following Brinton (1996), the present study will use the term "pragmatic marker". As she recognizes, the term "discourse marker", which is proposed by Schiffrin (1987), would be the most common name (Brinton, 1996:29). However, the term "pragmatic" is preferable to the term "discourse" since it better captures the range of functions, namely the interpersonal and the textual functions, performed by these expressions. The word "marker" is used in order to include phrases as well as individual words (Brinton, 1996:29–30).

Pragmatic marker is defined as an expression whose pragmatic functions fall into two categories, interpersonal and textual, two of the three modes or functions of language which Halliday (1970, 1979) identifies (Brinton, 1996:38–40).[42] Brinton explains these modes as follows:[43]

> The "interpersonal" mode is the expression of the speaker's attitudes, evaluations, judgements, expectations, and demands, as well as of the nature of the social exchange, the role of the speaker and the role assigned to the hearer. ... In the "textual" mode, the speaker structures meaning as text, creating cohesive passages of discourse; it is "language as relevance", using language in a way that is relevant to context.   (Brinton, 1996:38)

In short, a pragmatic marker has interpersonal and/or text-structuring functions.[44]

Although opinions vary as to which items are to be analyzed under the name of pragmatic markers, attention has been paid to interjections such as *oh*, *well*, conjunctions such *so*, *then*, and adverbial phrases such as *you know* and *I mean* in the study of pragmatic markers. In the present study, we focus on two types of conjuncts, namely, the subordinate conjunction *because* in English and the *zyuui-setuzoku-zyosi* 'subordinate conjunctive particle' *kara* in Japanese. The notion of pragmatic markers offers the key to a comprehensive understanding of the phenomena of functional extension of *because*-clauses and *kara*-clauses from subordinate to independent clauses in PDE and PDJ.

First, let us expand the notion of pragmatic markers into the case of *because*-clauses. It has been reported that *because*-clauses do not necessarily accompany their main clause in colloquial discourse in PDE (see 3.2.1.2 for detail). Consider (40) below. Irene and Henry are arguing about a religious ritual. After Irene describes a series of religious acts, she says the following words to Henry, who is defending the ritual.

(40) Irene: (describing a series of acts) ... That's asinine, Henry.
Henry: *Because* you don't understand, see, because ith– it was done that way – =
Irene: I don't understand WHAT? ...   (Schiffrin, 1987:200)

In (40), no "main" clause associated with the *because*-clause appears in Henry's utterance.[45] *Because* does not link the propositional contents of the two utterances, but it does link a speaker's turn with the previous speaker's through a challenge to the previous utterance. It functions in the textual mode. Henry challenges Irene by saying that her opinion rests on her lack of understanding. It functions as expressing the speaker's attitudes toward the hearer, i.e., a challenge in this case, in the interpersonal mode. Thus, it seems reasonable to analyze the *because*-clause in (40) as a pragmatic marker plus a single clause as shown in (40'). Compare it with the schema of a canonical *because*-clause as in (26').

(40') [Independent *because*-clause]
    (you say so)   *because*   you don't understand
    [ø   PM   CL   ]

(26') [Subordinate *because*-clause]
    John came back   *because*   he loved her
    [[CL1   [SCM   CL2   ]]

We will examine in detail *because*-clauses used as independent clauses in 3.2.1.2.

2.3.2.2 Pragmatic markers in Japanese

Next, we will extend the notion of pragmatic markers to a case of conjunctive particles in Japanese. Japanese has a group of particles appearing in utterance-final position, thus, called *syuuzyosi* 'final particles' (Martin, 1975:914; Shibatani, 1990:334).[46] They do not contribute to the propositional meaning of the sentences or utterances that they attach to but "express the speaker's emotion or attitude toward the hearer in a conversational situation (Makino and Tsutsui, 1986:45)". Martin (1975:914) explains that they "impart some additional hint of the speaker's attitude toward what he is saying – doubt, conviction, caution, inquiry, confirmation or request for confirmation, recollection, etc." Concerning *ne* and *yo*, the most commonly used final particles in PDJ, Alfonso (1980:1142) notes that they are used to signal "sentiments of sympathy, or persuasion, of agreement, of strong feeling".[47] In other words, they are particles functioning in interpersonal mode in the sense given by Halliday (1970, 1979). Thus, they can be regarded as what Brinton (1996) calls pragmatic markers.

It has been pointed out that Japanese *kara*-clauses appear without an accompanying grammatically associated "main" clause in colloquial discourse (see 4.2.3 for details). For example, let us assume that a customer dashes to the supermarket when it is about to close. A shop assistant would say (41), trying to stop the customer:

(41) sumimasen ga, moo owari desu *kara*.
     excuse.me but now end COP KARA
    '(Lit.) Excuse me, but *because* we close now.'

(Alfonso, 1980:1203)

In (41), there is no "main" clause that associates with the *kara*-clause. In this case, the *kara*-clause in (41) can be analyzed as a single clause plus a final particle since *kara* is used exactly where a final particle usually appears.[48]

(41') sumimasen ga,   moo   owari   desu   *yo/ne*/etc.
     excuse.me   but already   end   COP   FP

Moreover, the *kara* in (41) contributes to text-structuring and/or interpersonal functions. As a text-structuring function, it can be interpreted as linking the utterance to the speaker's implicit message such as "don't enter", "come again tomorrow", "you may shop just for a few minutes", etc. In addition, it can be regarded as being used as marking the transition of a turn (Ohori, 1997a). In the interpersonal mode, the *kara*-clause can be interpreted as serving the function of softly expressing a caution or a persuasion. Accordingly, the *kara*-clause in (41) can be anaslyzed as a single clause plus a pragmatic marker. The schema for an ordinary *kara*-clause is given in (37').

(41") [Independent *kara*-clause]
      moo   owari   desu   *kara*.
      now   end   COP   KARA
      [CL   PM   ]
      '(Lit.) *because* we close now' = 'we are closing now, you know/so'

(37') [Subordinate *kara*-clause]
      kare   wa   ii   koto   ga   atta   *kara*,   ukiuki-siteiru.
      he   TOP   good   incident   NOM   happened   KARA   happy-be
      [[CL1   SCM]   CL2   ]
      '(Lit.) *Because* something good happened (to him), he (looks) happy.'

We will examine *kara*-clauses used as independent clauses in more detail in 4.2.3.

So far we have seen cases where *because* and *kara*, which are generally labeled as subordinate clause markers (i.e., so-called subordinating conjunction in English and conjunctive particle in Japanese) can better be analyzed as a pragmatic marker in the sense of Brinton (1996) when *because*-clauses and *kara*-clauses appear independently, especially in colloquial discourse. In sum, they can be schematized as follows:

(42) *Because*-clauses and *kara*-clauses as subordinate and independent clauses

	English			Japanese		
Subordinate:	CL1	*because*	CL2	CL1	*kara*	CL2
	[CL1	[SCM	CL2]]	[[CL1	SCM]	CL2]
Independent:	ø	*because*	CL	CL	*kara*	ø
	[PM	CL]		[CL	PM]	

It follows from (42) that causal clauses in both languages are extending in the same direction, i.e., from dependent to independent clauses, although they are unrelated languages in terms of linguistic typology. The functional extension under discussion can be considered yet another instance of reanalysis of subordinate clauses as independent (Evance, 1988; Ohori, 1995a, 1997a) and pragmatic(al)ization (Erman and Kotsinas, 1993; Onodera, 2000, 2004; Aijmer, 2002) of clause-initial and clause-final elements in PDE and PDJ.[49] We will return to these points in 3.5.4 and 4.5.4 below.

2.3.3 Summary

In 2.3, we have reviewed some earlier studies and shown rather heterogeneous characteristics of *because*-clauses in PDE and *kara*-clauses in PDJ, both of which are generally categorized as subordinate clauses of cause or reason. Section 2.3.1 considered the range of meaning expressed in causal clauses and pointed out that both *because*-clauses and *kara*-clauses can be divided into three different types. Section 2.3.2 proposed that *because* and *kara*, so-called subordinate clause markers, can be analyzed as pragmatic markers when clauses marked by them appear without an accompanying "main" clause. From the viewpoint of grammaticalization, the questions that may arise are how these clauses have come to acquire multiple functions and what are the motivations behind such an extension. Bearing this question in mind, we will trace the developmental pathways of these clauses in Chapters 3 and 4.

2.4 A note on the methodology and sources of the present study

This section gives some notes on the methodology and the data that will be used in the present study. When we trace the developmental process of English *because*-clauses and Japanese *kara*-clauses and consider the motivations behind the development under investigation, we examine the diachronic and synchronic text of novels and plays in colloquial language as well as transcripts of conversation in English and Japanese for comparison purposes.

2.4.1 The methodology of collecting data

As for the diachronic sources, we collect data from the dialogue portions of novels and play scripts from different periods (Onodera, 1993, 1995, 1996, 2000, 2004; R. Suzuki, 1998a, 1999a). With regard to synchronic sources, both conversational portions of novels and transcripts of conversation are used. Following the methodology adopted in R. Suzuki (1998a, 1999a), no more than the first 10 tokens are collected from each source in order to minimize any bias in sampling. No more than two excerpts of novels or plays written by the same author are used whenever alternative works are available in order to minimize weighting authors' preferences for choosing words or style. The expressions are grouped together in periods of 50 years. Although we admit that these sources have some problems, they are the best sources available for the present study at this point.

Each group of expressions in each period of 50 years is further subdivided into four in the following way in order to examine the transition in structural function of *because*-clauses and *kara*-clauses (see 3.4.2 and 4.4.2 for further details).

(43) Basic classification of *because*-clauses and *kara*-clauses in the present study

  (a) [CL1 *because* CL2]   (a) [CL1 *kara* CL2]
  (b) [*Because* CL1, CL2]   (b) [CL1, CL2 *kara*]
  (c) [*Because* CL1]   (c) [CL *kara*]
  (d) others   (d) others

The classifications (a)–(c) will be basically subdivided into three according to expressions that overtly lead to epistemic and speech-act conjunction interpretation in the sense of Sweetser (1990) in order to observe the shift of *because*-clauses and *kara*-clauses in semantic/pragmatic function (see 3.4.3 and 4.4.3 for further details).

(44) Subdivision of (43) according to overt expressions of epistemic and speech-act
   conjunction interpretation
   (i) clauses with an overt expression of epistemic conjunction
   (ii) clauses with an overt expression of speech-act conjunction
   (iii) others

2.4.2 The sources of the present study
2.4.2.1 Data for English

A variety of electronic corpora are currently available for research on the English language.[50] We make use of electronic corpora, novels, and play scripts in the present study. We limit ourselves to Southern British English in collecting data.

 In order to collect data from diachronic texts in colloquial English, we sample from conversational portions of novels and play scripts. The diachronic component of the Helsinki Corpus (henceforth HC) is used as a supplement.[51] We choose diachronic texts of novels and play scripts written by the authors who were either born or educated in Southern Britain. From the HC, only the data from the texts categorized as imaginative fiction (fiction, romance, drama, and private correspondence) are used in order to compare the data collected from conversational portions of novels and play scripts.

As representing text data in colloquial language in present-day British English, the British National Corpus (henceforth BNC) is consulted. It comprises written and spoken components. The data in the BNC is available through the sample search. It seems that the BNC consists of texts written or recorded in the 1980s and 1990s. Regarding the expressions from the written component of the BNC, only dialogue portions of newspapers and magazines are used.

With regard to transcripts of conversation in present-day British English, we use the data from the spoken component of the BNC and the London-Lund Corpus of Spoken English (henceforth LLC).[52] The LLC contains 100 texts of conversation recorded from 1953 to 1976. The present study uses 10 texts of conversation between equals recorded in the 1960s and 1970s.

2.4.2.2 Data for Japanese

In the same way as English, conversational portions of novels and play scripts written in the Edo/Tokyo dialect are used in order to collect data in colloquial Japanese. We choose the novels and play scripts during the Edo Period (1603–1868) which are said to be written in Edo spoken language. After the Edo Period up to present, we consult novels and play scripts written by the authors who were either born or educated in Tokyo and the neighboring districts.

Regarding transcripts of conversation in present-day Japanese, we make use of the conversation transcripts given in Lee (2000) and *Nihongo Journal* (1999–2000). The speakers in the transcripts were born in Tokyo and the neighboring districts (Chiba, Kanagawa, and Saitama).

Notes

1. The term "grammaticalization" is also called "grammaticization" or "grammatiation" (Heine et al., 1991a:3; Hopper, 1991:34 Note 2; Traugott and Heine, 1991:1–2; Hopper and Traugott, 2003:xv–xvi). The present study will use "grammaticalization" except for citations from elsewhere with no special feelings or implications.
2. Krug (2000:13) notes that recent studies in grammaticalization focus on more complex constructions.

3. In recent years, we are confronted by a debate over which phenomena are to be discussed in terms of grammaticalization (see 2.2.2 below).
4. Hopper and Traugott (1993:xv) defines grammaticalization as the "process" whereby lexical items and constructions come in certain linguistic contexts to serve grammatical functions, and, once grammaticalized, continue to develop new grammatical functions. As work on grammaticalization progresses, "it has become clear that the definition of grammaticalization as 'process' has been misleading" (Hopper and Traugott, 2003:xv). To avoid terminological confusion, it is now defined as a "change".
5. Rissanen (1997a) proposes that "[the] types of grammaticalization can be divided into 'primary' and 'secondary', on the basis of whether or not they involve radical changes in the word class or structural properties of the items (p. 4)." The cases of *because*-clauses and *kara*-clauses belong to "secondary" grammaticalization in his sense.
6. The history of research in grammaticalization reviewed here is mainly based on Heine et al. (1991), Hopper and Traugott (1993, 2003), Matsumoto (1996), Ramat and Hopper (1998), and Ohori (2002a). For a more detailed historical survey of the theory of grammaticalization, see Lehmann (1995 [1982]:1–8), Heine et al. (1991a:5–23), Hopper and Traugott (2003:19–38), Harris and Campbell (1995:14-47), Hopper (1996), and Krug (2000:11-18). For a full account of the framework of grammaticalization, see Lehmann (1985, 1995 [1982]), Heine and Reh (1984), Heine et al. (1991a), Hopper and Traugott (1993, 2003), Bybee et al. (1994), and Heine (2003).
7. Not all historical linguists grant special status to grammaticalization as an approach to language change (e.g., Harris and Campbell, 1995).
8. For current studies in grammaticalization, see, e.g., Axmaker et al. (1988), Traugott and Heine (1991), Pagliuca (1994), Hopper (1996), Traugott (1996), Ramat and Hopper (1998), Comrie (1998), Croft (2000:Ch. 6.3), *Language Sciences* (vol. 23, no. 2-3, 2001), Ohori (2002a:Ch. 9), Wischer and Diewald (2002), Joseph and Janda (2003: Part VI), Hopper and Traugott (2003:Ch. 2.4), Akimoto et al. (2004), Fischer et al. (2004), and Heine and Kuteva (2005). For recent studies on grammaticalization in English, see, e.g., Rissanen et al. (1997), Fischer et al. (2000), Krug (2000), Akimoto (2001, 2002), Traugott and Dasher (2002), and Lindquist and Mair (2004). For studies on grammaticalization in Japanese, see, e.g., Dasher (1983, 1995), Matsumoto (1988, 1998), Shibatani (1991), Onodera (1993, 1995, 1996, 2000, 2004), Ohori (ed. 1998, 2004, 2005), R. Suzuki (1998, 1999a, 1999b), Hino (2001), Traugott and Dasher (2002: Ch. 6), and *Nihongo no Kenkyu [Studies in the Japanese Language]* (vol. 1, no. 3, 2005).
9. More studies of grammaticalization from the synchronic perspective have been made in

recent years. See, e.g., Heine and Reh (1984), Heine et al. (1991a) for the languages in Africa, Romaine and Lange (1991), Thompson and Mulac (1991), etc., for English, and Nakayama and Ichihashi-Nakayama (1997), Horie (1998, 2001), Fujii (2000), etc., for Japanese.

10. Hopper (1991:20-21) summarizes these parameters besides attrition as follows. For further details of attrition, see Lehmann (1986:6–7).
    — Paradigmatization (the tendency for grammaticized forms to be arranged into paradigms)
    — Obligatorification (the tendency for optional forms to become obligatory)
    — Condensation (the shortening of forms)
    — Coalescence (collapsing together of adjacent forms)
    — Fixation (free linear orders becoming fixed ones)
11. Tabor and Traugott (1998) suggest using the following three hallmarks to identify change episodes as grammaticalization.
    1. Morphosyntactic change
    2. Pragmatic/Semantic change
    3. Gradualness in the sense that some subtypes of a new construction become possible before others.
12. The illustration here is based on Hopper (1991) and Hopper and Traugott (2003:1–3). There are many example of grammaticalization of auxiliary verbs o such as *iru* 'be' > *te-iru* (stative, continuous) and *dasu* 'take out' > [infinitive verbal form + *dasu*] (inceptive) in Japanese. For a study of *oku* 'place, put' > *te-oku* (completive) > *toku*, and *simau* 'put back' > *te-simau* (completive) > *tyau* from the perspective of grammaticalization, see T. Ono (1992). Matsumoto (1998) discusses the grammaticalization of verbs into postpositions in Japanese.
13. The example here is based on Hopper (1991), and Hopper and Traugott (2003:65–66, 117–118).
14. For a full account of reanalysis and analogy in grammaticalization, see Hopper and Traugott (2003:Ch. 3) and Bybee et al. (1994:Ch. 8). See Haspelmath (1998) for an argument against reanalysis as a major account for grammaticalization.
15. For a full account of pragmatic factors in grammaticalization, see Hopper and Traugott (2003:Ch. 4) and Heine et al. (1991:Ch. 2-3).
16. For further details of unidirectional hypothesis in the study of grammaticalization, see Hopper and Traugott (2003:Ch. 5–7). See also Haspelmath (1999), Beths (1999), and Lass (2000) for further discussions of unidirectionality in grammaticalization.
17. For counter-examples to the hypothesis of unidirectionality, see Matsumoto (1988),

some of the papers in Traugott and Heine (1991) and in Ramat and Hopper (eds. 1998), some referred to by Tabor and Traugott (1998:230-231), Traugott (2001), Hopper and Traugott (2003:Ch. 5–7), Fischer et al. (2004), etc. Craig (1991) discusses a case of polygrammaticalization. For a discussion of polygrammaticalization in Chinese, see Lamarre (2002a). Frajzyngier (1996) gives instances of bidirectional grammaticalization. P. Ramat (1992) takes up the phenomenon of degrammaticalization.

18. For further details of recent studies of complex sentence structures, see Foley and Van Valin (1984), Shopen (1985), Thompson (1987), Haiman and Thompson (1988), Van Valin (1993, 2005), Van Valin and LaPolla (1997), Whaley (1997), Ohori (2000), Croft (2001:Ch. 9), etc.

19. Note that "hypotaxis" in (7) is not "cosubordination" (+ dependent, – embedded) in Role and Reference Grammar (Hopper and Traugott, 2003:236 Note 1 in Ch. 7). For further details of Role and Reference Grammar, see, for example, Foley and Van Valin (1984), Van Valin (1993, 2005), and Van Valin and LaPolla (1997). I thank John Roberts for the following comments. Whereas hypotaxis includes *because*-clauses, Van Valin and LaPolla (1997:454) say specifically that adverbial clauses like *because*-clauses are subordinate. They distinguish two types of structurally dependent clauses: arguments (nominal clauses) and modifiers (relative clauses and adverbial clauses). See also Van Valin (2005:183).

20. The present study classifies the *which*-clause in (i) as "subordination" although it labels *John read but Mary didn't* in the *which*-clause as "coordination". I thank Kinsuke Hasaga for drawing my attention to this point. However, an examination of such examples lies outside the scope of this study.

    (i) the book which John read but Mary didn't

21. For examples of the development of complex sentence constructions, see Hopper and Traugott (2003:Ch. 7.4). For counte-examples to the unidirectionality in clause-combining constructions, see Matsumoto (1988), Harris and Campbell (1995), Leuschner (1998), Evance (1988), Günthner (1996), A. Ramat (1998), and Hopper and Traugott (2003:Ch. 7.6). Harris and Campbell (1995:282–286) suggest that the traditional view that hypotaxis is developed out of parataxis explains little.

22. For further details of the sources of *because* and *kara*, see 3.3.2 and 4.3.2 respectively.

23. Schwenter and Traugott (1995) note that "the ordering of the Tendencies is too specific (p. 263)" to adequately account for some instances of semantic/pragmatic changes in the process of grammaticalization and that "metalingusitic meanings tend to arise last (p. 263)". See, for example, Sweetser (1990), Powell (1992), and Aijmer (1997) for the discussion of the rise of metalinguistic meanings.

24. "Subjectivity" broadly refers to "expression of self and the representation of a speaker's (or, more generally, a locutionary agent's) perspective or point of view in discourse – what has been called a speaker's imprint" (Finegan, 1995:1). See also Lyons (1993) for a discussion of subjectivity. For the latest formalization of semantic change, see Traugott and Dasher (2002). For the history of the study of subjectification, see Finegan (1995). Carey (1995) discusses the difference of "subjectification" in the sense between Traugott (1989, 1995a) and Langacker (1990). For further details of the difference, see Traugott and Dasher (2002:97–99).

    Herring (1991) illustrates that subjectification is a bi-directional process based on the observation of rhetorical questions in Tamil, which have developed into causal conjunctions, a relativizer and a tag question marker. Rissanen (1997a) suggests that subjectification seems "too strong a factor in the analysis of grammaticalization (p. 3)" and "the more general starting-point of pragmatic inferencing, ... and the dichotomy 'expressive/routinalization' (Hopper and Traugott, 1993:63–93) offers a less problematic starting-point (pp. 3–4)".

25. Traugott and Dasher (2002) view subjectification as "typical of semantic change in general and [is] not limited to grammaticalization. This is also true of intersubjectification (pp. 89–90)". The term "intersubjectification" is defined as "a change which results in the development of meanings that explicitly reveal recipient design: the designing of utterances for an intended audience ... at the discourse level (Traugott and Dasher, 2002:31)". It can be considered to be "an extension of subjectification (Traugott 2003b:134)". Traugott (2003b) presents the following hypothesis about semantic unidirectionality: nonsubjective > subjective > intersubjective. It is interesting to follow up the hypothesis further based on the data to be used in the present study, but I limt the discussion to "subjectification" in what follows.

26. We are not concerned here with participle clauses with causal meaning. See Uchida (2002) for the study of consequential participle clauses in English and French from the viewpoint of cognitive semantics.

27. The set of distinctions according to whether the information in the causal clause is assumed to be known/given or not is one possible distinction among causal clauses (Traugott, 1992:252). To go into details about this distinction is beyond the scope of the present study.

28. Non-referential meaning is often regarded as including social and/or expressive meaning (Schiffrin, 1987:62, 187–188). It is pointed out that the distinction between social and expressive meaning is not clear-cut (Lyons, 1977:50-56).

29. Halliday and Hassan (1976) recognize that "the distinction between the external and the internal types of cohesion tends to be a little less clearcut in the context of causal relationships than it is in the other contexts, probably because the notion of cause already involves some degree of interpretation by the speaker (p. 257)".
30. See also Altenberg (1984) for a similar view of causal meaning.
31. Schiffrin (1987:337n) notes that the three-way distinction she proposes is similar to a three-way distinction often referred to as the functions of language: referential (fact), expressive (knowledge), and social (actions). She states that her distinction is an expansion of Halliday and Hassan's (1976) distinction between external meaning and internal meaning. She considers knowledge-based and action-based to be subsumed under internal meaning.
32. For a discussion of cases where more than one relationship is simultaneously realized, see Schiffrin (1987:210–217) and Sweetser (1990:77–78).

    I thank Wesley M. Jacobsen for the following comment on the ambiguity of *because*-clause in (i) below depending on the intonation given.

    (i) Are you going to the post office, *because* I have some letters to send?

    Jacobsen (p.c.) points out: (a) If question intonation is added after *post office* together with falling intonation at the end of the *because*-clause, the *because*-clause would be taken as an explanation of why I am asking the question. I would use it in a situation where the relevance of the question *Are you going to the post office* might not otherwise be clear to the person to whom I am talking, and where the question might otherwise sound abrupt or nosy. (b) If question intonation occurs at the end of the *because*-clause (and no pause is inserted prior to the clause), this will be interpreted as a question why you are going to the post office (e.g., in a situation where I thought you had other business at the post office, but have just realized that maybe you are making a special trip for me). This interpretation, though probably less common than (a), is certainly possible, but would probably be written without a comma in the written form. We will introduce some intonational characteristics of *because*-clauses in 3.2.3.
33. For a discussion of the three types of domain, see Shimokawa (1978), Sweetser (1982, 1990), Dancygier (1992, 1998), Dancygier and Sweetser (1996, 2000), Couper-Kuhlen and Kortmann (2000), etc. Ohori and Uno (2001) give a review article of Dancygier (1998). Beside the three types of domain distinguished in Sweetser (1990), Dancygeir (1992, 1998) discusses another type called metatextual domain.

    The following idiomatic phrases or clichés may be counted as "metatextual" *kara*-clauses in the sense of Dancygier (1992, 1998). Since such examples lies outside the scope of the present study, we will classify them as "others" in 4.4 below, if any.

(i) onegai da   *kara*/   gosyoo   da   *kara*/
    wish   is   KARA   heaven   is   KARA
    tanomu *kara*, sizukani site!
    ask   KARA   quiet   do

   'For pity's sake, will you be quiet!'

Kyratzis et al. (1990) also divide causal clauses into three in a similar way as Sweetser (1990) based on data consisting of children's spoken discourse.

34. Uno (1997) examines Japanese *kara*-clauses in the content domain and subcategorizes them into four.
35. Strictly speaking, what van Dijk (1977) calls "explanation", i.e., the example (22) above, is slightly different from the other corresponding terms in (32) in the sense that it refers to an explanation for the action that was already done at a moment of speech while the others are involved in an explanation for the speech-act being performed through the "main" clause (also Traugott (1992:252) on the use of *for*-clauses in PDE). Moreover, what is termed "rhetorical" by Traugott (1992) can also be different from the other corresponding terms in (32) in that it is pointed out to be "restricted to pre-main clause position (p. 252)". To follow up this matter further, however, would take us beyond the scope of the present study. It is necessary to inquire further into how meanings and functions expressed by one construction should be distinguished on what grounds. For further details of this point, see Dancygier (1992, 1998) and Uno (1997, 2001), for example. I thank Kinsuke Hasegawa and Toshio Ohori for drawing my attention to this point. So far as the examinations of English *because*-clauses and Japanese *kara*-clauses in 3.4 and 4.4 below are concerned, we may say that it suffices to distinguish referential from non-referential, i.e., a two-way distinction, to show that the direction of their semantic/pragmatic extension is toward more subjective meanings, i.e., toward non-referential meanings, along with grammaticalization.
36. The square brackets in (33) and (34), which indicate the scope of the modal expression *desyoo* 'guess', are originally in Takubo (1987).
37. Kambayashi (1989, 1991) and Iwasaki (1995) emphasize the importance of studying *kara* and *node* not from the traditional viewpoint, i.e., "subjective" or "objective", but from Takubo's (1989).
38. The examples from Alfonso (1980) are transcribed in the *Kunrei* system here.
39. Shirakawa (1995) defines what he calls a non-reason clause as a clause that is not felicitous in the following context.

    Titi: Sumanai   kedo,   zisyo   o   totte.kite-kure.
    Father: excuse.me but   dictionary ACC   take.come-give.IMP

'Father: Excuse me, but (go and) fetch the dictionary (for me).'

Musume: Doosite?
Daughter: Why
'Daughter: Why?'

| Titi: | *Syosai | no | tukue | no | ue | ni | aru | *kara*. |
| Father: | study | in | desk | of | top | on | exist | KARA |

'Father:*Because it is on the desk in the study.'

(Shirakawa, 1995:190)

It is not really clear, based on this definition alone, whether non-reason clauses in Shirakawa (1995) fall into the class of speech-act conjunction in Sweetser's (1990) sense or not. Some of them may be classified as epistemic conjunctions. For a discussion of non-reason *kara*-clauses, see also Maruyama (1996, 1997), Nagata (2000), and Y. Suzuki (2000).

40. For further details of the content and epistemic conjunction interpretations in Japanese causal clauses, see Uno (1997, 2001). See also Maeda (2000) for a similar three-way distinction of causal clauses in PDJ.
41. For further details, see, e.g., Schiffrin (1987:332 Note 1 for Chapter 2, 2001), Brinton (1996:29–40, 2001), Fraser (1996), Aijmer (2002), and Blakemore (2004).
42. Östman (1982:150–152) suggests that pragmatic markers may operate simultaneously on two different levels: on the structural and the pragmatic levels, i.e., the textual and the interpersonal modes according to Halliday's (1970, 1979) term.
43. Halliday's third mode, which Brinton (1996) calls "propositional" mode based on Traugott (1982), is "the expression of content of the speaker's experience of both the outside and the inside world, including happenings, participants, and circumstances. It is realized in elemental structures in the constituent structure of language" (Brinton, 1996:38).
44. For the case where interpersonal and text-structuring functions merge, see Schiffrin (1987:210–216) and Schleppegrell (1991:332–333).
45. The present study uses the traditional terms "main" and "subordinate" clauses only for the sake of convenience.
46. They are also called "particles signaling sentiments" (Alfonso, 1980), "sentence-final particles" (e.g., Makino and Tsutsui, 1986; Cook, 1990), or "interactional particles" (e.g., Maynard, 1990). See Maynard (1989a, 1993, etc.) for a discussion of these expressions in conversation in Japanese.
47. See, for example, Kokuritsu Kokugo Kenkyujo (1951), Makino and Tsutsui (1986), and Masuoka and Takubo (1992) for more examples of final particles. See Kamio (1990,

1994, 1997, 2002) for the discussion of final particles from the perspective of the theory of the territory of information.
48. I thank Toshio Ohori for his comment that no other linear order than [*kara* + *yo* + *ne*] is accepted.
49. For further details of the historical perspective in pragmatics, see Jacobs and Jucker (1995), Arnovick (1999), Brinton (2001), Traugott (2004), and *Journal of Historical Pragmatics*.
50. For details of corpus-based studies, see Rissanen et al. (1993), Kennedy (1998), for example. Krug (2000) is one of the latest corpus-based approaches to grammaticalization.
51. See Rissanen et al. (1993) for further information on the HC.
52. See Svartvik (1990) for further information on LLC. For problems of LLC, see Kennedy (1998:32).

Chapter 3

Development of English *because*-clauses

3.1 Introduction

This chapter explores the functional extension of *because*-clauses in the history of English. It will be demonstrated that the direction of the syntactic extension under investigation is from more to less integrated clause-combining constructions and that of semantic/pragmatic extension is toward subjectification (Traugott, 1989, 1995a, 1997, etc.; and Traugott and Dasher, 2002) (See 2.2.6).

Because-clauses are generally characterized as causal subordinate clauses in PDE.

(1) [Subordinate *because*-clause]
John came back *because* he loved her.

(Sweetser, 1990:77)

Many studies, however, have been devoted to non-subordinate uses of *because*-clauses, especially in spoken discourse (Chafe, 1984, 1988; Altenberg, 1984; Schiffrin, 1987; Schleppegrell, 1991; Ford, 1993; Couper-Kuhlen, 1996; Stenström and Andersen, 1996; Stenström, 1998, among others). For example, the *because*-clause in (2) is more like a paratactic clause than a subordinate clause. It is separated from the "main" clause by the comma, indicative of its loose connection to the "main" clause orthographically. In addition, it is pragmatically linked to the prior discourse, merely further elaborating the previous discourse.

(2) [Paratactic *because*-clause]

What are you doing tonight, *because* there's a good movie on.

(Sweetser, 1990:77)

In the following example, the *because*-clause can be analyzed as an independent clause since no grammatically associated "main" clause is present. Instead, it is pragmatically related to the speech act in the preceding utterance.

(3) [Independent *because*-clause]

Irene: (describing a series of acts) ... That's asinine, Henry.

Henry: *Because* you don't understand, see, because ith– it was done that way – =

Irene: I don't understand WHAT?

(Schiffrin, 1987:200)

This chapter will detail the diachronic functional extension of English *because*-clauses, which will be compared with that of Japanese *kara*-clauses. Sections 3.2 and 3.3 introduce earlier studies on *because*-clauses: synchronic studies in 3.2 and diachronic studies in 3.3. Section 3.4 examines the developmental process of *because*-clauses from subordinate to non-subordinate clauses. Section 3.5 discusses the findings of this chapter from the perspective of grammaticalization.

3.2 *Because*-clauses in present-day English

The present section is intended as a review of earlier studies on *because*-clauses in PDE. We will have a look at their characteristics from the syntactic, semantic/ pragmatic, and prosodic aspects. Syntactically, *because*-clauses can be distinguished as subordinate (i.e., hypotactic in the sense of Hopper and Traugott, 2003), non-subordinate (i.e., paratactic in the sense of Hopper and Traugott, 2003), and single independent clauses. From the semantic/pragmatic point of view, there is a correlation between the interpretations of *because*-clauses and their syntactic properties. From the viewpoint of prosody, it is pointed out that the syntactic independence of *because*-clauses from their "main" clause is reflected in the intonational pattern. These studies will show us the diverse functions of *because*-clauses in PDE.

3.2.1 Syntactic aspects of *because*-clauses in present-day English

This subsection discusses earlier studies on the syntactic functions of *because*-clauses in PDE. Although they have not reached complete agreement upon the grammatical functions of *because*-clauses in PDE, recent studies note that *because*-clauses can be differentiated into subordinate, non-subordinate, and independent clauses based on some syntactic differences among them.

3.2.1.1 *Because*-clauses as subordinate and paratactic clauses

Because is generally classified as a subordinate clause marker with causal meaning in PDE.[1] In general, a "subordinate" clause is described as a clause that is incorporated within a superordinate clause (e.g., Lehmann, 1988:182; Quirk et al., 1972:720, 1985:1070–1074). According to Quirk et al. (1985:1072–1074), a *because*-clause can be either an adjunct clause, as in (4), or a disjunct clause, as in (5).

(4) [adjunct]
    She parked the car *because* her father told her to.

                                             (Stenström, 1998:128)

(5) [disjunct]
    She parked the car, *because* I was watching her.

                                             (Stenström, 1998:128)

In both examples, the *because*-clauses can be analyzed as constituents of the superodinate clause "she parked the car" in a different way. Adjunct clauses, as in (4), are "similar in the weight and balance of their sentence role to other sentence elements," whereas disjunct clauses, as in (5), are "in some sense 'superordinate', in that they seem to have a scope that extends over the sentence as a whole (Quirk et al.,

1985:52, 813, 1070)".

A number of studies have proposed several syntactic tests which make a distinction between adjunct and disjunct *because*-clauses and point to the non-subordinating roles of *because* in PDE (e.g., Green, 1976; Bolinger, 1977; Stubbs, 1983:81; Lakoff, 1984; Quirk et al., 1985:1070–1071; Couper-Kuhlen, 1996:403–404; Stenström and Andersen, 1996:192; Stenström, 1998:128–129). Stenström makes a useful summary of these tests. Consider the following tests and examples that are adapted from Stenström (1998:128–129).

1. only *because('cos)* adjunct clauses can be the focus of a cleft sentence;
    (6a) [adjunct] It was *because* her father told her to that she parked the car.
    (6b) [disjunct] *It was *because* I was watching her that she parked the car.

2. only *because('cos)* adjunct clauses can be the focus of a variant of the pseudo-cleft;
    (7a) [adjunct] The reason she parked the car is *because* her father told her to.
    (7b) [disjunct] *The reason she parked the car is *because* I was watching her.

3. only *because('cos)* adjunct clauses can answer a *wh*-question formed from the matrix clause;
    (8a) [adjunct] Why did she park the car? *Because* her father told her to.
    (8b) [disjunct] *Why did she park the car? *Because* I was watching her.

4. only *because('cos)* adjunct clauses can occur in the sentence-initial position;
    (9a) [adjunct] *Because* her father told her to she parked the car.
    (9b) [disjunct]**Because* I was watching her, she parked the car.

5. *because('cos)* adjuncts can be either restrictive or non-restrictive, whereas *because('cos)* disjuncts are always non-restrictive. A subordinate clause is described as 'restrictive' when it is "required to complete the description of the

situation in the matrix clause (Quirk et al., 1985:1076)";

(10) [adjunct, restrictive]

She didn't park the car *because* she was tired.

'It wasn't *because* she was tired that she parked the car.'

(11) [adjunct, non-restrictive]

She didn't park the car, *because* she was tired.

'She didn't park the car, and the reason was that she was tired.'

(12) [disjunct, non-restrictive]

She parked the car, *because* I've been watching her.

'I know that she didn't park the car, *because* I was watching her.'

The following summarizes the syntactic tests introduced so far. They indicate that the syntactic relationship between a *because* disjunct clause and its "main" clause is different from that between a *because* adjunct clause and its "main" clause. *Because* disjunct clauses (and some *because* adjunct clauses) are not necessarily referred to as an element of the superordinate clause.

(13) A summary of the syntactic tests which distinguish a *because* adjunct clause from a *because* disjunct clause:

		***because* adjunct**	***because* disjunct**
1	cleft	yes	no
2	pseudo-clefting	yes	no
3	answering to *wh*-question	yes	no
4	reversal	yes	no
5	restrictiveness	restrictive	
		non-restrictive	non-restrictive

A variety of earlier studies have long recognized that all *because*-clauses cannot necessarily be described as subordinate clauses, especially in spoken discourse, in PDE. For example, Quirk et al. (1972:795) state that "a conjunction like *because*, which occurs almost exclusively in final-position clauses in colloquial language, is ... nearer to coordinator than to subordinator." Halliday (1985:197) suggests that *because* often carries out what seems closer to a paratactic function. Chafe (1988) casts doubt on the grammatical status of *because* as 'subordinator' in spoken language.[2] In sum, the *because*-clause can be a subordinate clause or a non-subordinate clause in PDE.[3] We will make a diachronic examination of the process of such extensions undergone by *because*-clauses in 3.4 below.

3.2.1.2 *Because*-clauses as independent clauses

Various studies have pointed to the non-subordinate, paratactic uses of *because*-clauses, i.e., the structural independence of a *because*-clause from its "main" clause, especially in spoken discourse, in PDE.[4] For example, Altenberg (1984) examines causal expressions in spoken and written British English and shows the loose linkage of causal clauses in spoken discourse.[5] He illustrates their looseness by indicating the similarity in use and function of *because*- and *so*-sequences, both of which exhibit great frequency in the spoken discourse. They are "communicatively equivalent in most respects except causal order. ... The fact that *because* is formally a subordinator and *so* a non-structural cohesive adverbial seems to be of little practical significance (p. 48)". Altenberg (1984:49–50) points out the following signs of the loose linkage, i.e., the structural independence, of *because*-clauses, emphasizing their pragmatic function.[6]

(14) Signs of the loose linkage of *because*-clauses pointed out in Altenberg (1984):

    1. *because*-clauses are nearly always set off by a prosodic break, often manifested as a pause of varying length

    2. *because*-clauses are easily separated from their main clause by an intrusive element, and they are frequently added after some hesitation, as an afterthought

    3. in cases where *because*-clauses have pragmatic function, no grammatical main clause is present but *because*-clauses is related to a previous speech

act or to an implied assumption, belief, etc.
4. pragmatic *because*-clauses may even function as questions

Based on a detailed description of non-subordinating, paratactic uses of the *because*-clause in conversational discourse, Schleppegrell (1991) differentiates subordinate *because* from non-subordinate *because*. The former creates "local links within the sentences" whereas the latter creates larger links and builds "cohesion in discourse". She further classifies the latter into three.[7]

(15) Non-subordinate, paratactic uses of *because*-clauses in Schleppegrell (1991):
    1. a discourse-reflexive textual link which introduces a reason for or explanation of a prior statement such as (16)
    2. an expressive, non-causal link which introduces further elaboration of a prior statement such as (17)
    3. a discourse marker which indicates continuation and response such as (18)

Let us now look at each example. The *because*-clause in (16) provides a statement about how he knows that the others don't like his partner, not a reason why they don't like her.

(16) (Responding to a question about the speaker's math partner)
    Well like I have a partner that hardly anybody likes *because* they make fun of her name
                                                (adapted from Schleppegrell, 1991:326)

In (17) below, the *because*-clause elaborates the prior statement that he "only knows how to count a little" by providing a further specification of what he knows in Spanish. It gives neither a reason for nor an explanation of the prior statement.

(17) (Matthew is reporting how much he knows in Spanish)
    Matthew: I only know how to count a little.
    Interviewer: But we'll go back to English.
    Sara: Where are you from?
    Matthew: *Because* my name in Spanish is Mateo and I can only count uno, dos, tres, cuatro, cinco, seis, that's all I can ...

(adapted from Schleppegrell, 1991:327–328)

The *'cause* in (18) functions as a marker of continuation. Challenged by the interviewer, Sara begins to justify her statement that she is "not so smart" with *'cause*. Although she has no justification for her statement, she holds the floor and repeats her statement.

(18) Sara: ... I'm not so smart.
    Interviewer: Oh listen to her?
    Sara: I'm not, I don't think so *'cause* um ...
    Interviewer: Listen to her? Yes, you are.
    Sara: *'cause* I don't – I don't think so, ...

(adapted from Schleppegrell, 1991:329)

Schleppegrell argues that "in addition to using *because* as a subordinating conjunction with causal meaning, speakers use *because* as a wide-scope discourse marker (p. 333)".[8]

Similarly, Stenström and Andersen (1996) and Stenström (1998) consider non-subordinate *because* as a discourse marker. They focus on the difference between *because* and its phonologically reduced form *'cos* in spoken British English. They investigate the Bergen Corpus of London Teenage Language (COLT), which compiles the language of London teenagers, and the London-Lund Corpus of Spoken English (LLC), which records the language of London adults mostly in academia, and demonstrate that *'cos* and *because* differ in frequency and function.

1. *'cos* is more frequent than *because* in COLT, as shown below.

   (19) Frequency of *'cos* and *because* in COLT and LLC

Item	COLT	LLC
'cos	63%	21%
because	37%	56%

   (adapted from Stenström and Andersen, 1996:191 and Stenström, 1998:137)

2. *'cos* is used as a non-subordinator more often than *because*, and twice as often in COLT as in LLC, as shown below.

   (20) Function of *'cos* and *because* in COLT and LLC

Item	Subordinator COLT	LLC	Non-subordinator COLT	LLC
'cos	51%	75%	49%	25%
because	66%	97%	34%	03%

   (adapted from Stenström, 1998:138)

Stenström and Andersen (1996) and Stenström (1998) concludes that *'cos* appears to be developing a new function, i.e., "undergoing a change from grammatical subordinator, introducing a clause of cause or reason, to discourse marker, the function of which is ultimately to serve as a take-off for further talk (Stenström, 1998:144)".[9]

We have so far seen cases where the so-called subordinate clause marker *because* functions as a pragmatic marker when *because*-clauses appear independently. This points toward a possible functional extension of *because*-clauses in progress in PDE. We will inquire into when and how independent *because*-clauses come into use in 3.4 below.

In this subsection, we have reviewed some earlier studies that have long discussed the syntactic status of *because*-clauses in PDE. These studies propose to distinguish *because*-clauses as subordinate, hypotactic clauses from non-subordinate, paratactic clauses. They also report that *because*-clauses do appear independently and *because* functions as a pragmatic marker in PDE.

3.2.2 Semantic/pragmatic aspects of *because*-clauses in present-day English

This subsection considers the relationship between syntactic and semantic/pragmatic functions of *because*-clauses. As discussed in 2.3.1 above, interpretation of *because*-clauses can be differentiated into three. A *because*-clause can be interpreted as being connected to its "main" clause in the content domain (i.e., connection in the real world), in the epistemic domain (i.e., connection in the epistemic domain), and in the speech-act domain (i.e., connection in the conversational domain).[10]

It has been pointed out in the literature that the differences in interpretation of *because*-clauses correlate with their syntactic properties.[11] Couper-Kuhlen (1996) gives a good account of the correlation on the basis of the following syntactic transformations. Although they are almost same as the syntactic tests mentioned in 3.2.1 above, it is helpful at this point to carry out these transformations one by one according to the types of interpretations.

1. In cases where *because* is interpreted as marking "a direct causal relation between two events or states of affairs" (content conjunction interpretation), the *because*-clause is subjected to certain syntactic transformations.

(21) [Content conjunction]
   I wasn't that concerned about the time, *because* I'm not a fast runner.

   (Couper-Kuhlen, 1996:403)

   a. [reversal]
      Because I'm not a fast runner, I wasn't that concerned about the time.
   b. [an answer to a *wh*-question]
      Why were you not concerned about the time?
      – *Because* I'm not a fast runner.

c. [*it*-clefting]

It's *because* I'm not a fast runner that I wasn't that concerned about the time.

2. In cases where *because* is interpreted as marking "an indirect cause or reason", i.e., as accounting for "why a speaker knows or believes what is expressed in a prior clause" (epistemic conjunction interpretation) or "why a speaker has carried out some particular speech act in the prior clause" (speech-act conjunction interpretation), the *because*-clause is not subjected to certain syntactic transformations

(22) [Epistemic conjunction]

She doesn't know she's seventeen and a half, *because* she still chases the squirrels.

(Couper-Kuhlen, 1996:404)

a. [reversal]

*Because she still chases the squirrels, she doesn't know she's seventeen and a half.

b. [an answer to a *wh*-question]

*Why does she not know she's seventeen and a half?

– *Because* she still chases the squirrels.

c. [*it*-clefting]

*It's *because* she still chases the squirrels that she doesn't know she's seventeen and a half.

(23) [Speech-act conjunction]

What are you doing tonight, *because* there's a good movie on.

(Sweetser, 1990:77)

a. [reversal]

*Because there's a good movie on, what are you doing tonight.

b. [an answer to a *wh*-question]

*What are you doing tonight? = *Because* there's a good movie on.

c. [*it*-clefting]

*It's *because* there's a good movie on that what are you doing tonight.

It follows from the above-mentioned transformations and some others proposed in earlier studies that interpretations of *because*-clauses are reflected in their syntax in PDE in the following way:

(24) Correlation between interpretation of *because*-clauses and their syntactic properties in PDE

1. In the case of content conjunction interpretation, a *because*-clause is a subordinate, hypotactic clause.
2. In the case of epistemic and speech-act conjunction interpretation, a *because*-clause is a non-subordinate, paratactic clause.

As it turned out, this study postulates the schematization of each interpretation as follows. The following are canonical examples of content, epistemic, and speech-act conjunction interpretation in PDE respectively. Each one of them is followed by the schematization.

(25) [Content conjunction]

John came back *because* he loved her.

[John came back [*because* he loved her]]

(Sweetser, 1990:77)

(26) [Epistemic conjunction]

a. John loved her, *because* he came back.

[John loved her][*because* he came back]

(Sweetser, 1990:77)

b. He must be here *because* his bicycle is outside.

   [He must be here][*because* his bicycle is outside]

$\hspace{20em}$ (Traugott, 1992:252)

(27) [Speech-act conjunction]

   What are you doing tonight, *because* there's a good movie on.

   [What are you doing tonight] [*because* there's a good movie on]

$\hspace{20em}$ (Sweetser, 1990:77)

The schematization of (25) represents that the *because*-clause is subordinate to its grammatically associated "main" clause whereas those of (26) and (27) show the non-subordinate, paratactic relationship of the *because*-clause to its "main" clause. As for epistemic conjunction, we here take up the following two types: one without an epistemic expression in the "main" clause as shown in (26a) and the other with an overt epistemic expression in the "main" clause as shown (26b). As for speech-act conjunction, a *because*-clause usually follows its "main" clause in which a speech-act is performed. Based on the earlier studies reviewed in this section, the schematization (25)–(27) can be elaborated upon by indicating the relationship between the two clauses in the following way.

(25') [Content conjunction]

   [John came back [*because* he loved her]]

(26') [Epistemic conjunction]

    a. [(I believe/conclude/etc.) John loved her][*because* (I know/see/etc.) he came back]

    b. [(I believe/conclude/etc.) he is here][*because* (I know/see/etc.) his bicycle is outside]

(27') [Speech-act conjunction]

    [(I ask) what you are doing tonight][*because* (my motive for asking is that) there's a good movie on]

(25') shows that the *because*-clause is associated with the main verb in the "main" clause. (26') indicates that the *because*-clause is related not to the main verb but to the speaker's belief or conclusion that is expressed in the "main" clause, whether it is overtly indicated or not. (27') represents the semantic/pragmatic relationship between the *because*-clause and the speech-act expressed in the "main" clause. In sum, we can make an assumption that the *because*-clause is associated with the main verb in the "main" clause in content conjunction interpretation whereas it is related to the speech-act performed in its "main" clause in epistemic and speech-act conjunction interpretation. We will make use of some types of expressions that overtly mark epistemic and speech-act conjunction interpretations when we observe the developmental process of the *because*-clause in 3.4.2 below.

    Further, as we have seen in 3.2.1.2 above, there are cases in PDE where the grammatical "main" clause is absent and *because* can be regarded as a pragmatic marker. In the earlier studies, *because* is viewed as a marker of subordinate idea units in the discourse (Schiffrin, 1987), an indicator of "continuation and response in conversational interaction" (Schleppegrell, 1991:323), "a means of doing continuation" (Couper-Kuhlen, 1996:423), or a signal of "a take-off for further talk"

(Stenström, 1998:144).[12] The functions of *because* as a pragmatic marker have not been entirely agreed upon in the literature, but it is not our present purpose to enter into a detailed description of them here. We limit ourselves to mentioning here that *because* comes to acquire alternative pragmatic functions other than expressing a cause or reason as *because*-clauses come to have a looser syntactic relationship to their associated "main" clause. We will consider motivations behind such structural and semantic/pragmatic extensions in 3.5.

In sum, this subsection reviewed some earlier studies on the correlation between syntactic functions of *because*-clauses and their semantic/pragmatic functions in PDE. An interpretation of *because*-clauses as content conjunctions typically corresponds to a subordinate *because*-clause whereas that of epistemic/speech-act conjunctions tends to be associated with a non-subordinate *because*-clause. Moreover, *because* may serve as a pragmatic marker when a *because*-clause appears as an independent clause.

3.2.3 Prosodic aspects of *because*-clauses in present-day English

This section introduces earlier studies on the relationship between the syntactic independence of *because*-clauses and their prosodic characteristics. They report that its syntactic independence tends to be reflected in the intonation.

It is useful to consult Quirk et al. (1985:1076–1077) for the difference in intonation in *because*-clauses. According to them, the difference is realized in intonation in the following way.[13]

(28) [adjunct, restrictive]
    She didn't park the car *because* she was tired.
    She didn't park the car *because* she was T\IRED#

(29) [adjunct, non-restrictive]
    She didn't park the car, *because* she was tired.
    She didn't park the C\AR# *because* she was T\IRED#

(30) [disjunct, non-restrictive (only)]

She parked the car, *because* I've been watching her.

She didn't park the C\AR#. *Because* I was W\ATCHING her#

As the tone unit boundary (#), together with the falling intonation (\) indicates, both the main clause and the restrictive adjunct clause in (28) are pronounced in one tone unit. The non-restrictive adjunct clause in (29) is pronounced in a separate tone unit, which is set off from the main clause by a tone unit boundary. The non-restrictive disjunct clause in (30) is also pronounced in a separate tone unit, which is followed by a brief pause (.). In short, a subordinate *because*-clause is pronounced in one tone unit whereas a non-subordinate *because*-clause is pronounced in a separate tone unit. The separated tone unit is considered an indication of the independence of non-subordinate *because*-clauses.[14]

Chafe (1984, 1988) makes a similar observation on English adverbial clauses as a group. Chafe (1984) studies cases where "the main clause is actually closed off with sentence-final intonation, and the following adverbial clause has the intonation of a separate sentence (1984:446)". An example with a *because*-clause is as follows.

(31) And I feel a little bad.

Because in some sense her ... I mean her kid's really a ... I think a great kid.

(Chafe, 1984:446)

He argues that in such cases adverbial clauses often "occur as intonationally separate afterthoughts (1984:448)". In Chafe (1988) where the falling pitch is called a "period" intonation and the non-falling pitch a "comma" intonation, he claims that "forward linking virtually requires a comma intonation at the end of the first clause, [while] backward linking has no such requirement" (1988:19). He reports that *because* is the most common linking device among backward linkings in his data.[15]

In line with Chafe's distinction in adverbial clauses, Ford (1993) studies adverbial clauses in American English conversation. She classifies them into initial clauses, final clauses with continuous intonation, and final clauses after ending intonation. In regard to *because*-clauses, her findings are summarized as follows (Ford, 1993:63–65, 85–101, 102ff).

(32) *Because*-clauses and intonation summarized in Ford (1993)
   1. *Because*-clauses follow final falling intonation more frequently than do temporal and conditional clauses. (p. 90)
   2. *Because*-clauses after ending intonation function as introducing "background, motivating, or explanatory material," which is most likely to appear in a separate intonation contour. (p. 103)

Couper-Kuhlen (1996), however, casts doubt on distinguishing the different uses of *because*-clauses in discourse based on the contrast between comma/continuous and period/ending intonation.[16] She claims that it is "declination reset or lack of it which distinguishes the realization of the *because*-clauses (p. 398)". The term "declination reset" refers to "the gradual decrease of the fundamental frequency values of comparable phonological events in an intonation phrase over the course of time (p. 363)". Based on the auditory and instrumental phonetic analysis of the use of *because*-clauses in British and American spoken discourse, she finds a regular correspondence between *because*-clauses of direct reason (approximately corresponding to "subordinate *because*-clauses") and the absence of declination reset, as well as between clauses of indirect reason ("non-subordinate *because*-clauses") and presence of declination reset. Although it is admittedly fruitful to analyze the use of *because*-clauses in terms of "declination reset", this criterion cannot be used in the analysis of the diachronic data collected for the present study since no information on intonational aspects of *because*-clauses is available.

This section has introduced some intonational characteristics of *because*-clauses. It is reported in some earlier studies that syntactic independence of *because*-clauses is reflected in their intonational pattern.[17]

3.2.4 Summary

In 3.2, we have seen a general picture of *because*-clauses in PDE from the viewpoint of syntax, semantics/pragmatics, and intonation. From the viewpoint of syntax, *because*-clauses can be distinguished as subordinate, non-subordinate, and independent clauses in PDE. To put it differently, *because* can be viewed as extending its function from a subordinate clause marker to a pragmatic marker. From the viewpoint of semantics/pragmatics, it was pointed out that there is a correlation between interpretations of *because*-clauses and their syntactic characteristics. *Because*-clauses are subordinate in the case of content conjunction interpretation while they are non-subordinate, paratactic in the case of epistemic/speech-act conjunction interpretation. From the viewpoint of intonation, it was shown that the syntactic independence of *because*-clauses is reflected in the intonational pattern. As a whole, the earlier studies reviewed in this section pointed toward a potential functional extension of *because*-clauses in PDE from less to more paratactic clause-combining constructions with an increase in pragmatic meanings. Viewed in this light, it may safely be assumed that they are extending from subordinate via paratactic to independent clause-combining constructions with an increase in subjective meanings in PDE. The following summarizes the characteristics of PDE *because*-clauses reviewed in this section:

(33) A summary of the characteristics of PDE *because*-clauses

Syntax:	subordinate, hypotactic [CL1 [*because* CL2]]	non-subordinate, paratactic [CL1] [*because* CL2]	independent [*because* CL]
Function of *because*:	subordinate clause marker	conjunction-like clause marker	pragmatic marker
Semantics/ pragmatics:	content-conjunction	epistemic conjunction speech-act conjunction	
Intonation:	one tone unit separate tone unit	separate tone unit	separate tone unit

3.3 History of *because*-clauses

This section introduces earlier studies on *because*-clauses from a diachronic perspective.[18] Before tracing the history of *because*-clauses, it is helpful to take a brief look at the history of causal clauses in English in order to understand the relative position of *because*-clauses to other causal clauses in the history of English.[19]

3.3.1 A note on the history of causal clauses in English

The typical causal clause in Old English (OE) is one that is introduced by [*for* + demonstrative pronoun + the optional subordinate particle *þe*].[20] It is frequently found in the form of *for þæm/þam/þan/þon (þe)* and sometimes in the form of *for þy/þi (þe)*.[21] (34) gives an example of *for þan þe*.

(34) [*for þan þe* in OE]

for ði	him (DAT)	ofhreow	þæs	mannes (GEN)	*for þan þe*
for that	to-him	pitied	of-that	man	for that PT
he wæs	bepæht	smid	þæs	deoflees	searocræftum
he was	deceived	by	that	devil's	wiles

'he was sorry for the man because he (the man) was deceived by the devil's wiles.'

(c.1000 *ÆCHom* I, 13 192.16 [*CHEL* vol. I:212])

Other OE causal expressions which do not survive in PDE includes *þæs (þe), þy/þe, (swa) þæt(te), swelc/seice(e), þær (þær), þonne (þonne, þe)*, etc.

It is well known that a temporal expression can give rise to a causal interpretation (Geise and Zwicky, 1971; Traugott and König, 1991:194–199; Hopper and Traugott, 2003:78–84; *CHEL*, vol. II:347, etc.). In OE, the temporal adverb *nu (þæt)* 'now (that)' is used as a causal clause marker as in (35).[22]

(35) [*nu (þæt)* in OE]

Untwylice	þu	lyhst	þæt	þu	God	sy.
Without.doubt	thou	liest	that	thou	God	art
nu	þu	nast		manna	geþohtas	
now	thou	not.knowest		of.men	thoughts	

'Certainly you lie saying that you are God, since you do not know men's thought.'

(c.1000 *ÆCHom* I, 26 378.6 [*CHEL* vol. I:255])

Other temporal expressions such as *þa* 'than', *þonne* 'then', and *siþþan* 'after' can occasionally be interpreted with a causal meaning in OE.

In Early Middle English (EME), a causal clause is frequently introduced by *for (that)* as in (36). It is presumably an elliptic form of OE *for þæm (þe)*. The various causal constructions with *for* in OE are simplified to *for (that)* in the Middle English period.[23]

(36) [*for (that)* in EME]

ac	hit	naht	ne	beheld,		
but	it	nothing	not	kept		
for	se	biscop	of	Særesbyrig	wæs	strang ...
for	the	bishop	of	Salisbury	was	strong

'but it had no effect because the bishop of Salisbury was powerful ...'

(c.1121–1155 *PC* (Ld) an.1123; 43.30–1 [*CHEL* vol. II:291])

That (< possibly OE *þæs (þe)*), the correlatives *for ... for-thi/therfore*, and *now (that)* (< OE *nu (þæt)*) also indicate cause in EME. A causal interpretation with *sith(en)/sin (that)*, which come from OE temporal *siþþan* 'after', develops rapidly in this period. (37) illustrates a causal use of *syn*.

(37) [*syn* in EME]

What sholde I tellen hem, *syn* they been tolde?

'Why should I then re-tell what has been told?'

(c.1387–1400 *CT* III.56 [2:56] [*CHEL* vol. II:347])

It is in the Late Middle English (LME) period that *because* comes into use and spreads rapidly. It originates in the phrasal expressions *by (the) cause that, for the cause that*, etc. The development of *because* is reviewed in more detail in 3.3.2 below.

In Early Modern English (EModE), *for* is the most common causal clause marker.

(38) [*for* in LME]

Nor *for* he sweld with ire was she affraid.

'Neither was she afraid because he was angry.'

(1600 FAIRFAX *Tasso* II. xix [*OED*])

In this period, *for* gradually developed toward a coordinate conjunction while *for that*, which is classified as a subordinate conjunction, becomes obsolete. From the point of view of clause combining, this can be regarded as an extension from subordinate to non-subordinate, i.e., paratactic clause combining. *Because* is beginning to catch up with *for* in frequency during the seventeenth century.[24]

Temporal expressions such as *sith(ence)/since* (< ME *sith(en)/sin (that)*, < OE *sippan*) and *as* can express a causal meaning in the EModE period.[25]

(39) [*sins* in EModE]

Sins it is not yet dinner tyme, let vs walke about.

(1577 B. GOOGE *Heresbach's Husb*. I. (1586) 7 b [*OED*])

(40) [*as* in EModE]

> Lete me fro this deth fle, *As* I dede nevyr no trespace.
>
> (1400 *Cov. Myst.* 281 [*OED*])

The following summarizes the history of causal clause markers taken up in this section:[26]

(41) The causal clause markers from Old English to Present-Day English (adapted from Kortmann, 1997:331)

OE	ME	EModE	PDE
for þæm (þe)	for (that)	for	--- [coord.]**
þæs (þe)	that	---	---
nu (þæt)	now (that)	now (that)	now (that)
[siþþan 'after']*	sith(en)/sin (that)	sith(ence)/since	since
[þonne 'then']*	---	---	---
[þa 'than']*	---	---	---
	for ... for-thi/therfore	---	---
	by (the) cause (that)	because (that)	because
		as	as

3.3.2 A note on the history of *because*

The ancestor of *because* is said to be the LME phrasal construction *by (the) cause (that)*, which is a borrowing from Old French *par cause de*.[27] It becomes popular in the fourteenth century. In its earlier stage, it appears in various forms.[28] See the following examples:

(42) [*because* in LME]

    a. And *by the cause that* they sholde ryse Erly ... Vnto hir reste went they.

       'And because they had to get up early, they went to bed.'

                                (c.1385 Chaucer *CT.Kn.* A. 2488 [*MED*])

    b. I moste seie forþ my seruise ... *Bi-cause whi* hit is clerkes wyse ... Forte synge Deo Gracias.   (c.1390 *In a Chirche* 36 [*MED*])

    c. And it is drye & no thing fructuous *be cause þat* it hath no moysture ...

                                (c.1400 *Mandev.* (Tit) 26.23-4 [*CHEL* vol. II, 346])

    d. Putt hym away *by cause* he is danugerous.

                                (1477 *Paston Lett.* 794 III. 186 [*OED*])

That gradually falls into disuse, leaving *because* only.[29] From the fifteenth century onward, *because that* is on the decrease and became archaic or dialectal in the Late Modern English (LModE) period. We may note, in passing, that the remnants of *that*, a general marker of subordination, can be seen in the subordinate use of *because*-clauses in PDE.

In EModE, *because* spreads rapidly.[30] It gains popularity in the sixteenth century, and it is beginning to gain on *for* in frequency during the seventeenth century.[31] According to Rissanen (1999:306–307), the ratio between *because* and *for* is 1:15 in the texts of the Helsinki Corpus dating between 1420 and 1500, while it is 1:3 between 1500 and 1640.

(43) The change in number and ratio between *because* and *for*

    (adopted from Rissanen 1999:306–307)

	approximate ratio between *because* and *for*	approximate number of instances *because*/*for*
+1420–1500 (LME)	1:15	50/750
1500–1640 (EModE)	1:3	350/1000

Because catches up with *for* and takes the lead in frequency in LModE. It becomes one of the typical causal clause markers in PDE. The following are examples of *because* in EModE and LModE respectively:

(44) [*because* in EModE]

Nor am I so vaine ... *bycause* I am not worth so much.

(1616 SIR R. DUDLEY in *Fortesc. Papers* 17 [*OED*])

(45) [*because* in LModE]

We wonder *because* we are ignorant and we fear *because* we are weak.

(1857 BUCKLE *Civilis*. I. S. 616 [*OED*])

The historical development of *because* can be summarized in the following way:

(46) [*because* from LME to PDE]

LME	EModE	LModE	PDE
by (the) cause (that), etc. >	because (that) >	because	because
phrasal construction		> single function word	

As Hopper and Traugott (2003:4) state:

When a content word assumes the grammatical characteristics of a function word, the form is said to be "grammaticalized." Quite often what is grammaticalized is not a single content word but an entire construction that includes that word, ...

From the standpoint of grammaticalization, the change under investigation can be viewed as the process whereby a phrasal construction that includes the content word *cause* developed into a single function word that works as a "causal" clause marker.

3.3.3 Summary

In 3.3 we reviewed earlier studies on the history of English causal clauses and the historical development of *because*. We saw that a former phrasal construction in various forms develops into a single grammatical marker *because*. In the process, it comes to take over *for*, the causal subordinate clause marker that survives from OE.

We mentioned that *that*, a general marker of subordination, fell into disuse with *because* in the course of time. However, we can see the remnants of *that* in *because*-clauses in PDE. It was observed in 3.2.1 that *because*-clauses in PDE can be differentiated into subordination and non-subordination on the basis of their syntactic behavior. The subordinate use of *because*-clauses in PDE can be viewed as the syntactic remainder of *that*.

3.4 Developmental path of *because*-clauses

We have reviewed a synchronic diversity of *because*-clauses in 3.2 and their diachronic transition in 3.3. Given the synchronic and diachronic state of *because*-clauses that was pointed out in those sections, it seems reasonable to suppose the developmental pathway of *because*-clauses from LME to PDE in the following way:[32]

(47) *Because*-clauses from LME to PDE

LME: CL1 *by (the) cause (that)* CL2
　　　　[CL1 [*by (the) cause (that)* CL2]]

　　　　CL2: subordinate
　　　　by (the) cause (that): phrasal
　　　　　　　　↓
EModE: CL1 *because (that)* CL2
　　　　[CL1 [*because (that)* CL2]]

CL2: subordinate

because (that): single CM

↓

LModE: CL1 *because* CL2

[CL1 [*because* CL2]]

CL2: subordinate

because: single CM

↓   ↘   ↘

PDE: CL1 *because* CL2   CL1 *because* CL2   *because*/'*cos* CL

[CL1 [*because* CL2]]   [CL1] [*because* CL2]   [*because*/'*cos* CL]

CL2: subordinate   CL2: non-subordinate   CL: independent

because: single CM   *because*: single CM   *because*: PM

In the light of the development of clause-combining constructions, (47) shows a developmental process of *because*-clauses from subordinate to independent clauses. It may safely be assumed that PDE is an intermediary stage in which subordinate (i.e., hypotactic), non-subordinate (i.e., paratactic), and independent *because*-clauses coexist from the perspective of grammaticalization. In the light of the development of a clause marker, it indicates a developmental path of *because* from a phrasal causal expression in various forms via a single causal clause marker to a pragmatic marker.

Our concern in this section is to trace an ongoing developmental process of *because*-clauses in more detail. We confine our attention to discourse indications that seem relevant to the inception of *because*-clauses in transition. Section 3.4.1 notes the data that will be used for this section. Section 3.4.2 details a diachronic process of *because*-clauses in terms of clause-combining constructions. Section 3.4.3 makes a diachronic survey of *because*-clauses in terms of the correlation between syntactic and semantic/pragmatic functions. Section 3.4.4 gives a summary of the findings in this section.

3.4.1 A note on the English data for this section

We use the diachronic component of the Helsinki Corpus (HC) for a preliminary survey. (48) shows the number of data collected from the HC for this survey.[33]

(48) The data collected from the HC for a preliminary survey:

LME:	ME3 (1350–1420)	1	
	ME4 (1420–1500)	12	
EModE:	EMBE1 (1500–1570)	30	
	EMBE2 (1570–1640)	32	
	EMBE3 (1640–1710)	19	
TOTAL:		94	

For the main purpose of the present study, we examine the written colloquial data collected from conversational parts of novels and play scripts, and the written component of the British National Corpus (BNC). We also examine the spoken data taken from the spoken component of the BNC and the London-Lund Corpus of Spoken English (LLC). There are a total of 313 *because*-clauses in the diachronic data and a total of 268 in the synchronic data as shown in (49).[34]

(49) The main data of *because*-clauses for the present study

Diachronic data (written colloquial)

–1600	18
1600–1650	29
1650–1700	17
1700–1750	16
1750–1800	32
1800–1850	56
1850–1900	61
1900–1950	84
TOTAL (diachronic data):	313

Synchronic data (written colloquial: from the BNC)

1950–2000	61

Synchronic data (spoken: from the BNC)

1950–2000	63

Synchronic data (spoken: from the LLC)

1950–2000	144
TOTAL (synchronic data):	268

We pointed out in 3.3 above that *because*-clauses gain in frequency from the sixteenth century onward. In our diachronic data, the earliest examples of *because*-clauses are found in the text written in the 1590s.

(50) Looke where he goes, but see, he comes again *Because* I stay:
> (c.1590 *Tamburlaine the Great, Part 2*: act 5, scene 3, line 75)

The data collected for the present study are originally grouped in periods of 50 years, as indicated in (49) above, for the purpose of comparing them with the Japanese data in section 4.4. However, they are regrouped at intervals of 100 years, if necessary, in the following subsections. It turns out, for example, that an instance of independent *because*-clauses is sporadically found in the diachronic data and it is hard to show the transition clearly.

The examples of *because*-clauses are basically classified into the following four groups. Each group will be divided into subgroups, if necessary.

(51) Basic classification of *because*-clauses in the present study

 (a) [CL1 *because* CL2]

 (b) [*Because* CL1, CL2]

 (c) [*Because* CL]

 (d) Others

[Examples of (a)–(c) from the diachronic data]

(a-1)

FERDINAND. … like the irregular crab,

    Which, thoug't goes backward, thinks that it goes right

    Because it goes its own way:

      (1612–1613 *The Duchesse of Malfi*, Act I, Scene II)

(a-2)

It cannot choose, *because* it comes from you

    (c.1590 *Tamburlaine the Great, Part 1*, act 1, scene 1, line 56)

(a-3)

I've been cadging boots – in particular – for days. *Because* I was sick of them.

    (1897 *The invisible man*, Chapter 9)

(b-1)

ANTONIO. *Because* you would not seem to appear to th' world

    Puff'd up with your preferment, you continue

    This out-of-fashion melancholy:

      (1612–1613 *The Duchesse of Malfi*, Act II, Scene I)

(b-2)

..., and imagine that, *because* they are sated with others, they know the delight of loneliness.

(1834 *The last days of Pmpeii*, Book the first, Chapter II)

(c)

FURTIVO

And no man but will admire to hear of his virtues—

LATRONELLO

[Aside] *Because* he ne'er had any in all his life.

FALSO

You write all down, Latronello?

(1603–1604 *The Phoenix*, III.i.)

(51a–c) indicates the relative position of a *because*-clause to its associated "main" clause in discourse. Thus, (51a) includes [CL1, *because* CL2], such as (a-2), and [CL1. *because* CL2], such as (a-3), for example. The initial capital letter of *because* in (51b) and (51c) expresses the beginning of a clause for the sake of convenience here. Thus, for instance, [*because* CL1, CL2], such as (b-2), is classified as (51b) as long as the *because*-clause is interpreted as being semantically related to CL2. A *because*-clause is classified as (51c) when it appears turn-initially and is clearly separated from the following clause, if any, by punctuation.[35] A *because*-clause serving as answer to a *wh*-question is classified as (51d). In all cases, we try our best to observe and interpret the data in discourse context. Whenever there is a risk of misjudgment, they are classified as (51d).

3.4.2 From subordinate to independent clauses

This subsection looks more carefully into the developmental process of *because*-clauses in terms of clause-combining constructions. It points out that the trend is toward increased *because*-clause independence from its "main" clause in PDE.

To begin with, it is helpful to make a preliminary survey using the Helsinki

Corpus (HC). We noted in 3.3.2 above that the phrasal expression *by (the) cause (that)* and its variants came into use in the LME period. As (52) below shows, various forms of *because* are used from ME3 to EMBE2, whereas no variant is found in EMBE3 in the HC. Notice that they are gradually standardized by EMBE3.[36]

(52) Various forms of *because* in the HC

period	forms of *because*	number	percentage *because*
ME3 (1350–1420)	by cause that	1	0
ME4 (1420–1500)	by cause	6	
	because	3	25
	bicause	1	
	bycause	1	
	because that	1	
EMBE1 (1500–1570)	because	19	63.3
	bicause	9	
	bycause	1	
	forbicause	1	
EMBE2 (1570–1640)	because	29	90.6
	beecause	2	
	becawse	1	
EMBE3 (1640–1710)	because	19	100

We also mentioned in 3.3.2 that *that* gradually falls into disuse with *because* from the fifteenth century on (i.e., in the LME period in the present study). As (52) above shows, no example of *because that* is found in the EMBE1–3 (i.e., in the EModE period in the present study).

Turning now to the main task, we look closely at a developmental process of *because*-clauses from EModE to PDE. Table 3.1 shows the transition of the distribution of *because*-clauses from EModE to PDE in the main data for the present study.

Table 3.1: The transition of the distribution of *because*-clauses by position

	−1650	−1750	−1850	−1950	−2000 (wr) (BNC)	−2000 (sp) (BNC)	−2000 (sp) (LLC)
(a) CL1 *because* CL2	30	22	61	86	46	44	115
	(63.8%)	(66.7%)	(69.3%)	(59.3%)	(75.4%)	(69.8%)	(79.9%)
(b) *Because* CL1, CL2	2	4	3	5	2	7	5
	(4.3%)	(12.1%)	(3.4%)	(3.5%)	(3.3%)	(11.1%)	(3.5%)
(c) *Because* CL	1	0	3	7	10	6	18
	(2.1%)	(0%)	(3.4%)	(4.8%)	(16.4%)	(9.5%)	(12.5%)
(d) Others	14	7	21	47	3	6	6
	(29.8%)	(21.2%)	(23.9%)	(32.6%)	(4.9%)	(9.5%)	(4.2%)
TOTAL	47	33	88	145	61	63	144
TOTAL				313			268

What may be noted from Table 3.1 is as follows. First, as (c) shows, independent *because*-clauses gradually increase in proportion. In view of clause-combining constructions, we can see that the trend is toward a looser structural relationship between a *because*-clause and its "main" clause. Second, independent *because*-clauses develop in the last 50 years. These observations support the arguments for the emergence of independent *because*-clauses made by earlier studies in 3.2.1.2 above. Lastly, the inversion of a *because*-clause and its "main" clause, i.e., type (b), does not seem to have a close correlation with the development of independent *because*-clauses in English.[37]

In this subsection, we have examined the developmental process of *because*-clauses in terms of clause-combining constructions. By analyzing the HC, we recognized that various forms of *because* are gradually standardized by around 1650. Further, based on the diachronic and synchronic data that were originally collected for the present study, we showed that *because*-clauses have gradually become more and more paratactic clause-combining constructions.

3.4.3 From content to epistemic/speech-act conjunction interpretation

This subsection observes the developmental process of *because*-clauses in the light of semantic/pragmatic interpretation. It points out that the trend is from content to epistemic/speech-act conjunction interpretation in PDE.

In 3.2.2 above, we touched upon some earlier studies that pointed out the correlation between syntactic and semantic/pragmatic functions of *because*-clauses in PDE (Couper-Kuhlen, 1996). The correlation can be summarized in the following way.

(53) Syntactic and semantic/pragmatic functions of *because*-clauses in PDE

syntax:	subordinate	non-subordinate, paratactic
	[CL1 [*because* CL2]]	[CL1] [*because* CL2]
semantics/	content conjunction	epistemic conjunction
pragmatics:		speech-act conjunction

In this subsection, we attempt to examine the above correlation synchronically and diachronically. The point to observe here is some types of expressions that overtly appear in both *because*-clauses and their "main" clauses in epistemic and speech-act conjunction interpretation (see also 4.4.3 below). The motivations to observe these expressions are as follows. First, Yoshii's (1977) survey on Japanese *kara*-clauses shows that their "main" clauses without these expressions gradually decrease proportionately over the course of time (see 4.3.2.3 below for further details). In other words, his survey suggests the tendency of *kara*-clauses toward epistemic/speech-act conjunction interpretation. Thus, we will make use of these expressions in examining the above-mentioned correlation synchronically and diachronically in English. Second, we try to answer the question of whether independent *because*-clauses have such expressions. We can posit that the more paratactic the syntactic relationship between a *because*-clause and its "main" clause becomes, the less they share such an expression. We predict that both a *because*-clause and its "main" clause acquire such an expression in the course of time.

(54) gives the subdivisions of (51a) [CL1 *because* CL2] according to noticeable overt expressions of epistemic and speech-act conjunction interpretation and the instances found in the synchronic data. Instances with an overt expression other than (i) and (ii) and those without one are classified as (iii) in the following surveys.[38]

(54) Subdivisions of (51a) according to overt expressions of epistemic and speech-act conjunction
    (i-1) epistemic conjunction: with an epistemic modality [with EM]
    (i-2) epistemic conjunction: with an epistemic expression [with EE]
    (i-3) epistemic conjunction: with an adjective [with A]
    (i-4) epistemic conjunction: with a noun [with N]
    (ii-1) speech-act conjunction: with an expression of speech-act [with SA]
    (ii-2) speech-act conjunction: with a speech-act verb [with SAV]
    (iii) others

[Examples of (i-1)–(ii-2) in the synchronic data][39]
    (i-1) epistemic conjunction: with an epistemic modality [with EM]
        but they (= the university presses) <u>would be</u> worth approaching#
        because that again is a technical# or unremunerative type of book#
                                      (LLC: 2 1 24 3190–3240)

    (i-2) epistemic conjunction: with an epistemic expression [with EE]
        <u>I know</u> it is Innocent the Fourth# <u>I'm sure</u>#
        because I know I've seen the portrait in lectures on Velasquez
                                      (LLC: 1 4 40 6040–6070)

    (i-3) epistemic conjunction: with an adjective [with A]
        <u>that's absurd</u> *because* that's absolutely international
                                      (LLC: 1 10 36 2750–2760)

    (i-4) epistemic conjunction: with a noun [with N]
        <u>it's a shame</u> you don't drive *because* then that way you will have your Saturdays free
                                      (BNC (sp): KCP4577)

(ii-1) speech-act conjunction: with an expression of speech-act [with SA]

    <u>do you</u> want somewhere to warm to work# at the weekends#

    because there's my place you can

                                                   (LLC: 2 4a 42 4440–4470)

(ii-2) speech-act conjunction: with a speech-act verb [with SAV]

    yes <u>I wish</u> we could do that again# *cos* that was really child's play wasn't it#

                                                   (LLC: 2 4a 42 4440–4470)

With regard to a total of 205 examples of (51a) [CL1 *because* CL2] in the synchronic data, the distribution of overt expressions specified in (54) in the "main" clause (CL1) is given in Table 3.2 and those in the *because*-clause (CL2) in Table 3.3.

Table 3.2: The distribution of (54) in "main" clauses in the synchronic data

Main clause (CL1)	–2000 (wr) (BNC)	–2000 (sp) (BNC)	–2000 (sp) (LLC)	TOTAL
(i-1) with EM	0	1	9	10 (4.9%)
(i-2) with EE	3	7	0	10 (4.9%)
(i-3) with A	0	3	13	16 (7.8%)
(i-4) with N	4	2	8	14 (6.8%)
TOTAL of (i)	7 (15.2%)	13 (29.5%)	30 (26.1%)	50 (24.4%)
(ii-1) with SA	8	9	9	26 (12.8%)
(ii-2) with SAV	2	3	12	17 (8.3%)
TOTAL of (ii)	10 (21.7%)	12 (27.3%)	21 (18.3%)	43 (21.0%)
(iii) Others	29 (63.0%)	19 (43.2%)	64 (55.7%)	112 (54.6%)
TOTAL	46	44	115	205

Table 3.3: The distribution of (54) in *because*-clauses in the synchronic data

Because-clause (CL2)	–2000 (wr) (BNC)	–2000 (sp) (BNC)	–2000 (sp) (LLC)	TOTAL
(i-1) with EM	1	4	4	9 (4.4%)
(i-2) with EE	4	5	0	9 (4.4%)
(i-3) with A	4	1	5	10 (4.9%)
(i-4) with N	3	2	5	10 (6.8%)
TOTAL of (i)	12 (26.1%)	12 (27.3%)	14 (12.2%)	38 (18.5%)
(ii-1) with SA	2	2	5	9 (4.4%)
(ii-2) with SAV	1	2	3	6 (2.9%)
TOTAL of (ii)	3 (6.5%)	4 (9.1%)	8 (7.0%)	15 (7.3%)
(iii) Others	31 (67.4%)	28 (63.6%)	93 (80.9%)	152 (74.1%)
TOTAL	46	44	115	205

Of the 205 "main" clauses, 24.4% of them have overt expressions of epistemic conjunction interpretation and 21.0% of them speech-act conjunction interpretation. Roughly speaking, as far as the data for the present study is concerned, 45% of the "main" clauses have overt expressions of epistemic or speech-act conjunction interpretation in PDE. As for *because*-clauses, 18.5% of them have overt expressions of epistemic conjunction interpretation and 7.3% of them speech-act conjunction interpretation. Approximately, a quarter of *because*-clauses have overt expressions of epistemic or speech-act conjunction interpretation in PDE.[40]

Having observed the distribution of (54) in PDE, we go on to observe the transition of the distribution of these overt expressions based on both the diachronic and synchronic data. In comparison with the synchronic data, instances in each type are sporadic and small in number in the periods of 50 years throughout the diachronic data. In order to see a general trend in the transition of the distribution, let us concentrate on the totals in both data here. A total of 199 examples of (51a) [CL1 *because* CL2] in the diachronic data (from 1590s to 1950, about 350 years) are compared to the 205 examples in the synchronic data (1950–2000, about 50 years) in Tables 3.4 and 3.5. The following are examples of overt expressions of epistemic and speech-act conjunction interpretation from the diachronic data.

(55) [Examples of (i-1)–(ii-2) in the diachronic data]
    (i-1) epistemic conjunction: with an epistemic modality [with EM]
        Juliet   … Lest in this marriage he <u>should</u> be dishonour'd
        Because he married me before to Romeo?
                            (1594–5 *Romeo and Juliet*, Act IV, Scene iii)
    (i-2) epistemic conjunction: with an epistemic expression [with EE]
        "It was alive four days after, <u>I know</u>, and down a grating in Great Titchfield Street; *because* I saw a crowd round the place, trying to see whence the miaowing came."   (1897 *The invisible man*, Chapter 20)
    (i-3) epistemic conjunction: with an adjective [with A]
        "…, and <u>it is good</u> for them, *because* they handle a lot of diverse wares and get to   learn about them, …" (1891 *News from nowhere*, p. 44)
    (i-4) epistemic conjunction: with a noun [with N]
        Hell. … <u>that will be our Destiny</u>, *because* we are both of one humour;
                              (1677 *The Rover*, Act III, Scene I)
    (ii-1) speech-act conjunction: with an expression of speech-act [with SA]
        Grace him as he deserves, And <u>let</u> him not be entertain'd the worse *Because* he favours me.   (1633 *The Jew of Malta*, Act I, Scene I)

(ii-2) speech-act conjunction: with a speech-act verb [with SAV]

    Barabas

    No, but <u>I grieve</u> *because* she liv'd so long.

                          (1633 *The Jew of Malta*, Act IV, Scene I)

Table 3.4: The comparison of the distribution of (54) in "main" clauses between the diachronic and synchronic data

Main clause (CL1)	Diachronic (1590–1950)	Synchronic (1950–2000)
(i-1) with EM	18 (9.0%)	10 (4.9%)
(i-2) with EE	14 (7.0%)	10 (4.9%)
(i-3) with A	1 (0.5%)	16 (7.8%)
(i-4) with N	2 (1.0%)	14 (6.8%)
TOTAL of (i)	35 (17.6%)	50 (24.4%)
(b-1) with SA	14 (7.0%)	26 (12.8%)
(b-2) with SAV	17 (8.5%)	17 (8.3%)
TOTAL of (ii)	31 (15.6%)	43 (21.0%)
(iii) Others	133 (66.8%)	112 (54.6%)
TOTAL	199	205

Table 3.5: The comparison of the distribution of (54) in *because*-clauses between the diachronic and synchronic data

Because-clause (CL2)	Diachronic (1590–1950)	Synchronic (1950–2000)
(i-1) with EM	6 (3.0%)	9 (4.4%)
(i-2) with EE	20 (10.1%)	9 (4.4%)
(i-3) with A	0 (0%)	10 (4.9%)
(i-4) with N	3 (1.5%)	10 (6.8%)
TOTAL of (i)	29 (14.6%)	38 (18.5%)
(i-1) with SA	3 (1.5%)	9 (4.4%)
(i-2) with SAV	2 (1.0%)	6 (2.9%)
TOTAL of (ii)	5 (2.5%)	15 (7.3%)
(iii) Others	165 (82.9%)	152 (74.1%)
TOTAL	199	205

Of the 199 "main" clauses in the diachronic data, 17.6% of them have overt expressions of epistemic conjunction interpretation and 15.6% of them speech-act conjunction interpretation. When we compare these percentages with those in the synchronic data, i.e., 24.4% and 21.0% respectively, we can be fairly certain that the overt expressions of these types of interpretation in "main" clauses increase proportionately over the past 50 years. As regards *because*-clauses in the diachronic data, 14.6% of them have overt expressions of epistemic conjunction interpretation and 2.5% of them speech-act conjunction interpretation. When these percentages are compared with those in the synchronic data, i.e., 18.5% and 7.3% respectively, we can say that the overt expressions of these types of interpretation in *because*-clauses are also on the increase during the past 50 years. What is noticeable in Tables 3.4 and 3.5 is that overt expressions of these types of interpretation increase proportionately in both clauses in PDE. In other words, the correlation between syntactic and semantic/pragmatic functions of *because*-clauses becomes overtly expressed in PDE.[41]

Next, we extend the observation made so far to that of the independent *because*-clauses, i.e., (51c) [*Because* CL], and compare the distribution of the overt expressions listed in (54) above. There are a total of 11 examples in the diachronic data (from 1770s to 1950, about 180 years) and a total of 34 examples in the synchronic data (from 1950 to 2000, about 50 years).[42]

(56) [Examples of (51c) in the diachronic data]

    a. FURTIVO

    No, 'tis well known, sir, I have a master the very picture of wisdom—

    LATRONELLO

    [Aside] for indeed he speaks not one wise word

    FURTIVO

    and no man but will admire to hear of his virtues—

    LATRONELLO

    [Aside] *Because* he ne'er had any in all his life.

    FALSO

    You write all down, Latronello?

                                     (1603–4 *The Phoenix*, III.i.)

    b. SURFACE

    Surely Land Sneerwell I am the greatest Sufferer – yet you see I bear the accident with Calmness.

    LADY SNEERWELL

    Because the Disappointment hasn't reached your HEART – your interest only attached you to Maria – had you felt for her …

                                  (1777 *The school for scandal*, ACT II. SCENE II)

(57) [Examples of (51c) in the synchronic data][43]

    (i-1) epistemic conjunction: with an epistemic modality [with EM]

        a: how soon do you want these back?

        A: I don't know# doesn't really

        a: *because* it <u>may</u> take us a month or so to sort of sort through them and decide you know whether we wish to approach you to ask if we make use of them

        A: yeah#

                                             (LLC: 2 2a 36 2090–37 2130)

    (i-2) epistemic conjunction: with an epistemic expression [with EE]

        A: ... and I think Sall's started buying it as a result of that#

        a: has she

        (A: *because* there still <u>seems</u> to be some in the box#)

        A: and

        a: yeah

                                                  (LLC: 1 7 9 840–10 880)

    (ii-1) speech-act conjunction: with an expression of speech-act [with SA]

        (a: it's all covered by the mortgage#)

        b: but the mortgage# is doing you quite well on that one# <u>isn't it</u>#?

        cos I saw a piece of paper# in your bedroom#

        a: how do you mean# doing us quite well#?

                                                  (LLC: 4 2 16 2220–2290)

    (ii-2) speech-act conjunction: with a speech-act verb [with SAV]

        B: I hope you'll accept my word on this #

        a: yes

        B: because <u>I mean</u> it#

        a: all right I will

                                                  (LLC: 2 1 13 1710–1740)

Table 3.6: The comparison of the distribution of (54) in (51c) [*Because* CL] between the diachronic and synchronic data

	Diachronic (1770–1950)	Synchronic (1950–2000)
(i-1) with EM	0 -	3 (8.8%)
(i-2) with EE	0 -	5 (14.7%)
(i-3) with A	0 -	0 (0%)
(i-4) with N	0 -	0 (0%)
TOTAL of (i)	0 (0%)	10 (29.4%)
(b-1) with SA	0 -	3 (8.8%)
(b-2) with SAV	0 -	2 (2.9%)
TOTAL of (ii)	0 -	5 (14.7%)
(iii) Others	11 (100%)	19 (55.9%)
TOTAL	11	34

Table 3.6 shows the increase in overt expressions of (54) in independent *because*-clauses in PDE. Of the 11 examples in the diachronic data, we find no instances with an overt expression of epistemic/speech-act conjunction interpretation.[44] Of the 34 examples in the synchronic data, there are 10 clauses (29.4%) with an overt expression of epistemic conjunction interpretation and 5 (14.7%) with that of speech-act conjunction interpretation. As far as the data for the present study is concerned, independent *because*-clauses acquire an overt expression of epistemic and speech-act conjunction interpretation in PDE.

In this subsection, we have observed the transition of the correlation between syntactic and semantic/pragmatic functions of *because*-clauses. We found that *because*-clause constructions with content conjunction interpretation are on the decrease, whereas those with epistemic/speech-act conjunction interpretation are on the increase in PDE. From the viewpoint of semantic/pragmatic functions, the trend is from content to epistemic/speech-act conjunction interpretation in PDE.

3.4.4 Summary

Section 3.4 examined the developmental process of *because*-clauses mainly from EModE to PDE. Section 3.4.1 presented the data used for this section in detail. From the viewpoint of clause-combining constructions, 3.4.2 examined the development of *because*-clauses in detail and showed the ongoing process toward independent clauses. From the viewpoint of the correlation between syntactic and semantic/ pragmatic functions, 3.4.3 inquired into the transition of the correlation. It demonstrated that the correlation becomes overtly expressed and the interpretation of *because*-clauses tends toward epistemic/speech-act conjunction in PDE.

Based on the observations in this section, together with what is pointed out in the previous studies taken up in 3.2 and 3.3 above, we can summarize the developmental process of *because*-clauses from LME to PDE in the following way:

(58) The developmental path of *because*-clauses from LME to PDE

    LME: CL1 *by (the) cause (that)* CL2
               [CL1 [*by (the) cause (that)* CL2]]

               CL1+CL2: subordination
               CL2: subordinate
               CM: phrasal SCM
                    ↓
    EModE: CL1 *because (that)* CL2
               [CL1 [*because (that)* CL2]]

CL1+CL2: subordination/hypotaxis

CL2: subordinate/hypotactic

CM: phrasal (?)/single SCM

    ↓

LModE: CL1 *because* CL2

[CL1 [*because* CL2]]

CL1+CL2: hypotaxis

CL2: hypotactic

CM: single SCM

    ↓   ↘   ↘

PDE: CL1 *because* CL2   CL1 *because* CL2   ø *because/'cos* CL

[CL1 [*because* CL2]] [CL1] [*because* CL2] ø [*because/'cos* CL]

CL1+CL2: hypotaxis	CL1+CL2: parataxis	ø+CL: parataxis
CL2: hypotactic	CL2: paratactic	CL: independent
CM: single SCM	CM: conjunction-like single CM	CM: single PM
	Interpretation:	
Interpretation:	epistemic conjunction/	
content conjunction	speech-act conjunction	

We limit our attention to the following two points for the purpose of considering the developmental process of *because*-clauses from the perspective of grammaticalization in the next section.[45]

First, we consider the development of *because*-clauses in terms of structural function. [CL1+CL2] in (58) above represents a distinction in clause-combining constructions posited by Hopper and Traugott (2003:176–184) (see 2.2.5 above). It shows that the relationship between the "main" clauses and *because*-clauses have developed from subordination via hypotaxis to parataxis. As "CL2" indicates, *because*-clauses have extended from subordinate via hypotactic to paratactic clauses. Then, they come to be more paratactic, i.e., independent, in PDE. "CM" shows that *because* has developed from phrasal expressions in various forms to a single subordinate clause marker. Then, the function of *because* comes to be a conjunction-like clause marker and a pragmatic marker (see 2.3.2.1 above). The developmental paths under investigation can be summarized in the following way:

(59) The development of *because*-clauses in structural function:
    a. clause-combining constructions:
        subordination > hypotaxis > parataxis
    b. *because*-clauses:
        subordinate > hypotactic > paratactic > independent
    c. *because*:
        phrasal expression > subordinate clause marker >
        conjunction-like clause marker > pragmatic marker

Second, it is important to note the development of *because*-clauses in view of semantic/pragmatic function. "Interpretation" in PDE shows an interpretation of *because*-clauses that is correlated with each structure (see 2.3.1.1). The trend of the semantic/pragmatic function of *because*-clauses is toward epistemic/speech-act conjunction interpretation in PDE. It can be summarized in the following way:

(60) The development of *because*-clauses in semantic/pragmatic function:
    content conjunction > epistemic/speech-act conjunction

In the following section, we will discuss the development of *because*-clauses in the light of grammaticalization.

3.5 Discussion

This section discusses the structural and semantic/pragmatic extensions of *because*-clauses from the perspective of grammaticalization. Section 3.5.1 focuses on multiple functions of *because*-clauses in PDE and considers the motivations behind such diversity. Section 3.5.2 shows that the diachronic process and synchronic diversity of *because*-clauses can be viewed as a case of grammaticalization. Section 3.5.3 raises the issue of the unidirectional hypothesis in terms of structure and semantics/pragmatics. Section 3.5.4 introduces some analogous cases in the history of the English language.

3.5.1 Multiple functions of *because*-clauses in present-day English

In the preceding section, it was found that independent *because*-clauses increase proportionately in PDE (see Table 3.1) and those with an overt expression of epistemic/speech-act conjunction interpretation are on the increase over the past 50 years (see Table 3.4 and 3.5). Based on these observations, it seems reasonable to suppose that *because*-clauses have developed toward being independent of their "main" clauses and come to be used to express more subjective meanings in PDE. In other words, *because*-clauses in PDE can be viewed as being in the process of being reanalyzed as independent main clauses with a clause-initial pragmatic marker. The reanalysis of subordinate *because*-clauses as independent can be schematized as follows (see 2.3.2.1 and 3.2.1.2):

(61) Reanalysis of *because*-clauses as independent in PDE:

      Subordinate   **Independent**

      CL1 *because* CL2   ø   *because* CL

      [CL1 + [SCM + CL2]]   ø   [PM + CL]

In addition, it was observed in the preceding section that both "main" clauses and *because*-clauses acquire an overt expression of epistemic/speech-act conjunction interpretation in PDE (see Tables 3.2 and 3.3). Insofar as *because*-clauses can be viewed as being related to the speech-act performed in their "main" clauses, *because*-clause constructions with epistemic/speech-act conjunction interpretation tend to be more paratactic than those with content conjunction interpretation (see 3.2.1.1 and 3.2.2). Hence, we can postulate that *because*-clauses acquire multiple functions in PDE in the following way:

(62) Structural and semantic/pragmatic extension of *because*-clause constructions in PDE:

Subordinate	**Paratactic**	**Independent**
[CL1 [*because* CL2]] ⟶	[CL1] [*because* CL2] ⟶	ø [*because* CL]
content conjunction	epistemic/speech-act conjunction	pragmatically invited (or imposed) conjunction

Let us now consider motivations behind the extension. As Tables 3.2 and 3.3 show, *because*-clause constructions with epistemic/speech-act conjunction interpretation are on the increase in their developmental process. As such constructions become frequently used, the association between the construction and epistemic/speech-act conjunction interpretation becomes stronger. Once such an association is conventionalized as part of *because*-clause constructions, the speaker can expect the hearer to interpret a paratactic *because*-clause construction as being pragmatically linked to the preceding (or sometimes following) clause. We may speculate that it is linked to the speech-act performed in its pragmatically associated "main" clause. Furthermore, as paratactic constructions come to be frequently used in such discourse context, the association between such constructions and the interpretation becomes stronger and gradually conventionalized as part of *because*-clause constructions. As Table 3.4 indicates, independent *because*-clauses that have overt expressions of epistemic/speech-act conjunction have increased during the past 50 years. It seems that the association is being conventionalized and the speaker may assume the hearer to interpret an independent *because*-clause as being pragmatically linked to the preceding (or following) context. In other words, we can say that a *because*-clause is in the process of being reanalyzed (or grammaticalized) as a clause-initial pragmatic marker plus a single independent clause in PDE. Indeed, *because* begins to give rise to a pragmatic function such as an indicator of "continuation and response in conversational interaction" (Schleppegrell, 1991), "a means of doing continuation" (Couper-Kuhlen, 1996), "a take-off for further talk" (Stenström, 1998), etc. The pragmatic characteristics of *because* become stronger as the stages in (62) progress. Therefore, it seems reasonable to suppose that *because* is in the process of developing into a clause-initial pragmatic marker in PDE.[46] On these grounds, we may reasonably conclude that the development of *because*-clauses from subordinate to independent clauses is motivated by conventionalization of pragmatic meanings.[47]

3.5.2 Development of *because*-clauses as an instance of grammaticalization

We have to inquire into whether the development of *because*-clauses from subordinate to independent clauses is an instance of grammaticalization. Here, reference is made to the five principles of grammaticalization proposed by Hopper (1991) (see 2.2.3 above).[48] While the development under investigation is not necessarily a textbook case of grammaticalization, i.e., the change from a lexical to a grammatical item, it does share characteristics associated with grammaticalization (Brinton, 2001).

First, the coexistence of subordinate, paratactic, and independent uses of *because*-clauses in PDE can be counted as an example of "layering", the coexistence of older and new layers.[49] In respect of clause markers, the following cases of "layering" are found in the diachronic and synchronic data; (i) the coexistence of several competing forms, such as *by cause that*, *bycause*, *bicause*, etc., from LME to EModE (see (52) in 3.4.2), (ii) the coexistence of the functions of *because* as a subordinate clause marker, a conjunction-like clause marker, and a pragmatic marker in PDE (see (58) in 3.4.4), and (iii) the coexistence of *because* and *'cos* in PDE conversation (see 3.2.1).

Second, the correlation between syntactic and semantic/pragmatic functions of *because*-clauses in PDE can be interpreted as an instance of "divergence", which "results in pairs or multiples of forms having a common etymology, but diverging functionally" (Hopper, 1991:24).[50] In 3.2, we reviewed that an interpretation of *because*-clauses as content conjunction typically corresponds to a subordinate *because*-clause whereas that as epistemic/speech-act conjunction tends to be associated with a paratactic *because*-clause in PDE. In 3.4.2, we showed the transition of *because*-clauses from less to more paratactic clause-combining constructions. In 3.4.3, we pointed out the trend of the interpretation of *because*-clauses from content to epistemic/speech-act conjunction. The functional diversity observed in PDE *because*-clauses can be regarded as an incipient stage where one form diverges functionally.

In the light of the causal clause markers, the existence of the clause marker *because* and the noun *cause* in PDE is easily referred to as an instance of "divergence". The single causal clause marker *because* in PDE is traced back to the several forms of phrasal expressions in LME which comprise the lexical form *cause*. Moreover, the original lexical form still remains as an autonomous element in PDE. The existence of *because* and *'cos* in PDE also exemplifies "divergence". They diverge functionally in the sense that the latter is observable mostly in spoken or written colloquial discourse. Moreover, the latter tends to mark paratactic relationship to a prior clause (Couper-Kuhlen, 1996; Stenström and Andersen, 1996; and Stenström, 1998, among others). To put it differently, *because* can be considered as in the process of diverging into a causal subordinate clause marker, a conjunction-like paratactic clause marker, and a pragmatic marker in PDE.

Third, the process whereby several forms of phrasal expressions that include the lexical form *cause* in LME developed into the single "causal" clause marker *because* in PDE illustrates "persistence". It refers to retention of the original lexical meanings in the grammaticalized form. Moreover, the "causal" meaning is retained in the variety of semantic/pragmatic functions of *because*-clauses (see 2.3.1.1) as well as the function of *because* as a pragmatic marker in the case of independent *because*-clauses (see 2.3.2.1 and 3.2.2) in PDE. These observations illustrate that "grammaticalized construction is constrained by its origins (Hopper and Traugott, 2003:121)".

Lastly, the development from several forms of the phrasal expressions containing the noun *cause*, i.e., a full member of a major grammatical category, to the causal clause marker *because* and the pragmatic marker *because/'cos*, i.e., members of a minor grammatical category, can be understood as an example of "de-categorialization".[51]

Following Hopper's (1991) principles of grammaticalization, we have so far demonstrated that the diachronic process and synchronic functional diversity of *because*-clauses share some characteristics associated with grammaticalization. They can be properly treated as a case of grammaticalization.

3.5.3 Development of *because*-clauses and the hypothesis of unidirectionality

We then consider the hypothesis of unidirectionality in grammaticalization. It is generally hypothesized in the literature that the direction of structural change is toward increase in bondedness whereas that of semantic/pragmatic change is toward increase in subjectivity (see 2.2.4). We confine our attention to two kinds of unidirectionality, namely the cline of clause-combining constructions (see 2.2.5) and subjectification (see 2.2.6).

First, we examine the cline of clause-combining constructions. It postulates that the development of clause combining goes along the following cline in the process of grammaticalization.

(63) A cline of clause-combining construction in grammaticalization

    parataxis   >   hypotaxis   >   subordination

(Hopper and Traugott, 2003:177)

The cline predicts that the direction of the development is from more to less paratactic clause-combining constructions along with grammaticalization. On the contrary, it was shown in 3.4.2 that *because*-clauses are developing from less to more paratactic clause-combining constructions. Moreover, the increase in proportion of independent *because*-clause in PDE points toward much looser clause-combining constructions. Given that an independent *because*-clause is paratactic to the preceding (or sometimes following) discourse, the development of *because*-clauses can be summarized as follows:[52]

(64) The development of *because*-clauses in terms of clause-combining constructions:
    (subordination)   >   hypotaxis   >   parataxis   >   paratactic to discourse

Therefore, we claim that the developmental path of *because*-clauses poses another counter-example to the unidirectional cline of clause-combining constructions in grammaticalization.

Next, we consider the hypothesis of semantic/pragmatic unidirectionality in the process of grammaticalization, i.e., subjectification.[53] It is defined as "the historical pragmatic-semantic process whereby meanings become increasingly based in the speaker's subjective belief state, or attitude toward what is said" (Traugott, 1997:185). We can say that causality in the epistemic/speech-act domain is more subjective than that in content domain in the sense that the former concerns the "speaker's subjective belief state, or attitude", whereas the latter involves causality in real world. Thus, the gradual increase of *because*-clauses associated with epistemic/speech-act conjunction interpretation in their developmental process (see 3.4.3) is considered to be an example of subjectification.

In addition, the function of *because* as a pragmatic marker in the case of independent *because*-clauses (see 2.3.2.1 and 3.2.2) can be counted as another example of subjectification. Here, R. Suzuki's (1998a) discussion on the development of *wake* 'reason' from a lexical noun to a pragmatic particle in Japanese helps account for subjectification in the case of *because* functioning as a pragmatic marker. She argues that "the speaker seems to invite the hearer (or impose on the hearer) to accept there is a logical relationship between the *wake*-clause and its preceding discourse" (R. Suzuki, 1998a:80) when the *wake* clause appears independently. The same account holds for the function of *because* as a pragmatic marker. In the case of subordinate and paratactic *because*-clauses, there is a causal relation between the *because*-clause and its preceding (or following) clause whether it is interpreted as content or epistemic/speech-act conjunction. In the case of an independent *because*-clause, the speaker may expect the hearer to interpret it as being logically related to the preceding (or following) discourse.[54] In this sense, it seems reasonable to suppose that the function of *because* as a pragmatic marker is more subjective than that as a subordinate or paratactic clause marker. Accordingly, the increase of independent *because*-clauses in PDE (see 3.4.2) can be regarded as an example of subjectification.

Viewed in this light, the direction of the semantic/pragmatic development undergone by *because*-clauses is toward an increase in subjectivity along with grammaticalization. It can be summarized in the following way:

(65) The development of *because*-clauses in terms of semantic/pragmatic functions:

	content conjunction	less subjective
>	epistemic/speech-act conjunction	↓
>	pragmatically invited (or imposed) conjunction to discourse	more subjective

We can say that the semantic/pragmatic aspect of the development of *because*-clauses is in accord with the hypothesis of semantic/pragmatic unidirectionality.

We have so far shown that the development of *because*-clauses from subordinate to independent clauses poses a counter-example to the unidirectional cline of clause-combining constructions whereas it supports the hypothesis of semantic/pragmatic unidirectionality in the process of grammaticalization.

3.5.4 Other analogous cases in English

In this subsection, we introduce some other analogous cases in the history of the English language in order to show that structural and semantic/pragmatic extensions in the developmental process of *because*-clauses are not exceptional, but commonly found in English.

First, the semantic/pragmatic trend toward an increase in subjective meanings is found in the development of other causal clauses in the history of English.[55] Kortmann (1997:291–335) comprehensively studies the history of adverbial subordinators in English and points out:

> The most general tendency that can be identified is that "semantic changes involving CCC relations (notably Condition, Cause, Concession, Concessive Condition, Result, and Purpose) seem to be unidirectional ... This tendency shows up time and again in accounts of directions of semantic change which have variously been described in terms of "concrete > abstract", "propositional > textual > expressive" ... or a conventionalization of conversational implicatures.
>
> (Kortmann, 1997:319)

Sweetser (1991) also reports that "*since* already has a strong tendency towards an epistemic or a speech-act reading, rather than towards a content-conjunction reading" (1991:82) in PDE. Assuming that this tendency shows inception of semantic/pragmatic extension, we may reasonably say that *since*-clauses will increasingly tend toward epistemic/speech-act conjunction interpretation, i.e., toward an increase in subjective meanings in the future, much as the interpretation of *because*-clauses has become more subjective in PDE.

However, we must note the functional differentiation between a *because*-clause and a *since*-clause in PDE. It is pointed out that causal clauses in PDE are often distinguished according to whether the information in the causal clause is assumed to be known/given or not (Traugott, 1992:252). The causal *since* is usually used for a "given" causal and it cannot be used in answer to a *why* question. Moreover, it is usually placed in pre-main clause position.

(66) a. *Since* I missed the bus, I am late.

    b. Why are you late? *Since I missed the bus.

(adapted from Traugott, 1992:252)

On the other hand, a *because*-clause is mostly placed in post-main clause position (see Table 3.1). It is not necessarily used for a "given" causal. In view of "given" information or not, it is likely that a *since*-clause is used for a piece of "given" information in pre-main clause position whereas a *because*-clause conveys a piece of "new" information in post-main clause position in PDE. In other words, these clauses are functionally differentiated in PDE. Thus, *since* in place of *because* in post-main clause position sounds puzzling to a native speaker of English, if not ungrammatical.[56]

(67) Are you going to the post office, *since* I have some letters to send?

Paul J. Hopper (p.c.) interprets (67) as suggesting that the listener would know already that the speaker has some letters to send, and the speaker is reminding him or her of that fact. It sounds as if the speaker is saying "since, as you are aware, I have some letters to send". For this reason, *since* sounds a little as if the speaker is angry or exasperated. *Because* in place of *since* would not imply any previous knowledge, but it is a newly added explanation. It would be a polite request and would not imply anger or exasperation. Further research on *because*-clauses, *since*-clauses, and some other causal clauses such as *for* and *as* from the viewpoint of "given" or "new" information and of pre-main or post-main clause position will clarify the functional differentiation and pragmatic effects among them in PDE.[57]

Second, the shift of causal clauses from less to more paratactic relationship to their "main" clauses is attested in the development of *for*-clauses. As we mentioned in passing in 3.3.1, various causal constructions with *for* in OE are simplified to *for (that)* in ME, and then the optional *that* becomes obsolete by the end of the seventeenth century. In EModE, "clauses introduced by causative *for* lose some of their subordinate characteristics" (Rissanen, 1999:282). In PDE, a *for*-clause is generally analyzed as a conjunction plus a coordinate clause, i.e., a clause-initial coordinate clause marker plus a single independent clause in our terms, which appears in written or rather archaic discourse in PDE. Thus, we can say that *for*-clauses have already undergone the change from subordinate to paratactic relationship to their "main" clauses. We predict that this will be the path taken by *because*-clauses in the future based on the their synchronic diversity.[58]

Third, there are some other cases of ongoing reanalysis of subordinate clauses as independent in PDE. Based on the analysis of conversations in the present-day American English, Thompson and Mulac (1991) explain the phenomenon of "*that*-deletion" from the multi-clause construction *I/you think* or *I/you guess* plus a clause in terms of grammaticalization of "epistemic phrases".[59]

(68) I think *0* exercise is really beneficial, to anybody [*sic*]

(Thompson and Mulac, 1991:313)

(69) It's just your point of view you know what you like to do in your spare time *I think* [*sic*] (Thompson and Mulac, 1991:313)

They suggest that *I think* in the above examples "is an epistemic phrase, expressing the degree of speaker commitment, functioning approximately as an epistemic adverb such as *maybe* with respect to the clause it is associated with" (Thompson and Mulac, 1991:313). Viewed in this light, the multiclause construction in (68) can be viewed as being reanalyzed as a clause-initial pragmatic marker plus a single clause and that in (69) as a single clause plus a clause-final pragmatic marker in PDE.[60] The phenomenon analyzed by Thompson and Mulac (1991) provides yet another example of subordinate clauses that can be regarded as main in PDE.

Lastly, the phenomenon of pragmatic markers developing from other types of clause-initial items is frequently attested to in the history of English.[61] For example, Traugott and Dasher (2002: Ch. 4) make a diachronic examination of *indeed, in fact,* and *actually*, and show that a clause-internal adverb has developed into an epistemic sentential adverb and then into a pragmatic marker.[62] They also discuss the development of *well* and *let's* as pragmatic markers.[63] These cases are also counted as instances of subjectification. The functional extension of *because* as a pragmatic marker in the case of independent *because*-clauses in PDE is analogous to the frequently attested development of pragmatic markers in English.

We have seen some instances of structural and semantic/pragmatic developments in English that appear to be parallel to those of *because*-clauses. They suggest that some types of structural and semantic/pragmatic processes undergone by *because*-clauses are recurrently found in the history of English.

In this chapter, we examined the developmental process of *because*-clauses in detail. After giving a general picture of *because*-clauses in PDE in 3.2 and introducing the history of *because*-clauses in 3.3, we traced the structural and semantic/pragmatic development of *because*-clauses in 3.4. Finally, we discussed the development from the perspective of grammaticalization in 3.5. It was suggested that *because*-clauses are in the process of being reanalyzed as a single independent clause with a clause-initial pragmatic marker in PDE. In addition, it was pointed out that the developmental process of *because*-clauses is an instance of grammaticalization although it is not a textbook case. Then, we examined the hypothesis of unidirectionality in grammaticalization. It was claimed that the development under investigation poses a counter-example to the hypothesis of structural unidirectionality while it is a case in support of the hypothesis of semantic/pragmatic unidirectionality in the process of grammaticalization. What has to be noticed in the developmental process of *because*-clauses is that it is motivated by conventionalization of pragmatic meanings.

I hope to have shown how *because*-clauses, so-called subordinate clauses, come to acquire multiple functions in PDE and that such an extension is not random but motivated. There is room for further investigation into independent *because*-clauses from this perspective in order to understand the mechanisms of grammaticalization and subjectification. In the following chapter, we examine the Japanese equivalent of English *because*-clauses, i.e., *kara*-clauses. The point to observe is that *kara*-clauses have developed in the same direction as *because*-clauses in both structural and semantic/pragmatic aspects.

Notes

1. In what follows, *because* and its phonologically reduced form such as *'cause* and *'cos* are represented by *because* unless otherwise noted.
2. For further discussion of the problem of 'subordination', see, for example, Haiman and Thompson (1984), Thompson and Longacre (1985), Matthiessen and Thompson (1988).
3. For other studies on non-subordinate uses of *because*-clauses, see, for example, Jespersen (1909–1946, Part V:394), Rutherford (1970), Kac (1972), Quirk et al. (1972, 1985), Green (1976), Bolinger (1977), Mittwoch (1977), McTear (1980), Levinson (1983), Stubbs (1983), Altenberg (1984), Chafe (1984, 1988), Lakoff (1984), Halliday (1985), Thorne (1986), Schleppegrell (1991), Ford (1993), Couper-Kuhlen (1996), Stenström and Andersen (1996), Stenström (1998), and S. Tanaka (2002).
4. In what follows, the term "discourse marker" is used if it is originally used in earlier studies. Otherwise, the term "pragmatic marker" will be used in the present study (see 2.3.2.1).
5. Altenberg (1984) points out that "the difference between 'sentence connection', coordination and subordination is often blurred, not only in speech where the sentence has doubtful grammatical status and where clauses introduced by a subordinator are often used independently, but also in writing where syntactic units are frequently separated by punctuation in an arbitrary way" (1984:41 Note 3).
6. Chafe (1984, 1988) and Couper-Kuhlen (1996) consider *because*-clauses as independent based on the examination of their prosodic characteristics. See 3.2.3 below for further details.
7. Schleppegrell (1991:332–333) examines a case where propositional (i.e., subordinating), textual (i.e., the first role of her differentiation), and interactional (i.e., the second and the third roles) roles of *because* merge and admits that they are not always separable. See Schiffrin (1987:210–216) for similar comments.
8. Schiffrin (1987:191–227) regards the function of *because* as a marker of subordinate idea units in the discourse, which reflects their grammatical function as a subordinator.
9. While the change of *'cos* from a subordinator to a discourse marker is regarded as a result of pragmaticalization in Stenström and Andersen (1996), Stenström (1998) maintains that it should be explained in terms of grammaticalization rather than pragmaticalization. In the present study, it will be shown that the functional extension of *because*-clauses as a whole can be regarded as grammaticalization involving subjectification (Traugott, 1989, 1995a, 1997, etc.; and Traugott and Dasher, 2002).
10. According to Sweetser (1990:78), the ambiguities in the three domains are the clearest for the class of causal and adversative conjunctions although the ambiguities "are

present in the usage of a much larger class of lexical items."
11. See Stubbs (1983:80–81) for a similar discussion on the correlation between syntactic and semantic/pragmatic properties of *because*-clauses.
12. Altenberg (1984:49–50) makes a similar observation on the pragmatic functions of independent *because*-clauses.
13. Examples (28)–(30) are adapted from Stenström (1998:128–129).
14. The distinction between subordinate and non-subordinate *because*-clauses from the viewpoint of intonation is also given in Schleppegrell (1991). She explains that the former is "intonationally integrated with a prior clause" whereas the latter is "preceded by a pause and new intonatinal contour" (p. 325). Similar intonational grounds for the distinction between subordinate and non-subordinate *because*-clauses have been suggested in the literature. See Jespersen (1909–1949, Part V, 394) and Bolinger (1984), for example. For the distinction in *because*-clauses based on intonation and the presuppositionality, see Rutherford (1970) and Thorne (1986), for example.

    We can make use of prosodic characteristics discussed in Quirk et al. (1985) above only when we analyzed the data from LLC in 3.4 below.

    It is pointed out that whether a *because*-clause is restrictive or non-restrictive is also reflected in punctuation, although it is not always consistent (Quirk et al., 1985:1628; Stenström, 1998:129–130).
15. Based on Chafe (1984), Sweetser (1991:82–86) discusses the relationship between the intonation and the interpretation of causal conjunctions. She points out that a commaless intonation-pattern (i.e., bound, integrated intonation in one tone unit) is impossible for epistemic-domain and speech-act-domain causal conjunctions such as *because* and *despite* (1991:83).
16. Couper-Kuhlen (1996) states that "reliance on pitch alone (or even on, pitch and syntax alone) as signals of turn completion may lead to faulty predictions (1996:395 Note 5) ".
17. Altenberg (1984) and Chafe (1984) pay attention to the reflection of syntactic units into punctuation. On the one hand, Altenberg states that "syntactic units are frequently separated by punctuation in an arbitrary way" (1984:41 Note 3) in writing. On the other hand, Chafe comments that "it is roughly true that the intonation units of speech are mimicked in writing by what I will call 'punctuation units'. A punctuation unit is any stretch of written language between punctuation marks. It seems that earlier writers of American English used punctuation to imitate intonation units more consistently than many recent writers do" (Chafe, 1984:438).
18. Approximate stages of English adopted in the present study are given in Page xi.
19. The history of causal clauses in English reviewed in this section is mainly based on *The*

Cambridge History of the English Language (*CHEL*), Kortmann (1997), and Rissanen (1998). The examples in this section are cited from *CHEL*, *Middle English Dictionary* (*MED*), and *The Oxford English Dictionary* (*OED*).

20. The causal clauses as well as other complex clause structures in OE are not apparently subordinate as in PDE. For further details of causal clauses in OE and ME, see *CHEL* (vol. I:219–222, 253, and vol. II:345–347). For detailed accounts of complex clause structures in OE and ME, see *CHEL* (vol. II:285–295).

21. The causal constructions with the subordinate particle *þe* "seem more likely than those without to express true source or cause rather than explanation" (*CHEL*, vol. I:253). This comment has much in common with the correlation between syntactic subordination and semantics/pragmatics of *because*-clauses discussed in 3.2 above.

22. *Nu (þæt)* is "already usually causal in Old English, but its temporal character remains prominent in its use in Middle English as is still the case today (where it could also still be purely temporal, as is still the case today)" (*CHEL*, vol. II:347).

23. In ME and EModE, *that* occasionally follows *for*. However, *for that* becomes obsolete by the end of the seventeenth century (Rissanen, 1999:303, 306). For further details of the optional *that/þæt*, see Rissanen (1997b, 1999:303–304, 2002, 2003), among others.

24. According to *CHEL*, the development of *because* "is due to the gradual development of *for* towards a coordinating conjunction, a development which underlines its use as an indicator of fairly loose, explanatory cause-effect relationship. Conversely, it can be argued that the emergence of a new clearly subordinating causal link may have accelerated the coordinator development of *for*" (vol. III:307).

25. For a discussion of semantic change from temporal *since* to causal *since* from the perspective of grammaticalization, see König and Traugott (1988), Traugott (1990), Traugott and König (1991), Kortmann (1997:320–321), Yonekura (2001), and Heine and Kuteva (2002:291), for example.

26. Note that the inventory is not exhaustive. The symbols for (41) are as follows.
    --- : obsolete
    * : the word in [ ] can occasionally be interpreted with causal meanings.
    ** : *for* in PDE is regarded as a coordinate conjunction.

    See Kortmann (1997:291–335) for further details of the development of adverbial subordinators in English.

27. Kortmann (1997:299–300) notes that a good number of borrowings (including loan translations) from French and, marginally, Old Norse are added to the ME inventory of adverbial subordinators. See Ohori (1997b) for a discussion of the history of *unless* (< Old French *à moins que*).

28. The history of *because*-clauses introduced in this section is based on *CHEL*, Jespersen (1909–1949, Part V:390), Kortmann (1997), and *OED*. The examples in this section are taken from *CHEL*, *MED*, and *OED*. We are not concerned with *because of* and the purposive function of *because* in the present study. For further details of the latter, see Kortmann (1997:323–324).
29. See Note 23 in Chapter 3.
30. Kortmann (1997:324) notes that the purposive function of *because* flourished from the 15th to the 17th centuries, but it has been dropped from modern usage. The present study does not concern itself with this function.
31. For the correlation between the increase of *because* in frequency and the development of *for* towards a coordinating conjunction, see Note 24 in Chapter 3.
32. *By (the) cause (that)* represents various forms in LME. *Because (that)* in EModE is described here as a single clause marker for the sake of convenience although it is admittedly not single in the form *because that*.
33. The data collected from the HC is colloquial although it is not necessarily taken from the conversational parts of the texts indicated by quotation marks.
34. See 2.4 above for further details of the methodology and sources of the present study.
35. A repetition of utterances made by a different speaker and an echo question is not included in (51c). When a *because*-clause appears halfway in one speaker's turns, it is included in (51c) only when it is clearly separated from the preceding or the following clause by punctuation. There are no instances of this in the written colloquial data for the present study. We can make use of the symbol for the tone unit boundary when we examine the spoken data from the LLC.
36. *Because that* is not included in the percentage of *because* in (52).
37. Ford (1993) points out that causal clauses (*because*, *'cause*, and *since*) mostly follow the "main" clauses in present-day American English conversation. On the other hand, the inversion of a *kara*-clause and its "main" clause (i.e., what is called non-canonical clause order in Japanese) seems to have a close correlation with the increase of independent uses. See 4.4.2 below for further details.
38. In this survey, a case where an epistemic expression does not overtly appear in a clause, e.g., "John loved her, *because* he came back" (Sweetser 1990:77), is classified as (iii) in order to avoid misinterpretation or biased interpretation when it is ambiguous. The construction [*it/that is* + adjective] [*it/that is* + noun] and their variants are classified as (i-3) and (i-4) respectively when they are clearly interpreted as expressing "speakers' (subjective) attitudes and opinions" (Bybee et al., 1994:176).

In what follows, most of the symbols in LLC are omitted for ease of reading. Note

that the symbol # indicates a tone unit boundary.
39. Here, we limit ourselves to giving examples of overt expressions of epistemic and speech-act conjunction that appear in "main" clauses. These expressions also appear in the *because*-clauses as shown in Tables 3.3, 3.5, and 3.6.
40. A closer study of each type in (54), based on a broader database from different genres (e.g., written/spoken language, written colloquial language/natural conversation, etc.), will be necessary to explore how *because*-clauses are used in PDE in different genres. However, it lies outside the scope of the present study.
41. We limit the discussion to an overview of the transition of the distribution of (51) here. A closer examination of the transition will tell us some other interesting characteristics of the history of *because*-clauses.
42. The instances of (51c) [*Because* CL] appear after the 1770s in the diachronic data for the present study, except for the one in 1600s such as (56a).
43. Here, we give some instances of independent *because*-clauses that appear with the overt expressions listed in (54) above. The labels epistemic and speech-act "conjunction" may be inappropriate for independent *because*-clauses since they are not "conjunction" within a single utterance or sentence but independent of their "main" clauses. However, we leave the labels here for the convenience of comparing the distribution of the overt expressions in independent *because*-clauses with that in subordinate *because*-clauses.
44. The following instance may be counted as (i-2) if we regard "you are going to tell" as an epistemic expression.
    (i) She fired when she asked the last question, and she slapped my face with such force as she had, when I answered it.
    'Now?' said she. 'You little coarse monster, what do you think of me now?'
    'I shall not tell you.'
    '*Because* you are going to tell, up-stairs. It that it?'
    'No,' said I, 'that's not it.'

    (1861 *Great expectations*, Chapter 11)
45. We have so far used the term "subordinate" in the traditional sense in this chapter. In (58), we use a set of terms defined for the cline of clause-combining constructions in grammaticalization (see 2.2.5). Thus, the subordinate *because*-clause in PDE is labeled as "hypotactic" here. What belongs to "subordinate" in (58) are the phrasal expression *by the cause that* and its variants in LME and *because that* in LModE.
46. See 5.2 for a discussion of the clause-initial and clause-final position as loci of the grammaticalization of pragmatic markers (Ohori 1997a).
47. For detailed arguments for conventionalization of pragmatic meanings in

grammaticalization, see, in particular, Traugott (1988, 1989, 1995a, 1997, etc.), Traugott and König (1991), König and Traugott (1988), Hopper and Traugott (1993, 2003), Levinson (2000), and Traugott and Dasher (2002).

48. Some principles of grammaticalization may not be applicable to developmental stages of *because*-clauses in a strict sense. We here attempt to find characteristics of grammaticalization that are shared by the development of *because*-clauses.

49. "Layers" in the principle of "layering" are intended as those within a functional domain, which is defined as "some general functional area such as tense/aspect/modality, case, reference, etc., of kind which frequently becomes grammaticized" (Hopper, 1991:23). For typical examples of "layering", see Hopper (1991:22–24) and Hopper and Traugott (2003:124–126). Strictly speaking, it is more appropriate to count the coexistence of several forms, such as a *because*-clause, a *since*-clause, a *for*-clause, etc., in the functional domain "causal clauses" in PDE as an example of "layering" than the coexistence of subordinate, paratactic, and independent *because*-clauses. Nevertheless, we here focus on the development of *because*-clauses only. It is beyond the scope of the present study to go into details of grammaticalization of causal clauses in English.

50. "Divergence is applicable to cases where one and the same autonomous lexical item becomes grammaticized in one context and does not become grammaticized in another" (Hopper, 1991:24). It is considered a special case of "layering" (Hopper, 1991:24). A textbook example of "divergence" is a lexical item undergoing grammaticalization to an auxiliary, clitic or affix (Hopper, 1991:24–25; Hopper and Traugott, 2003:118–122).

51. However, as Akimoto (2001:15–16, 2002:7–8, 2004:8–9) points out, it is difficult to judge whether the noun *cause* in the phrasal expression *by (the) cause (that)* is decategorized or not. It remains a noun in PDE and does not "lose the morphological and syntactic properties that would identify it as a full member of a major grammatical category such as noun or verb" (Hopper and Traugott, 2003:107). I thank Minoji Akimoto for drawing my attention to this point.

52. In this subsection, we have so far used the term "subordinate" in the traditional sense. In (64), we use a set of terms defined for the cline of clause-combining constructions in grammaticalization (see 2.2.5). Since we are not concerned here with the ancestor of *because* that appears in various forms with *that*, "subordination" is put in parentheses in (64).

53. The semantic change from the lexeme "cause" in the LME phrasal expressions *by (the) cause (that)*, etc., to the "causal" clause marker *because*, i.e., from concrete to abstract meanings, is typical of semantic change in general (Sweetser, 1990; Heine et al., 1991; Bybee et al., 1994, etc.). It is one of several kinds of unidirectionality summarized by

Tabor and Traugott (1998:229–230), i.e., the trend from less to more abstract meanings in the process of grammaticalization (see 2.2.4).

54. Blakemore (1987, 1992) claims that the connection between two utterances would not be left unspecified in actual discourse and that the speaker constrains the interpretation of utterances by means of discourse connectives, which are considered approximately corresponding to "pragmatic markers" in the present study. See Blakemore (2002) for a recent development of her study.

55. For further details of each item of causal clause markers, see, for example, the following studies: Jespersen (1901–1949, Part V:391–392), König and Traugott (1988), Traugott (1982, 1989, 1990), and Traugott and König (1991) for *since*, Traugott (1982) for *as*, and Rutherford (1970), Wiegand (1982), and Rissanen (1999) for *for*.

56. I thank Kinsuke Hasagawa for bringing example (67) to my attention.

57. Traugott (1992:252) notes that *for*-clauses are restricted to post-main clause position. For further details of adverbial clauses in pre-main versus post-main clause position, see Thompson (1985), Ford and Thompson (1986), Ford (1993), Diessel (2001, 2005), and Ohori (2002b), among others.

58. Taking into consideration the above-mentioned tendency of *since* and the loss of subordinate characteristics from *for*, a set of causal clause markers *because*, *for*, and *since* in PDE can be counted as an example of renewal, "a process whereby existing old meanings may take on new forms" (Hopper and Traugott, 1993:121).

59. In (68), *0* represents '*that*-deletion'. It would be easier to understand (69) with a comma in the following way.

(69') It's just your point of view, you know what you like to do in your spare time *I think*

I am indebted to Jane Boughton for the suggestions above.

60. For some arguments for *I think* developing into a discourse marker, see Aijmer (1997) and Kärkkäinen (2003). For a discussion of first-person epistemic parentheticals such as *I think/suppose/believe* etc. in ME, see Brinton (1995:Ch. 8).

See Ford (1993:136–139) for a discussion of *if*-clauses without an accompanying "main" clause.

61. Studies of various languages have reported on a similar phenomenon. See 4.5 for Japanese and 5.3 for other languages.

62. Traugott and Dasher (2002) use the term "discourse marker" for "pragmatic marker". For further details of the development of pragmatic markers in English, see, for example, Hanson (1987), Brinton (1990, 1995, 1996, 2001), Aijmer (1997), Rissanen (1997a), Tabor and Traugott (1998), Traugott (1995b, 1999a, 2003a), Schwenter and Traugott

(1995, 2000), and Kärkkäinen (2003).
63. The development of *let's* also exemplifies the reanalysis of biclausal construction as single clause construction with a clause-initial pragmatic marker in English. For further details of *let's*, see Hopper and Traugott (2003:10–15), and Traugott (1995a). Romaine and Lange (1991) study the use of *like* as pragmatic marker. Traugott (1995a) discuss the grammaticalization of *let alone* as a pragmatic marker.

Chapter 4

Development of Japanese *kara*-clauses

4.1 Introduction

The purpose of this chapter is to examine the functional extension of *kara*-clauses in the history of Japanese. We will show that the direction of the syntactic and semantic/ pragmatic extension under investigation is the same direction as that of English *because*-clauses. More specifically, the syntactic extension of *kara*-clauses is from more to less integrated clause-combining constructions, and the semantic/pragmatic extension of these clauses shows an increase in subjective meanings, i.e., subjectification (Traugott, 1989, 1995a, 1997, etc.; and Traugott and Dasher, 2002).

Generally, *kara*-clauses are treated indiscriminately as subordinate clauses with causal meaning such as (1) in PDJ.

(1) [Subordinate *kara*-clause with causal meaning]
    Taroo   wa   Hanako o   aisite-iru   kara   modotte-kita.
    Taro   TOP   Hanako ACC   love   KARA   came.back
    'Taro came back *because* he loved Hanako.'

However, some studies point out that *kara*-clauses can neither be considered to be subordinate nor to express cause or reason (Alfonso, 1980; Takubo, 1987; Shirakawa, 1995; Uno, 1996). For example, the *kara*-clause in (2) is more like a paratactic clause than a subordinate clause since it is out of the scope of the nominal marker *no* (Takubo, 1987). Moreover, it does not express cause or reason why Taroo loved Hanako but the speaker's knowledge from which he/she draws a conclusion that Taroo loved Hanako.

(2) [Non-subordinate *kara*-clause with non-causal meaning]
   Taroo wa modotte-kita *kara* Hanako o aisite-iru no daroo.
   Taro TOP came.back KARA Hanako ACC love NOMI guess
   'Taro loved Hanako, *because* he came back.' =
   'I believe/draw a conclusion that Taro loved Hanako based on my knowledge of Taro's coming back.'

In the following example, the *kara*-clause can be regarded as an independent clause since there is no grammatically associated "main" clause in discourse (Alfonso, 1980; Shirakawa, 1991). The function of *kara* in (3) is more similar to that of a pragmatic marker, i.e., *syuuzyosi* 'final particle', than that of a subordinate clause marker, i.e., *setuzoku-zyosi* 'conjunctive particle', as discussed in 2.3.2.2 (Ohori, 1995a, 1997a; Iguchi, 1998; Honda, 2001, 2005).

(3) [Independent *kara*-clause]
   sumimasen ga, moo owari desu *kara*.
   excuse.me but now end COP KARA
   ' (Lit.) Excuse me, but *because* we close now.' =
   ' Excuse me, but we are closing now, you know.'

(Alfonso, 1980:1203)

This chapter will explore the diachronic functional extension of Japanese *kara*-clauses. The developmental process of these clauses provides us with a more striking instance of reanalysis in progress of subordinate clauses as independent main clauses than that of the *because*-clauses observed in the preceding chapter. Section 4.2 introduces preceding studies on *kara*-clauses in PDJ. Section 4.3 reviews studies on the history of *kara* and *kara*-clauses. Section 4.4 traces the developmental pathway of *kara*-clauses in light of structural and semantic/pragmatic functions. Section 4.5 discusses the findings from the perspective of grammaticalization.

4.2 *Kara*-clauses in present-day Japanese

This section examines how *kara*-clauses are used in PDJ. After considering the relationship between the causal clause marker *kara* and the ablative case marker *kara*, we will review earlier studies on *kara*-clauses in PDJ. As we have seen in 3.2, a fairly large number of studies have been made on *because*-clauses in PDE over the past few decades. Relatively speaking, only a few attempts have so far been made at studying *kara*-clauses in PDJ. It has been pointed out that some types of *kara*-clauses cannot necessarily be labeled as causal subordinate clauses (see 2.3.1.2) and that the interpretation of *kara*-clauses and their syntactic characteristics correlate in a similar way as those of *because*-clauses (see 3.2.2). More recent studies focus on *kara*-clauses appearing without an accompanying grammatically associated "main" clause in colloquial discourse (see 2.3.2.2). In this section, we will review some earlier studies that discuss the great diversity of functions of *kara*-clauses in PDJ.

4.2.1 A note on *kara* as a case marker

In PDJ, *kara* is approximately differentiated into two groups according to whether it is affixed to a noun phrase or a clause. When *kara* is affixed to a noun phrase, it functions as an ablative case marker as in (4), but when it is affixed to a clause, it is called a *setuzoku-zyosi* 'conjunctive particle' and serves as a subordinate clause marker with causal meaning as in (5).

(4) [Ablative case marker *kara*]
    eki   kara   uti   made   aruite   zyuppun   desu.
    station KARA my.house to on.foot ten.minutes COP
    'It is a ten minute walk from the station to my house.'

(5) [Subordinate clause marker *kara* with causal meaning]
    Taroo wa Hanako o aisite-iru kara modotte-kita.
    Taroo TOP Hanako ACC love KARA came.back

'Taroo came back *because* he loved Hanako.'

The ablative case marker *kara* can be further differentiated into subcategories according to the meaning it expresses, such as source, agent, cause/reason, etc. There are also some complex expressions comprised of *kara*, such as [*te*-form of verbal (gerund) + *kara*] 'after doing' or 'ever since', *kara-ni-wa* 'since', etc. We will not be concerned with them any further in this section since they are beyond the scope of this study. For a detailed description of *kara*, see Martin (1975), for instance.

It is worth mentioning here the relationship of the ablative case marker *kara* to the causal clause marker *kara*. The latter is said to have developed from the former in the Early Modern Japanese (EModJ) period (see 4.3 for detail). The development from an ablative case marker to a causal clause marker is a case marker extension that is widely observed across languages. For example, Genetti (1986, 1991) investigates the Bodic branch of Tibeto-Burman languages and summarizes the extension of case markers to clause-linkage markers in the following way:

(6) Locative > if/although, when/while/after
     Ablative > when/while/after, because, non-final
     Allative > purpose
     Dative   > purpose
     Ergative/Instrumental > because, when, while

(Genetti, 1991:229)

The case of Japanese *kara* corresponds to the second extension observed in (6) (Ohori, 1995b). Similarly, Japanese grammarians observe that many of the PDJ conjunctive particles developed from case markers, which came from other grammatical categories such as nouns, other types of particle, verbal inflections, etc. Conjunctive particles in Japanese are said to have developed in the later stages of the history of Japanese (e.g., Konoshima, 1966, 1983; Sakakura, 1993; Yamaguchi, 1980, 1996, etc.). Thus, the relationship between the ablative case marker *kara* and the causal clause marker *kara* observed in PDJ follows the general tendencies in the extension of case markers to clause-linkage markers.[1]

4.2.2 *Kara*-clauses as subordinate and paratactic clauses

Let us turn to the causal clause marker *kara* in PDJ. We reviewed the earlier studies on *because*-clauses in PDE from the syntactic, semantic/pragmatic, and prosodic aspects in 3.2. In contrast to the studies on PDE *because*-clauses, there are not many earlier studies on PDJ *kara*-clauses. Roughly speaking, more attention has been paid to the following two subjects for decades. One is the distinctions among various causal clauses, such as *kara*-clauses, *node*-clauses, *tame*-clauses, *te*-forms of verbals (gerunds) when they are interpreted as expressing cause or reason (e.g., Mikami, 1972 [1953]:291–303; Nagano, 1979 [1952]; Takubo, 1987; Morita, 1989; Imao, 1991; Iwasaki, 1994, 1995; Masuoka, 1997:121–128).[2] The other is the classification of subordinate clauses based on syntactic properties (e.g., Minami, 1964, 1974, 1993; Y. Kato, 1992, 1994).[3] A close examination of these subjects is necessary, but here we limit ourselves to reviewing earlier studies on *kara*-clauses in PDJ.

As we discussed in 2.3.1.2 and elsewhere, there are cases where *kara*-clauses can neither be called subordinate clauses nor a means of expressing cause or reason. Further, it is pointed out that there is a correlation between the semantic/pragmatic interpretations of *kara*-clauses and their syntactic characteristics (Takubo, 1987; Uno, 1996) (see 2.3.1.2 above) in a way that is similar to in English *because*-clauses (see 3.2.2). It is helpful at this point to have a quick look at earlier studies that examine the correlation between these two aspects.

Takubo (1987) suggests that *kara*-clauses can fall into two of the three classes into which Minami (1974) differentiates subordinate clauses in Japanese.[4] Takubo notices the following correlation between the interpretation and syntactic behavior of *kara*-clauses.

(7) [Content conjunction]

    [kare ga itta *kara* kanozyo mo itta] no desyoo.
    he NOM went KARA she also went NOMI guess

    '(Lit.) I guess [because he went (there) she also did].' =
    'I guess [she also went (there) because he did].'

(8) [Epistemic conjunction]

    kare ga itta *kara* [kanozyo mo itta] desyoo.
    he NOM went KARA she also went guess

    '(Lit.) Because he went (there), I guess [she also did].' =
    'I guess [she also went (there)], because (I know) he did.'

(Takubo, 1987:43)

Example (7) expresses a real-world causal relation between the events described in the *kara*-clause and its associated main clause. The *kara*-clause in (7) serves as a restrictive clause since it is within the scope of the nominal marker *no* and is associated with the verb in the main clause. By contrast, the *kara*-clause in (8) is understood in such a way as to express the speaker's grounds for drawing the conclusion that "she also went there". It serves as an unrestrictive clause since it is associated not with the verb but with the modal expression *desyoo* 'I guess' in the main clause.

Further, Takubo notes that *kara*-clauses are unrestrictive when they express a motivation for the speech-act performed in the main clause.

(9) [Speech-act conjunction]

    gohan o tabeta *kara* sanpo ni iki-masyoo.
    meal ACC ate KARA walk to go-VOL

    '(Lit.) Because (we) have eaten, let's go for a walk.' =
    'My motivation for suggesting "let's go for a walk" is that we have eaten.'

(Alfonso, 1980:545)

The *kara*-clause in (9) is associated not with the stem of the verb *iki-* but with the speaker's suggestion expressed by the volitional form V-*masyoo* in the main clause. In sum, what Takubo points out is that the interpretation of *kara*-clauses as content conjunctions typically associates with subordination whereas that of epistemic/speech-act conjunctions associates with non-subordination. This is the same correlation that exists between the semantic/pragmatic interpretations of *because*-clauses and their syntactic characteristics demonstrated in 3.2.2 above.

Within Sweetser's (1990) framework, Uno (1997) examines *kara*-clauses with content and epistemic conjunction interpretation and points out that the former basically corresponds to subordinate clauses and the latter to coordinate clauses. She also suggests that *kara*-clauses with speech-act conjunction interpretation possibly correspond to coordination, although they are not within the scope of her study.

In the same way as *because*-clauses, the correlation can be summarized as follows:

(10) Correlation between interpretation of *kara*-clauses and their syntactic properties in PDJ
   1. In the case of content conjunction interpretation, a *kara*-clause is a subordinate clause.
   2. In the case of epistemic and speech-act conjunction interpretation, a *kara*-clause is a coordinate clause.

In addition, the present study posits the schematization of each interpretation in the same way as *because*-clauses. Examples (7)– (9) above may be schematized as follows.

(7') [Content conjunction]
    [[kare   ga   itta   *kara*]   kanozyo   mo   itta]
    he   NOM went   KARA   she   also went

(8') [Epistemic conjunction]

    [kare ga itta *kara*] [kanozyo mo itta desyoo]
    he NOM went KARA she also went guess

(9') [Speech-act conjunction]

    [gohan o tabeta *kara*] [sanpo ni iki-masyoo]
    meal ACC ate KARA walk to go-VOL

The schematization (7') represents the *kara*-clause as subordinate to its grammatically related "main" clause, and associated with the main verb in the "main" clause. By contrast, (8') shows that it is coordinated to the following "main" clause and is related not to the main verb but to the speaker's belief or conclusion that is usually expressed in the "main" clause.[5] Similarly, (9') indicates that it is related to the speech-act performed in the "main" clause. We will make use of some types of expressions that overtly mark epistemic and speech-act conjunction interpretations when we observe the developmental process of *kara*-clause in 4.4.2 below.

4.2.3 *Kara*-clauses as independent clauses

This subsection considers examples of *kara*-clauses whose grammatically associated "main" clauses are absent. It has been widely recognized that subordinate or embedded clauses do not necessarily have to be followed by "main" clauses, especially in colloquial discourse, in Japanese.[6] Recently, a few studies have focused on *kara*-clauses without an accompanying "main" clause in PDJ. As suggested in 2.3.2.2, such clauses can be analyzed as a single independent clause plus a pragmatic marker.

    Shirakawa (1991) observes independent *kara*-clauses in written colloquial PDJ and describes *kara* as expressing an implicit message "take notice of this information, and you will know what to do". According to him, the *kara*-clause in (11) conveys a piece of information that the speaker expects the addressee to take notice of in order to accomplish the action of "helping oneself" expressed in the main clause.

(11) soko ni soosu ga   arimasu kara   ziyuu-ni totte-kudasai
     there at sauce NOM exist   KARA   freely   take-please
  '(Lit.) Because the sauce is there, please help yourself.'

(Shirakawa, 1991:254)

The speaker may expect the addressee to infer from an independent *kara*-clause such as (11') what is implicitly meant in the main clause.

(11') soko ni soosu ga   arimasu kara
      there at sauce NOM exist   KARA
  '(Lit.) Because the sauce is there (you should know what to do).'

Shirakawa ascribes the use of independent *kara*-clauses to the omission of main clauses.

Ohori (1995a, 1997a), on the other hand, considers subordinate clauses with no following main clauses (suspended clauses) not as mere elliptical patterns but as independent grammatical constructions in their own right (Fillmore, 1988; Fillmore et al., 1988; Goldberg, 1995; etc.). He suggests that subordinate clause markers drift toward clause-final pragmatic particles in Japanese. For example, the *kara* in (12) marks the speaker's solicitation of the hearer's involvement (possibly sympathy in this case).[7]

(12) watasi nante motto taihen-dat-ta-n.da   kara ne.
     1sg   EMPH   more   troubled-PRED-PAST-PRED   KARA PRT
  'I was even more troubled' or 'I had an even tougher time, so …'

(Ohori, 1995a:211)

The inferential mechanism concerning *kara*-clauses is schematized in Ohori (1995a) in the following way:

(13) X-KARA, Y ('X, so Y') => X-KARA, ø ('X, so you know what,' or 'X, so it concerns me/you') (Ohori, 1995a:211)

Ohori (1997a) points out that Japanese suspended clause constructions "embody particular procedures for interpretation, namely preference for inference-intensive readings and reinforcement of inter-personal functions" (p. 478).

In Iguchi (1998), I show that *kara* has a variety of discourse-pragmatic functions when it appears in clause-final position based on the observation of written colloquial data in PDJ (see also Honda, 2001, 2005). I also suggest that *kara* in clause-final position can be seen not as a subordinate clause marker but as a pragmatic marker on the following grounds. First, it appears in clause-final position; second, it has some new discourse-pragmatic functions which cannot necessarily be regarded as being associated with the function of a subordinate clause marker with causal meaning.

These studies show that *kara*-clauses do appear independently in PDJ and *kara* in clause-final position takes on the characteristics of a pragmatic marker (see 2.3.2.2). *Kara*-clauses in PDJ can be reanalyzed as a single independent clause with a clause-final pragmatic marker when they are used independently. These studies are all based on observation of synchronic data. We will observe the ongoing process of reanalysis of subordinate *kara*-clauses as independent clauses on the basis of both synchronic and diachronic data in 4.4 below.

4.2.4 Summary

In 4.2, we have shown how *kara*-clauses are used in PDJ. Compared with PDE *because*-clauses, not many synchronic studies on *kara*-clauses have so far been made. Section 4.2.1 examined in passing the function of *kara* as an ablative case marker in PDJ. The parallel between the ablative case marker *kara* and the causal clause marker *kara* observed in PDJ is counted as one of the instances of the extension of case markers to clausal clause markers. Sections 4.2.2 and 4.2.3 considered various functions of *kara*-clauses in PDJ. Section 4.2.2 focused on the correlation between the semantic/pragmatic interpretations of *kara*-clauses and their syntactic characteristics. It is the same correlation observed in the case of *because*-clauses (see 3.2.2). Section 4.2.3 discussed cases where *kara*-clauses appear without an accompanying "main" clause and pointed out that they can be reanalyzed as a single independent clause plus a clause-final pragmatic marker. In sum, it is reasonably assumed that the functional expansion of *kara*-clauses is ongoing in PDJ. Presumably, they are extending from subordinate to non-subordinate, paratactic clause-combining constructions to independent clause constructions with an increase in subjective meanings in PDJ. The following summarizes the characteristics of PDJ *kara*-clauses reviewed in this section.

(14) A summary of the characteristics of PDJ *kara*-clauses

Syntax:	subordinate	non-subordinate	independent
	[[CL1 *kara*] CL2]	[CL1 *kara*] [CL2]	[CL *kara*]
Function of *kara*:	subordinate clause marker	conjunction-like clause marker	pragmatic marker
Semantics/pragmatics:	content-conjunction	epistemic conjunction speech-act conjunction	

4.3 History of *kara*-clauses

This section presents earlier studies on *kara*-clauses from a diachronic perspective.[8] Following a quick look at the history of causal clauses in Japanese, this section reviews the history of *kara* from a formal noun to an ablative case marker to a causal clause marker.

4.3.1 A note on the history of causal clauses in Japanese

There is a group of particles called *setuzoku-zyosi* 'conjunctive particle' in Japanese. Conjunctive particles (including phrasal expressions serving as a conjunctive particle) in PDJ are said to be a later development in the history of Japanese (Konoshima, 1966:122–125; 1983:125–127; Sakakura, 1993:58–60). We will have a quick look at the history of causal clauses in Japanese in what follows.[9]

In Old Japanese (OJ, Nara Period), the bare *izenkei* verbals 'perfective form' expresses causal meaning (Konoshima, 1983:126; McCullough, 1988:26) as in (15).[10]

(15) [Perfective form]

wagaseko	ga	kaku	*kohure*	koso
my.sweetheart	NOM	this.way	love	INT
nubatamano.ime	ni	mietutu	ineraezukere	
dream	in	can.see	could.not.sleep	

'because my sweetheart loved me so dearly, (I) was able to see him in my dream (and) could not sleep.'

(c.759 *Man'yoo* 4–639 [Konoshima, 1983:126])

It is the combination of the perfective verbals form suffixed by *ba* that is most commonly used to express causal relation in OJ.

(16) [Perfective form + *ba*: cause or reason]

… subemonaku	samuku	si	are	*ba*	katasiho	wo
… very	cold	INT	be	BA	lump.of.salt	ACC
toritudusirohi …						
eat.little.by.little						

'… because it is very cold, (I) (take and) eat a lump of salt little by little …'

(c.759 *Man'yoo* 5–892 [Konoshima, 1983:128])

The perfective form suffixed by *ba* is often called *kakutei-zyooken* 'confirmed conditional', expressing that "the preceding sequence is the condition under which the following sequence occurs (McCullough, 1988:27)". The perfective form followed by *ba* is usually interpreted as indicating that the preceding sequence is:

1. a cause of, or reason for, the following sequence (*hituzen-kakutei-zyooken* 'necessary confirmed conditional') as in (16) above, which can be translated as 'because' or 'since' in English;
2. a temporal condition for the following sequence (*guuzen-kakutei-zyooken* 'accidental confirmed conditional') as in (17) below, which can be translated as 'when' in English;
3. a regular condition of the following sequence (*koozyoo-kakutei-zyooken* 'constant confirmed conditional') as in (18) below, which can be translated as 'whenever' in English.

(17) [Perfective form + *ba*: temporal]

    sore wo mire *ba*, san.zun bakari naru hito,
    that ACC look BA three.inch about be person
    ito utukusiute witari
    very beautiful existed

    'when (the man) looked at (the bamboo), (he found) a beautiful girl who was about three inches high (there).'

                            (c.900 *Taketori* [H. Suzuki, 1952:892])

(18) [Perfective form + *ba*: conditional]

    ihe ni are *ba* ke ni moru ihi wo
    home at be BA bowl in serve rice ACC
    kusamakura.tabi ni si are ba sihinoha ni moru
    travel   at INT be because sii.leaf on serve

    'The rice (I) serve in a bowl whenever (I am) at home, (I) serve (it) on the *sihi* leaf because (I am) on my travels.'   (c.759 *Man'yoo* 2–142 [*ZDKZ*])

Other expressions of causal relation in OJ include, for example, *ahida* 'while' and *yuwe-ni* 'reason + dative case marker'.

(19) [*ahida*]¹¹

    amarini   mausi   susumuru   *ahida*,   kayauni   gensansitu

    very   say   recommend   AHIDA   this.way   have.granted.an.audience

    'because (he) recommended (me) (to see the master), (I have) granted an audience (to the master) this way.'

                                                                         (c.1218 *Heike* 1 [ZDKZ])

(20) [*yuwe-ni*]

    wagimoko   ga   niha   no   tatibana   ito   tikaku

    my.sweetheart   NOM   garden   in   tatibana.flower   very   near

    uwete   si   *yuwe-ni*   narazuha   yamazi

    plant   INT   YUWE-NI   not.bear.fruit   not.stop

    'because my sweetheart planted the *tatibana* flower taken from her garden nearby/ because (I) planted the *tatibana* flower taken from my sweetheart's garden nearby, it is impossible that it should not bear fruit.'

                                    (c.759 *Man'yoo* 3–411 [Yamaguchi, 1996:183])

In Late Old Japanese (LOJ, Heian Period), the perfective form suffixed by *ba* eventually replaces the verbals *mizenkei* 'irrealis form' suffixed by *ba* (called *katei-zyooken* 'hypothetical conditional') as the latter begins to decline.¹² From Late Middle Japanese (LMJ, Muromachi Period) to Early Modern Japanese (EModJ, Edo Period), as the former gradually begins to cover the ranges of meanings expressed by the latter and becomes polysemous, the causal relation marked by the former begins to be taken over by various other expressions such as *hodo-ni* and *ni-yotte*.¹³

(21) [*hodo-ni*]

… aruhiha	yo	wo	osore	aruhiha	hitome	wo
… some	world	ACC	fear	some	public.eye	ACC

tutumu	*hodo-ni*	tohi	toburahu	mono	hitori	mo	nasi
mind	HODO-NI	visit	inquire.after	person	one	INT	no

'… because some fear the world and some mind the public eye, no one visits (the master).'

(c.1218 *Heike* 2 [Konoshima, 1983:168])

(22) [*ni-yotte*]

onna	wa	tie	asou,	buenryona	*ni-yotte*,
woman	TOP	wisdom	shallow	imprudent	NI-YOTTE

ta	ni	moraite	ata	to	naru	zo
others	to	reveal	enemy	to	become	FP

'because a woman is unwise and imprudent, she reveals (a secret) to others and (it) brings about harm.'

(1593 *Isoho* 438-18/19/20 [C. Kobayashi, 1973])

It is from the LMJ to the EModJ period that *kara* begins to be used as a causal clause marker. In place of the perfective form suffixed by *ba*, which is polysemous in these periods, *kara* becomes widely used, especially in the eastern part of Japan. Yoshii (1977) reports that *kara* becomes overwhelmingly popular around 1760 and *node* comes to be constantly used after 1850.[14]

The following gives a summary of the history of causal clauses introduced in this section. Note that the inventory is not comprehensive.[15]

(23) A summary of causal clauses from OJ to PDJ:

OJ	MJ	LMJ	EModJ	ModJ	PDJ
perfective					
perfective+*ba*	perfective+*ba*	---[hypothetical]			
ahida	---[written]				
yuwe-ni	*yuwe-ni*	*yuwe-ni*			---[archaic]
		hodo-ni			
		ni-yotte			---[passive agent]
			kara	*kara*	*kara*
				node	*node*

4.3.2 A note on the history of *kara*
4.3.2.1 From a nominal to an ablative case marker

Kara in OJ is generally categorized as *keisiki-meisi* 'formal noun', which is defined here as a noun-like word which occurs "either typically or exclusively with adnominal modification" (Martin, 1975:664).[16] Examples of *kara* in OJ are given in (24)–(28) below.[17] Japanese historical grammarians regard *kara* in OJ as a formal noun on the following syntactic grounds. First, it follows the genitive case particle *no* or *ga*, which shows that *kara* is not a particle, as in (24), (25), and (27). Second, it is followed by the dative case particle *ni* or some other particles which follow nominals, as in (25), (27), and (28).[18]

(24) [Noun + Genitive *no/ga* + *kara* in OJ]

    ono.*ga*   mi   no   *kara*
    my   body GEN KARA

      (Lit.) 'following my body/soul'

                              (c.759 *Man'yoo* 16–3799 [Ishigaki, 1955:111])

(25) [Noun + Genitive *no/ga* + *kara* + Dative *ni* in OJ]

    wa   ga   kara   ni

    I   GEN   KARA   DAT

       (Lit.) 'following myself'

                                   (c.759 *Man'yoo* 20–4356 [Ishigaki, 1955:112])

(26) [Noun + *kara* in OJ]

    wa   ga   kokoro   *kara*

    I   GEN   heart   KARA

       (Lit.) 'following my heart'

                                   (c.759 *Man'yoo* 4–694 [Konoshima, 1983:119])

(27) [Adnominal verbal form + Genitive *ga* + *kara* + Dative *ni* in OJ]

    yama   koyuru   ga   kara   ni

    mountain   pass   GEN   KARA DAT

       (Lit.) 'passing the mountain'

                                   (c.759 *Man'yoo* 6–1038 [Konoshima 1983:119])

(28) [Adnominal verbal form + *kara* + Dative *ni* in OJ]

    hitoyo   hedatesi   *kara*   ni

    one.night   separate   KARA   DAT

       (Lit.) 'passing one night'

                                   (c.759 *Man'yoo* 4–683 [Konoshima, 1983:119])

The meaning of *kara* in OJ is said to be 'following', 'with', 'along', 'by way of', etc.[19]

By LOJ, *kara* gradually begins to appear without a genitive particle. In other words, types (24), (25), and (27) become obsolete and types (26) and (28) survive.

(29) [*Kara* from OJ to LOJ][20]

	OJ		**LOJ**
(24) N + GEN + *kara*	[N + N]		---
(25) N + GEN + *kara ni*	[N + N + P]		---
(26) N + *kara*	[N + N]	>	[N + P]
(27) ADN + GEN + *kara ni*	[CL + N + P]		---
(28) ADN + *kara ni*	[CL + N + P]	>	[CL + N (+ P)]

In his survey of texts written from LOJ to Early MJ (EMJ), Ishigaki (1955:130) finds only examples of *kara* directly following a noun or an adnominal verbal form. He suggests that *kara* begins to lose its nominal characteristic in LOJ. Konoshima (1966:107) also makes a similar suggestion, that *kara* behaves as a particle in the LOJ period. He finds few examples of *kara* which follow the genitive case particle *no* or *ga* and precede the dative case particle *ni* in some LOJ texts, which he investigates.

Japanese historical grammarians seem to agree on the idea that *kara* as an ablative case particle gradually developed from *kara* directly following a noun, i.e., type (26) above, from OJ to LOJ. Examples (30) and (31) provide good illustrations of the early stages of the development. Following a place noun, *kara* in these examples can be interpreted as meaning 'following' or 'by way of', from which a case particle meaning 'from time/space' is considered to have developed.[21]

(30) [PLACE + *kara* in OJ]

... yama   *kara*   si   ... kaha   *kara*   si
... mountain   KARA   INT   ... river   KARA   INT

'(Lit.) by way of the mountain, ... by way of the river, ...'

(c.759 *Man'yoo* 3–315 [Ishigaki, 1955:98])

(31) [PLACE + *kara* + verb of coming/going in OJ]

   a.   ... tada   ti   *kara*   ware   ha   kituredo
         just   road   KARA   I   TOP   have.come.although

'(Lit.)... although I have come (to see my sweetheart) just following the road ...'

(c.759 *Man'yoo* 11–2618 [Ishigaki, 1955:100])

b. ... hototogisu   unohanabe   kara   ... koyu ...
   little.cuckoo   unohana.flower.field   KARA   pass

'(Lit.) ... a little cuckoo ... passing the *unohana* flower field ...'

(c.759 *Man'yoo* 11–2360 [Ishigaki, 1955:100])

In LOJ, the widespread use of *kara* as a case particle meaning 'from time/space' is suppressed by *yori*, an ablative case particle which is widely used until the LMJ period, but there are a few examples of *kara* meaning 'from time/space'.[22]

(32) [*Kara* as an ablative case particle in LOJ]

a. kesa   kara
   this.morning   KARA

   'from this morning'

(c.905 *Kokin* 10 [Ishigaki, 1955:149; Konoshima, 1966:105])

b. oki   kara
   offing   KARA

   'from the offing'

(c.905 *Kokin* 10 [Konoshima, 1983:120])

Based on Ishigaki (1955:96–101, 149–160) and Konishima (1983:119), the development of a case particle from the formal noun, from OJ to Late OJ, can be summarized as follows:

(33) [*Kara* from OJ to LOJ: from a formal noun to a case particle]

OJ	LOJ
N + *kara* (formal noun)	N + *kara* (case particle)
[N + N] >	[N + P]
'along/via PLACE' >	'from TIME/SPACE' = *yori* 'from'

In OJ, *kara* functioning as a conjunctive particle never appears alone and is mostly used in phrasal expressions such as *kara-ni* and *mono-kara*.

(34) [*Kara* as a conjunctive particle in OJ]

a. te   ni   toru   ga   *kara-ni*   wasuru ...
    hand   in   take   GEN   KARA-NI   forget

'as soon as (I) take (it) in (my) hand, (I) forget ...'

(c.759 *Man'yoo* 7–1197 [Yamaguchi, 1980:221])

b. tamakadura   taenu   *mono-kara*   sanuraku   ha
    kazura.vine   end.not   MONO-KARA   sleep   TOP
    tosi   no   watari   ni   tada   hitoyo   nomi
    year   GEN   pass   at   just   one.night   only

'although our relationship never ends (just like a tendril of *kadura* vine), we sleep together once a year.'

(c.759 *Man'yoo* 10–2078 [ZDKZ])

On the one hand, *kara* in *kara-ni* is generally analyzed as a formal noun on the grounds that it precedes the dative case particle *ni*. Roughly speaking, *kara-ni* is interpreted as meaning 'as soon as', 'because', and 'although'.[23] In OJ, there are many examples of [verbal + genitive case particle *ga* + *kara-ni*] such as (34a) and (27) above, and a few without *ga*, such as (28) above. Thus, *kara* is generally regarded as a noun in OJ. In LOJ, the former type of *kara-ni* becomes obsolete, and the latter type increases as the use of *kara* as a case particle develops (Yamaguchi, 1966:221; Konoshima, 1966:109). On the other hand, *kara* in *mono-kara* can be analyzed as a case particle that follows a formal noun *mono* 'thing' (Yamaguchi, 1996:203). *Mono-kara* is said to mean 'although' in OJ, and is expanded to mean 'because' in MJ. Although *kara* used as an ablative case particle is generally considered to have developed from [noun + *kara*], *mono-kara* may have played a certain role in the reanalysis of *kara* as a particle (Yamaguchi, 1996:203).[24]

In sum, *kara* in OJ is usually analyzed as a formal noun. It gradually loses its nominal character and comes to behave as a case particle by LOJ. Japanese grammarians generally share the presumption that *kara* establishes its usage as an ablative case particle expressing source of time/space in LOJ, although there are not many incipient examples of such uses.

Through the MJ period, *kara* gradually develops in usage as an ablative case particle. In EMJ, however, the use of *kara* as a case particle expressing source remains overshadowed by *yori*, especially in written Japanese, but it continues to be used in spoken language and some dialects in eastern Japan (Ishigaki, 1955:166–170; Hojo, 1975; Hikosaka, 1997).[25] In LMJ, *kara* functioning as an ablative case particle overtakes *yori* and expands its range of meanings.[26] For example, Ishigaki (1955) traces the following different meanings of *kara* up to LMJ:

(35) [*Kara* functioning as an ablative case particle up to LMJ]
   a. TIME

      yonaka   mae   *kara*
      midnight before KARA
      'from before midnight'

                              (1593 *Isoho* [Ishigaki 1955: 172])

   b. SPACE

      yoso   *kara*
      distance KARA
      'from a distance'

                        (1592 *Amakusa Heike* 1-1 [Ishigaki 1955: 174])

c. SUBJECT

takoku	*kara*	hiraku	koto	ga	mareni	atta
opponent.country	KARA	disperse	COMP	NOM	rare	existed

to	kikoeta.
QUO	heard

'(I) heard that there were rare cases where opponent countries (first)dispersed.'

(1593 *Isoho* [Ishigaki 1955: 176])

d. PASSIVE AGENT

Kiso	*kara*	yurus-arete
Kiso	KARA	be.permitted

'(his younger brother) was permitted by Kiso'

(1592 *Amakusa Heike* 3-12 [Ishigaki 1955: 176])

e. PLACE OF ACTION

menuki	no	moto	*kara*	...	worete
sword.base	GEN	base	KARA		break

'(the sword) breaks off the base ...'

(c.1590 *Amakusa Heike* 2-5 [Ishigaki 1955: 177])

f. N1 *kara* N2 (*made*) 'from N1 to N2'

minami	no	mon	*kara*	yotuduka	*made*
south	GEN	gate	KARA	fourth.gate	to

'from the south gate to the fourth gate'

(c.1592 *Amakusa Heike* 4-19 [Ishigaki 1955: 178])

g. ABSTRACT/LOGICAL SOURCE

zihi	no	ue	*kara*
mercy	GEN	top	KARA

'for the sake of mercy'

(1593 *Isoho* [Ishigaki 1955: 178])

Ishigaki (1955:184) points out that the trend of the change of *kara* is from independent to dependent item and from concrete to abstract just as with other case particles in Japanese.

4.3.2.2 From ablative case marker to causal clause marker

In LMJ, *kara* also begins to follow adnominal verbal forms and to be interpreted as serving as a subordinate clause marker. The use of *kara* as a subordinate clause marker is said to come from its use as an ablative case particle expressing abstract/logical source in LMJ such as in (35g) above (Ishigaki, 1955:179–180; Konoshima, 1966:120–121; 1983:122; Yamaguchi, 1996:207; Yuzawa, 1958:265). Yuzawa (1958:265) states that *kara* is interpreted as expressing a source of action in LMJ, which is further extended to causal clause marking in the later period. However, he notes that it is too early to interpret such instances of *kara* as expressing a causal relation in LMJ. Some incipient examples of *kara* as a causal subordinate clause marker in LMJ are given in (36).[27]

(36) [Adnominal verbal form + *kara* in LMJ]

    a. muyouna   koto   o   ihu   *kara*   nana-koku   mo
       unnecessary word ACC say KARA seven-countries INT
       hansita zo
       rebel   FP

       'because (you) said unnecessary words, seven countries rebelled against us.'

                                                (1528–1532 *Moogyuusyoo* 9–43 [Yuzawa, 1958:265])

    b. tanosimi o   takumu   *kara*   …   mi-o-ayamatu mono   dya
       pleasure ACC   seek   KARA   go.wrong   COMP COP
       'because (people) seek pleasure, … (they) go wrong.'

                                                          (1593 *Isoho* [Ishigaki, 1955:179])

A new phrasal expression [*te*-form of verbal (gerund) + *kara*] comes into use in LMJ. It expresses a starting point in time, and then is expanded to mean "although/

but" and "even if" (Ishigaki, 1955:172–174).

(37) [*te*-form of verbal + *kara* in LMJ]

yo	ake*te*	*kara*	mata	sanzyuunin	amari	no	kubi	o
night	break	KARA	again	thirty.people	about	GEN	head	ACC

kiri ...
cut

'after the day breaks, (they) behead about thirty people again ...'

(1952 *Amakusa Heike* 3–3 [Ishigaki, 1955:172])

A more detailed study of the construction [*te*-form of verbal + *kara*] is outside the scope of the present study.

The development of *kara* in the MJ period can be summarized as follows:

(38) [*Kara* from EMJ to LMJ: from a case particle to a clause marker][28]

LOJ/EMJ	LMJ	LMJ/EModJ
<Structure>		
N + *kara*	N + *kara*	
[N + P]	> [N + P]	
ADN + *kara*		
	> [CL + CM]	
<Meaning>		
'from TIME/SPACE'	> 'from TIME/SPACE'	
	> 'from ABSTRACT SOURCE'	> 'BECAUSE'
	(see (35g))	

In EModJ, *kara* surpasses *yori* in expressing source, especially in eastern Japan (Edo, later called Tokyo), and its use as a causal subordinate clause marker also spreads over the Edo area. In the western part of Japan, *sakai(-ni/de)* is widely used instead of *kara* (Ishigaki, 1955; c. Kobayashi, 1977; Konoshima, 1966:121;

1983:162). As the adnominal verbal form gradually merges into the dictionary form (*syuusi-kei*), *kara* following the adnominal verbal form comes to be regarded as a subordinate clause marker following a dictionary verbal form (Yoshikawa, 1955, cited in Yoshii, 1977). An example of EModJ *kara* follows:

(39) [*Kara* functioning as a causal subordinate clause marker in EModJ]
    gozonzi-nai   *kara*   sayooni   ooseraruru
    know-not   KARA   this.way say
      'because (you) don't know, you say so.'
                                                    (1604–1608 *Rodriguez* [Ishigaki, 1955:179])

We have so far reviewed the change of *kara* from a formal noun to a case particle to a subordinate clause marker. The developmental pathway may be summarized as follows:

(40) [Development of *kara* from a formal noun to a clause marker]

OJ	LOJ	MJ	EModJ
formal noun	formal noun	(bound morpheme)[29]	
	case particle	case particle	case particle
			clause marker

4.3.2.3 Development of *kara* functioning as a causal clause marker

As mentioned at the end of 4.3.1, *kara* begins to function as a causal clause marker in the EModJ period. As we discussed in 2.3.1 and 4.2, the interpretation of *kara*-clauses in PDJ can be differentiated into content conjunction, epistemic conjunction, and speech-act conjunction in terms of semantic/pragmatic functions. Such a difference in interpretation can also be observed in *kara*-clauses in EModJ.

    For example, Yamaguchi (1996:207) notes that *kara*-clauses in EModJ express not only a reason/cause based on facts (i.e., content conjunction interpretation in the sense of Sweetser (1991)), but also a motivation for the speech act performed by the associated main clause (i.e., speech-act conjunction interpretation in the sense of Sweetser (1991)) such as an order as in (41a) or an invitation as in (41b).

(41) [Speech-act conjunction in EModJ]

a. Hatibei-san mo   ima de   wa   kakasan hitori da   *kara,*
    Hatibei   INT now in   TOP mother   one   COP   KARA
    zuibun   kookoo-si-nasai.
    very   dutiful-be-IMP
    'because, Hachibei-san, you only have a mother now, be very dutiful to her.'

    (1809–1813 *Ukiyoburo* 1 [Yamaguchi, 1996:207])

b. yo-zi   degozaimasu *kara* okusuri   o   mesiagari-masen
    four.o'clock   COP.POL   KARA   medicine ACC   take-not
    ka.
    Q
    'because it is four o'clock, won't you take the medicine?'

    (1886 *Settyubai* Zyoo-1 [Yamaguchi, 1996:207])

Yoshii (1977) observes the development of causal clauses in the Tokyo area from around 1700 to the first half of the twentieth century. He makes a close study of causal clauses, especially *kara*- and *node*-clauses, which appear in the conversational parts of novels written in spoken Japanese. He makes several important statements on the diachronic development of these clauses from EModJ to Modern Japanese (ModJ, Meizi, Taisho, and Showa Periods). For the present, we shall confine our attention to the following three points concerning *kara*.

First, *kara* begins to appear in conversation around 1700. It comes to be used in approximately 80% of all causal expressions around 1760.[30]

(42) The ratio of causal clause markers in ModJ (adapted from Yoshii, 1977:20)

	kara	node	others (approximate ratio)
1700–1730	9.6	0.9	89.5
1760–1780	79.5	0	20.5
1800–1820	90.5	0.4	9.1
1850–1870	83.0	5.9	11.1
1940–1960	83.0	13.3	4.7

Second, Yoshii inquires into what kinds of predicate appear in the grammatically associated "main" clause of *kara*-clauses. He differentiates the predicates into the following seven groups based on Nagano's (1979 [1952]) classification.[31]

(43) The classification of the expressions appearing in the "main" clause of *kara*-clauses (Yoshii, 1977:30)

    a. Conjecture   e.g., *daroo, zyanaika, kamosirenai*
    b. Opinion   e.g., V-*beki*
    c. Volition   e.g., V-*(y)oo*, V-*teitadaku*
    d. Order   e.g., imperative form, V-*nasai*
    e. Request   e.g., V-*tekure/tyoodai*, V-*naide*, V-*tewa*
    f. Question   e.g., *desyoo*
    g. Description of facts

The following are examples of (43) in Nagano (1979 [1952]).

(43') [Examples of (43)] in Nagano (1979 [1952])]

    a. Conjecture

Yuzuki	ga	kata	ga	warui	sooda	*kara,*	kyoo	wa
Yuzuki	NOM	shoulder	NOM	bad	I.hear	KARA	today	TOP
yahari	Takemasu			zya		nai	ka	na
certainly	Takemasu			COP.TOP		not	Q	SF

'Because I hear Yusuki has a bad shoulder, (I) wonder if Takematsu is going to be (a pitcher) today.'

b. Opinion

Kurohune no gi wa syoobai no koto dearu
the.Black.Ships of matter TOP business of matter COP
kara, tosituki o hete booeki ni kuru <u>beki</u> dearu.
KARA years ACC passing trade to come should COP

'Because the matter of the Black Ships is one of business, (they) should come to trade (with us) later.'

c. Volition

Tomoko ga kawaisoo da *kara* nagusamete age-<u>yoo</u>.
Tomoko NOM poor COP KARA cheer.up give-VOL

'Because (I feel) sorry for Tomoko, I will cheer her up.'

d. Order

haikyuu o yaru *kara* tori ni <u>koi</u>.
ration ACC give KARA receive to come

'Because (I'll) distribute the ration, come to receive it.'

e. Request

kon'ya oisii sityuu o tukuru *kara*,
this.evening good stew ACC make KARA
gyuunyuu <u>tyoodai</u> yo.
milk give FP

'Because (I'll) make good stew, give me (some) milk.'

f. Question[32]

Masui-san wa … hitori da *kara*
Masui-san TOP alone COP KARA
sonna hituyoo o kanzi-nai <u>desyoo</u>?
that necessity ACC feel-not guess

'Because, Masui-san, (you live) alone, (I) guess you don't feel you need that, (do you)?'

g. Description of facts

> kuuki ga kirei da *kara*, kenkoo ni yoi.
> air NOM clean be KARA health for good
>
> 'Because the air is clean, it is good for (our) health.'

The expressions (43a)–(43f) may be regarded as corresponding to epistemic and speech-act conjunctions and (43g) to content conjunctions in the sense of Sweetser (1991). Yoshii shows that (43g) gradually decreases in ratio whereas (43a)–(43f) increase.[33]

(44) The ratio of (43g):(43a)– (43g) in ModJ (adapted from Yoshii, 1977:30)

1700–1730	30.0
1760–1780	36.1
1800–1820	40.8
1850–1870	27.0
1900–1920	17.4
1920–1940	17.7
1940–1960	15.7

Third, Yoshii points out the rapid increase in ratio of *kara* in sentence-final position, especially in the twentieth century.

(45) The ratio of *kara* in sentence-final position to all occurrences of *kara* in ModJ
(adapted from Yoshii, 1977:30)

1700–1730	9.1
1760–1780	9.8
1800–1820	4.9
1850–1870	11.6
1900–1920	35.0
1920–1940	42.0
1940–1960	51.2

We have so far reviewed the development of *kara* functioning as a causal clause marker from EModJ to ModJ. It can be summarized in the following way:

(46) Development of *kara* functioning as a causal clause marker

EModJ	ModJ
content conjunction	on the decrease (being taken over by *node*)
epistemic conjunction	on the increase
speech-act conjunction	on the increase
	sentence-final use (pragmatic marker?)

Examining the developmental process in more detail, we will develop Yoshii's (1977) observation a little further in 4.4 below. However, the method of data collection will be clarified in the following two respects. First, it is not clear how many examples are taken from each source in his survey. In order to minimize the bias in data collection, we will limit ourselves to sampling the first 10 tokens from each source (see 2.4.1 for details). Second, the definition of "*kara* in sentence-final position" is not clarified in his paper. Whether it refers to the inversion of a *kara*-clause and its grammatically associated "main" clause and/or an independent *kara*-clause without an accompanying "main" clause is not specified. We will count the two types of "*kara* in sentence-final position" separately in the following section.

4.3.3 Summary

In 4.3, we introduced earlier studies on the history of causal clauses in Japanese and the historical development of *kara*. The function of *kara* develops from a formal noun to an ablative case marker, and then to a causal clause marker. In the ModJ period on, the focus of meanings expressed by the causal clause marker *kara* shifts from content to epistemic/speech-act conjunction in the sense of Sweetser (1991), and *kara* begins to appear in sentence-final position. We will examine the development of *kara*-clauses in progress in more detail in the following section.

4.4 Developmental path of *kara*-clauses

We have reviewed the functional diversity of PDJ *kara-clauses* in 4.2 and their diachronic development in 4.3. It follows from what has been reviewed in the preceding sections that the developmental process of causal *kara*-clauses from EModJ onward can be summarized as follows:

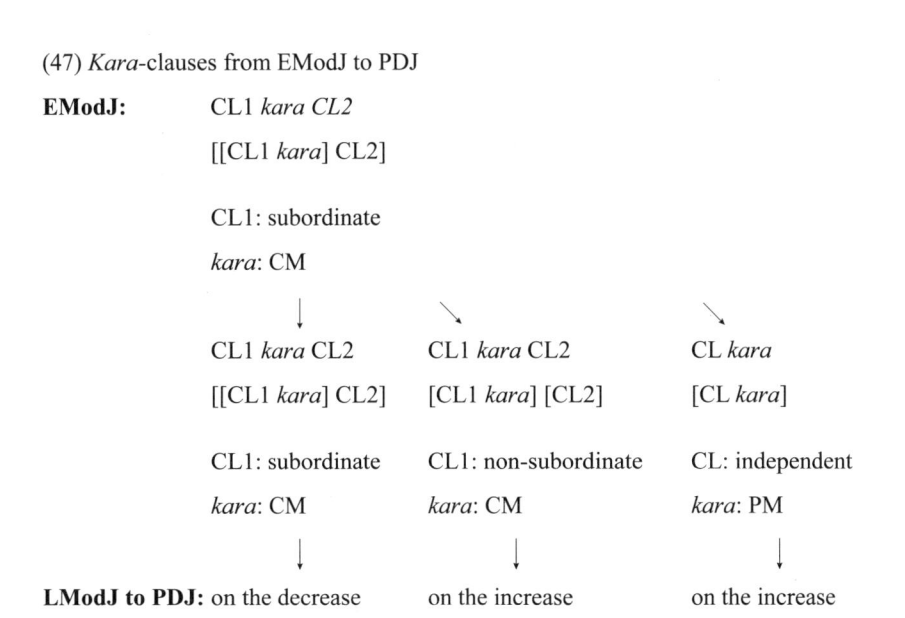

(47) *Kara*-clauses from EModJ to PDJ

EModJ: CL1 *kara* CL2

[[CL1 *kara*] CL2]

CL1: subordinate

kara: CM

CL1 *kara* CL2	CL1 *kara* CL2	CL *kara*
[[CL1 *kara*] CL2]	[CL1 *kara*] [CL2]	[CL *kara*]
CL1: subordinate	CL1: non-subordinate	CL: independent
kara: CM	*kara*: CM	*kara*: PM

LModJ to PDJ: on the decrease   on the increase   on the increase

In view of clause-combining constructions, (47) represents the transition of *kara*-clauses from subordinate to independent clauses from EModJ to PDJ. It seems reasonable to suppose that subordinate, non-subordinate, and independent *kara*-clauses begin to coexist in the later EModJ period and the latter two types show a tendency to proportionately increase in LModJ and PDJ. In view of the clause marker (*setuzoku-zyosi* 'conjunctive particle'), (47) assumes that the clause marker *kara* has gradually extended its function from a causal clause marker to a pragmatic marker (*syuuzyosi* 'final particle') in clause-final position.

The purpose of this section is to explore a little further the ongoing functional expansion of *kara*-clauses. We basically supplement Yoshii's (1977) observation by modifying his method of data collection (see 4.3.2 above) and by examining newer PDJ data. Section 4.4.1 presents a brief note on the data that will be used for this section. Section 4.4.2 observes the diachronic process of *kara*-clauses in the light of clause-combining constructions. Section 4.4.3 makes a diachronic examination of *kara*-clauses in the light of semantic/pragmatic functions. Section 4.4.4 summarizes the findings in this section.

4.4.1 A note on the Japanese data for this section

The diachronic and synchronic data for this section are collected from conversational parts of novels and play scripts in the Edo/Tokyo dialect. We also use the data taken from conversation scripts in PDJ. There are a total of 335 *kara*-clauses in the diachronic data and a total of 207 in the synchronic data as shown in (48).

(48) The main data of *kara-clauses* for the present study:

Diachronic data (written colloquial)

–1750	13
1750–1800	94
1800–1850	58
1850–1900	50
1900–1950	120
TOTAL (diachronic data):	335

Synchronic data (written colloquial)

1950–2000	100

Synchronic data (spoken)

1950–2000	107
TOTAL (synchronic data):	207

We noted in 4.3 above that *kara*-clauses came to be used as causal clauses in eastern Japan from the LMJ to the EModJ period. As long as the diachronic data for the present study are concerned, one of the earliest examples of *kara*-clauses is found in the text written in the 1700s. For instance, see (49a-2) below.

Following the classification of *because*-clauses in 3.4 above, we basically classify instances of *kara*-clauses into the following four groups. Each group will be divided into subgroups if necessary.

(49) Basic classification of *kara*-clauses in the present study

    (a) [CL1 *kara* CL2]
    (b) [CL1, CL2 *kara*]
    (c) [CL *kara*]
    (d) Others

[Examples of (a)–(c) from the diachronic data]

(a–1)

Yoshihide: tuker-areta   *kara*   ukkari   itta
          were.added   KARA   carelessly   said

'Because (the lines) were (wrongly) added, I said them carelessly.'

(1736 *Shibaraku*, p. 162)

(a-2)

Monbei: hate,   soo   sa   na.   Agemaki   ga   haha
        well   so   FP   FP   Agemaki   of   mother

        dearoo   *kara*,   Agemaki   ga   koto   o
        COP.guess   KARA   Agemaki   of   matter   ACC

        babaa   ni   nomikomasite   tanomu   no   da
        old.lady   DAT   understand-CAU   ask   NOMI   COP

        wa   yai.
        SF   SF

'Well, let me see. Because (I) guess (you) are Agemaki's mother, (let me) make (this) old lady understand what happened to Agemaki and ask you.'

(1713 *Sukeroku*, p. 67)

(b-1)

ikani   hisasiku   konai   tote,   miwasureta   kao
how   long.time   not.come   QUO   forgotten   face

wa   nei   wa.   sikasi   soo   daroo,   hisasiburi   da   *kara*.
INT   not   FP   but   so   guess   after.a.long.time COP   KARA

'I haven't come (here) for a long time, but how dare you say you don't recognize me. But (I) guess so, because (I have come here) after a long time.'

(1770 *Yuusi hoogen*, p. 281)

(b-2)

sukosi no   koto   wa   kikinogasi-ni-siyai   no.
trivial of   matter TOP   miss.IMP   FP
sore   sono kekkoo sugita   kara.
look   well very   went.too.far   KARA

'Forget trivial matters. Look, because you went too far (in your talk).'

(1721 *Sinzyuu yoigoosin,* p. 452)

(c)

Zyoroo: sukanee   ko   da   ga   nee.
        unpleasant person   COP   but   SF
'(I) don't like her.'

Onaka: mada   narenee   kara   sa.
       yet   unfamiliar   KARA   FP
'Because (you are) still unfamiliar (with her).'

(1770 *Tatumi no sono,* p. 307)

(49a–c) represents the relative position of a *kara*-clause to its associated "main" clause in discourse. Thus, (49a) includes "CL1 *kara*, CL2", as in (a-2), as long as the *kara*-clause is interpreted as being semantically related to CL2. (49b) includes "CL1, CL2 *kara*", as in (b-1), and "CL1. CL2 *kara*", as in (b-2), as long as they are uttered by a single speaker.[34] A *kara*-clause is classified as (49c) when it appears turn-initially and is clearly separated from the following clause, if any, by punctuation.[35] When a *kara*-clause appears halfway in one speaker's turns, it is included in (49c) as long as it is clearly separated from the preceding or the following clause by punctuation. All other types of *kara*-clauses, including those serving as an answer to a *wh*-question, are classified as (49d). In all cases, we try our best to observe and interpret the data in a discourse context and classify them as (49d) when there is a risk of misjudgement.

4.4.2 From subordinate to independent clauses

This subsection traces the developmental process of *kara*-clauses in more detail in terms of clause-combining constructions. It demonstrates that the trend is for a *kara*-clause to become more independent from its "main" clause in PDJ.

First of all, we observe the developmental process of *kara*-clauses by examining the diachronic and synchronic data given in (48) above. Table 4.1 shows the transition of the distribution of *kara*-clauses from EModJ to PDJ.

Table 4.1: The transition of the distribution of *kara*-clauses by position

	–1750	–1800	–1850	–1900	–1950	–2000 (wr)	–2000 (sp)
(a) CL1 *kara* CL2	9 (69.2%)	84 (89.4%)	50 (86.2%)	38 (76.0%)	67 (55.8%)	44 (44.0%)	48 (44.9%)
(b) CL1, CL2 *kara*	1 (7.7%)	3 (3.2%)	3 (5.2%)	8 (16.0%)	27 (22.5%)	35 (35.0%)	11 (10.3%)
(c) CL *kara*	0 (0%)	2 (2.1%)	0 (0%)	1 (2.0%)	17 (14.2%)	9 (9.0%)	45 (42.1%)
(d) Others	3 (23.0%)	5 (5.3%)	5 (8.6%)	3 (6.0%)	9 (7.5%)	12 (12.0%)	3 (2.8%)
TOTAL	13	94	58	50	120	100	107
TOTAL					335		207

First, we recognize from Table 4.1 that independent *kara*-clauses (i.e., (c)) increases in proportion in the twentieth century whereas the canonical use of these clauses (i.e., (a)) decreases from the nineteenth century onward. This observation diachronically supports the arguments for the emergence of independent *kara*-clauses made by previous studies in 4.2.3 above. Next, we can see from (b) in Table 4.1 that the inversion of a *kara*-clause and its "main" clause increases proportionately from the late nineteenth century. By putting (b) and (c) together, we can demonstrate that the proportion of "*kara* in the final position of sentences" increases rapidly in the twentieth century as Yoshii (1977:30) points out.

(50) The percentage of "*kara* in sentence-final position" in all *kara*'s

–1750	7.7
1750–1800	5.3
1800–1850	5.2
1850–1900	18.0
1900–1950	36.7
1950–2000 (wr)	44.0
1950–2000 (sp)	52.4

Viewed in this light, we may assume that the repeated use of inversion may lead to the use of independent *kara*-clauses in colloquial discourse in the twentieth century. From the viewpoint of clause-combining constructions, Table 4.1 clearly shows that the structural relation between a *kara*-clause and its grammatically associated "main" clause is becoming looser toward PDJ.

We now look for some indications that seem relevant to the inception of "*kara* in sentence-final position". The first point to observe is the inversion of a *kara*-clause and its "main" clause (i.e., (b)) diachronically. Table 4.1 above shows that (b) starts to increase around 1900. The increase in (b) can be interpreted as showing that a *kara*-clause becomes less integrated into the "main" clause and is on its way to becoming more independent from its "main" clause. There are a total of 77 examples of (b) in the written colloquial data. They can be subdivided into two groups by punctuation.[36] See (49) above for the instances of (b-1) and (b-2).

(51) Subdivision of (49b) by punctuation
    (b-1) [CL1, CL2 *kara*]
    (b-2) [CL1. CL2 *kara*]

Table 4.2 presents the distribution of *kara*-clauses of (49b) in the written colloquial data. In Table 4.2, we here focus on the distribution after the 1850s since the number of instances is not enough before that time.

Table 4.2: The transition of the distribution of (49b) in the written colloquial data

	–1750	–1800	–1850	–1900	–1950	–2000 (wr)	TOTAL
(b-1) CL1, CL2 *kara*	0 (0%)	2 (66.7%)	3 (100%)	7 (87.5%)	9 (33.3%)	4 (11.4%)	25
(b-2) CL1. CL2 *kara*	1 (100%)	1 (33.3%)	0 (0%)	1 (12.5%)	18 (66.7%)	31 (88.6%)	52
TOTAL	1	3	3	8	27	35	77

What is noticeable in Table 4.2 is that the proportion of (b-1) falls from the late nineteenth century onward whereas that of (b-2) rises in the twentieth century. We see that a *kara*-clause becomes more separate from the "main" clause in the early twentieth century, although we must admit that the punctuation in the diachronic data cannot be totally depended upon. From what we have observed in Tables 4.1 and 4.2, we may postulate the following pathway from less to more independent *kara*-clauses:

(52)

EModJ   **LModJ to PDJ**

(a) [[CL1 *kara*] CL2]

(b) [CL1 [CL2 *kara*]]   >   (b-1) [CL1, [CL2 *kara*]]

　　　　　　　　　　　　　(b-2) [CL1]. [CL2 *kara*]

(c)   ø   [CL *kara*]   >   [CL *kara*]

Another point to note is the correlation between an independent *kara*-clause and a *syuuzyosi* 'final particle' (see 2.3.2.2). It frequently appears in the utterance-final position in spoken discourse in Japanese. Table 4.3 shows the transition of instances of *kara*-clauses followed by the final particle *yo*, *ne*, and *sa*.

Table 4.3: The transition of the distribution of a *kara*-clause + FP

	−1750	−1800	−1850	−1900	−1950	−2000 (wr)	−2000 (sp)
[1] CL *kara*	13 (100%)	90 (95.7%)	57 (98.3%)	45 (90.0%)	102 (85.0%)	72 (72.0%)	90 (84.1%)
[2] CL *kara* FP	0 (0%)	4 (4.3%)	1 (1.7%)	5 (10.0%)	18 (15.0%)	28 (28.0%)	17 (15.9%)
TOTAL	13	94	58	50	120	100	107
TOTAL					335		207

Table 4.3 shows the gradual increase in *kara*-clauses followed by a final particle toward the twentieth century.[37]

Next, we focus on the written colloquial data from the 1850s to 2000 in order to observe the transition of the distribution of *kara*-clauses marked by a final particle in more detail. Each group in (49) above can be subdivided into two groups each according to whether the *kara*-clause is followed by a final particle or not (i.e., [1] or [2] in Table 4.3).

(53) Subdivision of (49) by a final particle following the *kara*-clause

    [1]   [2]

    (a) [CL1 *kara* CL2]   (a') [CL1 *kara* FP CL2]

    (b) [CL1, CL2 *kara*]   (b') [CL1, CL2 *kara* FP]

    (c) [CL *kara*]   (c') [CL *kara* FP]

    (d) Others   (d') Others with FP

[Examples of (b') and (c') from the diachronic data][38]

(b')

"nande   mata   konna   inaka   e   nagarekonde-kita   no   dai"
 why   INT   such   country to   drifted.into   NOMI   Q

'I wonder why you drifted into such a country as this?'

"tigee   nee,   danna   no   ossyaru   toori   da.
 wrong   not   you   NOM   say   as   COP

mattaku   nagarekonda   n   da   *kara*   <u>ne</u>.   ..."
really   drifted.into NOMI COP   KARA   SF

'That's it, you are right. Because I really drifted (here).'

(1906 *Kusamakura*, Ch. 5)

(c')[39]

"...   tonariatte   ita   mon   da   *kara*   watasi   made
       next.to   was   NOMI   COP   KARA   I   INT

hidoi   me   ni   awasarete   yo"
bitter   experience   DAT   had   SF

'... since I was next to (them), I had a bitter experience, too.'

"um,   karera   ga   koomanna   kao   o   siteiru   *kara*   <u>sa</u>. ..."
um   they   NOM   haughty   face   ACC   look   KARA   SF

'um, because they look high-and-mighty.'

(1897 *Konzikiyasya*, Ch. 2)

Table 4.4: The transition of the distribution of the *kara*-clause + FP after the 1850s

	–1900	–1950	–2000 (wr)
(a) CL1 *kara* CL2	38 (100%)	67 (100%)	43 (97.7%)
(a') CL1 *kara* FP CL2	0 (0%)	0 (0%)	1 (2.3%)
(a) + (a')	38	67	44
(b) CL1, CL2 *kara*	6 (75.0%)	19 (70.4%)	14 (40.0%)
(b') CL1, CL2 *kara* FP	2 (25.0%)	8 (29.6%)	21 (60.0%)
(b) + (b')	8	27	35
(c) CL *kara*	0 (0%)	8 (47.1%)	3 (33.3%)
(c') CL *kara* FP	1 (100%)	9 (52.9%)	6 (66.7%)
(c) + (c')	1	17	9
(d) Others	1	8	12
(d') Others FP	2	1	0
(d) + (d')	3	9	12
TOTAL of (a) – (d)	45	102	72
TOTAL of (a') – (d')	5	18	28
TOTAL	50	120	100

What is noteworthy is that (b') and (c') increase in proportion in the twentieth century. It is likely that the frequent use of final particles with *kara*-clauses adds a tone of finality to *kara*-clauses as a whole and has some influence upon the independence of *kara*-clauses from their "main" clauses. We can summarize the observation in the following way:

(54) Distribution of the *kara*-clause + FP after the 1850s
    (b) [CL1, CL2 *kara*]   on decrease
    (c) [CL *kara*]   on decrease

(b') [CL1, CL2 *kara* FP]   on increase
(c') [CL *kara* FP]   on increase

We may elaborate on (52) above and posit the following path of *kara*-clauses from subordinate to paratactic to independent clauses.[40]

(55)
EModJ   **LModJ to PDJ**
(a) [[CL1 *kara*] CL2]
(b) [CL1 [CL2 *kara*]]   >   (b) [CL1 [CL2 *kara*]]
                                (b') [CL1 [CL2 *kara* FP]   >   (b') [CL1] [CL2 *kara* FP]
                                                                    (c')   ø   [CL *kara* FP]

In this subsection, we have seen the transition of *kara*-clauses from less to more independent clause-combining constructions based on the diachronic and synchronic data. We have also observed the inception of the transition. We noticed that the inversion of *kara*-clauses and their "main" clauses frequently appears in LModJ and PDJ and that *kara*-clauses followed by a final particle gradually increase from LModJ onward. It is likely that these factors affect the paratactic and independent use of *kara*-clauses in PDJ. Taking into consideration cases where the "main" clause remains unspoken since it is understood from the context, we may posit the developmental process of *kara*-clauses from less to more independent clauses as follows:

(56) Development of *kara*-clauses from less to more independent clauses

EModJ   **LModJ to PDJ**

(a) [[CL1 *kara*] CL2]   (a) [[CL1 *kara*] CL2]

                                  [[CL1 *kara*] ø]   >   (c) [CL *kara*] ø

(b) [CL1 [CL2 *kara*]]   >   (b) [CL1 [CL2 *kara*]]

                                    ø [CL *kara*]   >   (c)   ø   [CL *kara*]

                                  (b') [CL1 [CL2 *kara* FP] >   (b') [CL1] [CL2 *kara* FP]

                                                                       (c')   ø   [CL *kara* FP]

4.4.3 From content to epistemic/speech-act conjunction interpretation

This subsection explores the developmental process of *kara*-clauses from the standpoint of semantic/pragmatic interpretation. It points out that the trend is toward epistemic/speech-act conjunction interpretation from EModJ to PDJ.

In 4.2.2 above, we reviewed Takubo (1987) and Uno (1997) who point out the correlation between syntactic and semantic/pragmatic functions of *kara*-clauses in PDJ. The correlation can be summarized in the following way:

(57) Syntactic and semantic/pragmatic functions of *kara*-clauses in PDJ

	subordinate	non-subordinate, paratactic
syntax:	[[CL1 *kara*] CL2]	[CL1 *kara*] [CL2]
semantics/	content conjunction	epistemic conjunction
pragmatics:		speech-act conjunction

We examine the above-mentioned correlation synchronically and diachronically in this subsection. We here focus on some types of expressions that overtly appear in both "main" clauses and *kara*-clauses in epistemic and speech-act conjunction interpretations. (58) below gives the subdivisions of (49a) [CL1 *kara* CL2] according to evident overt expressions of either epistemic, i.e., (i), or speech-act conjunction interpretation, i.e., (ii), and instances that are taken from the database for the present study.[41] Here, the simple past and non-past forms of verbs are classified as (iii) for the purpose of comparing Yoshii's (1977) survey (see the second point in Yoshii (1977), i.e., (44) and (45), in 4.3.2.3 above).[42] It turns out that clauses with the expression *n(o) da*, i.e., an auxiliary-like expression that follows a predicate and serves to add various semantic/pragmatic effects to the predicate, frequently appear in the twentieth century. They are classified as (iv) separately from the rest, but they are not explored here.[43] We need to mention here only that some examples of them may be regarded as overt expressions of speech-act conjunction interpretation. The instances with overt expressions other than (i)–(iv) and those without them are classified as (v) here.

(58) Subdivisions of (49a) according to overt expressions of epistemic and speech-act conjunctions

    (i-1) epistemic conjunction: with an epistemic modality [with EM]

    (i-2) epistemic conjunction: with an epistemic verb [with EV][44]

    (i-3) epistemic conjunction: with an adjective [with A]

    (i-4) epistemic conjunction: with a noun [with N]

    (ii) speech-act conjunction: with an expression of speech-act [with SA]

        (see (43b–f) in 4.3.2.3 above)

    (iii) with V

    (iv) with *n(o) da*

    (v) others

[Examples of (i-1)–(iv) in the diachronic data]

    (i-1) epistemic conjunction: with an epistemic modality [with EM]

Shinbei: naruhodo,	kisama	wa	Hakonezan	de
indeed	you	TOP	Mt. Hakone	at
gakumon	o	sasitta	*kara*,	
education	ACC	did	KARA	
yoo	sittegoza*roo*.			
well	know.guess			

'indeed, because you were educated at Mt. Hakone,

(I) suppose (you) know well.'

(1713 *Sukeroku*, p. 107)

(i-2) epistemic conjunction: with an epistemic verb [with EV]

Uki: … yonbe	mo	okyaku	ga,	tyootin	ga
last.evening	too	guest	NOM	paper.lantern	NOM
mettkaranee		totte		sagasassyaru	*kara*,
find.not		QUO		search.for	KARA
an	da	to	omot-tara,		
what	COP	QUO	wonder.then		
hinbukuro			no	koto	sa.
wick.of.stone.lantern			of	thing	FP

'… last night, too, because a guest said that (he could) not find a paper lantern and (he) searched for (it), (I) wondered what (it) was, and then (I found that what he meant was) the wick of a stone lantern.'

(1778 *Karuisawa*, p. 325)

(i-3) epistemic conjunction: with an adjective [with A]

Karu: mada isogasikanbee.
 still busy.guess

'(I) guess (you are) still busy.'

Saki: ai	mata	imani	omanma	o	dasimasu	*kara*,
yes	again	soon	meal	ACC	serve	KARA

isogasyuu-gozarimasu.
busy

'Yes, because we are about to serve a meal, (we are) busy.'

(1778 *Karuisawa*, p. 326)

(i-4) epistemic conjunction: with a noun [with N]

Motome:	site,	sono	okane	wa	donokurai	are-ba
	so	that	money	TOP	how.much	need.if
	yoi	no	degozarimasu.			
	good	NOMI	COP			

'so, how much do you need (for repaying his kindness)?'

Sagobei:	sorya	saki	kara	"kure"	to	iu
	that.TOP	him	from	give.me	QUO	say
	no	de	wa	nasi,	kottino	kokorozasi
	NOMI COP		INT	not	my	gratitude
	de	ageru	no	da	*kara*,	tatoeba
	with	give	NOMI	COP	KARA	for.exmple
	gozyuu-ryoo	demo	go-ryoo		demo,	
	fifty-ryo	be.if	five-ryoo		be.if	
	kokorozasi	wa	onazi	koto	zya.	
	gratitude		TOP	same	thing	COP

'It is not that he asked (me) "give me (some money)", but because (I) (will) give (him) with gratitude, it's all the same if (I give him), for example, 50-ryo or 5-ryo.'

(1859 *Kosode*, p. 299)

(ii) speech-act conjunction: with an expression of speech-act [with SA]

Raigen:	korya	omae	ni	kagiru	yaku	da.
	this.TOP	you	DAT	right	role	COP
	otoko	ga	itte	wa	ikenu	*kara*,
	man	NOM	go	TOP	not.good	KARA
	nantoka.katoka	yawarakani,		itiban	damasite	
	somehow	well		one.play	trick	
	okaeri	nasare.				
	go.home	do.IMP				

'This is a right role for you. Because it is not good for a man to go, somehow, you trick (them) and go home.'

(1736 *Shibaraku*, p. 156)

(iii) with V[45]

omae	ga	nannokano	to	iinasaru	*kara*
you	NOM	this.and .that	QUO	say	KARA

watasya	soba	de	ki-o-momiyasita.
I.TOP	beside	at	was.anxious.about

'Because you talked about this and that, I was anxious about (what you were going to say), (staying) beside you.'

(1736 *Tatumi no sono*, p. 311)

(iv) with *n(o) da*[46]

Fuzii: … godan-me	no	seihon	ga
… fifth.act	of	original.copy	NOM

hutokoro	ni	atta	*kara,*	matigeete
breast.pocket	in	existed	KARA	wrongly

tuketa	no	da
added	NOMI	COP

'Because I had the fifth act in the original copy (of the scenario) in my breast pocket, I carelessly added (the lines).

(1736 *Shibaraku*, p. 161)

[Examples of (i-1)–(iv) in the synchronic data]

(i-1) epistemic conjunction: with an epistemic modality [with EM]

omote	wa	syattaa	ga	simatteiru	*kara*
front	TOP	shutter	NOM	closed	KARA

haire	ya	sinai	daroo.
can.enter	INT	cannot	guess

'Because the front shutter is closed, (we) cannot go in.'

(1978 *Shimbashi*, Ch. 2)

(i-2) epistemic conjunction: with an epistemic verb [with EV]

    H: ... tuaa, bon-tte ryokoogaisya de
          tour bang-QUO travel.agency at
          tanonzyatte, omakase da *kara*,
          reserve leave COP KARA

    '... because (many people) just reserve (a package) tour at (a) travel agency with a bang and leave (everything to the agency)'

    S: un
       yes
    'yes'

    H: anmari ne, zikokuhyo katuyoosimasu tte
         rarely FP timetable make.use.of QUO
         iu hito, mezurasii to <u>omou</u>.
         say person rare QUO think

    'I think a person (like you) who makes use of a timetable is rare,'

                                        (1999 Conversation, NJ9911)

(i-3) epistemic conjunction: with an adjective [with A]

    Q: mukasi no nedan da *kara* takai yo
        old of price COP KARA expensive FP

    'because (it) is an old price, (it) is expensive.'

                                        (1995 Conversation, Z9515)

(i-4) epistemic conjunction: with a noun [with N]

    K: ... kodomo ga neteru aidani dekiru sigoto da
         child NOM sleeping while can.do work COP
      kara, Yamamura-san no sigoto wa, sooiu <u>are</u>
      KARA Yamamura of work TOP such that
      <u>desu</u> yo ne, genkoo o kaku, raitaa-san.
      COP FP FP article ACC write writer

    '... because (it) is work that (you) can do while (your) child is sleeping, Yamamura's work is like that, isn't it? writing an article, a writer.'

(1999 Conversation, NJ9909)

(ii) speech-act conjunction: with an expression of speech-act [with SA]

Q: de	ano	hito	hudan	okonnai	*kara*
then	that	person	usually	angry.not	KARA

kowaku-<u>nai?</u>

scary-not

'then because she doesn't usually get angry, she isn't scary, is she?'

(1995 Conversation, Z9512)

(iii) with V

Q: demo	hikkosityatta	*kara*	zenzen	<u>awanakunatte-kita</u>.
but	moved	KARA	at.all	see.not-came.to

'but because (she) moved (to some other town), (I) don't see her at all now.'

(1995 Conversation, Z9513)

(iv) with *n(o) da*

enpitu	no	motikata	ga	warui	*kara*
pencil	of	hold.way	NOM	bad	KARA

koo	naru	<u>no</u>	<u>da</u>
this	become	NOMI	COP

'because your way of holding the pencil is bad, you end up like this.'

(1970 *Kokoo no hito*, Ch. 1–2)

These expressions will be used as clues for examining (49a) [CL1 *kara* CL2], (49b) [CL1, CL2 *kara*], and (49c) [CL *kara*] in terms of the correlation between syntactic and semantic/pragmatic functions of *kara*-clauses in this subsection. As for (49a), we can observe the transition of the distribution of these expressions from EMod to PDJ. Since (49b) and (49c) start to appear in the twentieth century, we mainly compare the distribution trend with that of (49a).

There are a total of 248 examples of (49a) [CL1 *kara* CL2] in the diachronic data and a total of 92 examples in the synchronic data. It turned out that the number of instances before the 1750s is too small in comparison with the rest.[47] We focus on the transitions after 1750, i.e., a total of 239 examples in the diachronic data. Table 4.5 shows the distribution of overt expressions in (58) in the "main" clause (CL2) and Table 4.6 presents that in the *kara*-clause (CL1).

Table 4.5: The transition of the distribution of (49a) [CL1 *kara* CL2] in "main" clauses

Main clause (CL2)	–1800	–1850	–1900	–1950	–2000 (wr)	–2000 (sp)
(i-1) with EM	6	4	5	11	6	2
(i-2) with EV	5	3	2	4	2	15
(i-3) with A	7	4	3	3	2	5
(i-4) with N	2	4	4	3	2	1
TOTAL of (i)	20 (23.8%)	15 (30.0%)	14 (36.8%)	21 (31.3%)	12 (27.3%)	23 (47.9%)
(ii) with SA	35 (41.7%)	10 (20.0%)	12 (31.6%)	24 (35.8%)	15 (34.1%)	8 (16.7%)
(iii) with V	26 (31.0%)	22 (44.0%)	10 (26.3%)	12 (17.9%)	7 (15.9%)	12 (25.0%)
(iv) with *n(o) da*	1 (1.2%)	2 (4.0%)	2 (5.3%)	3 (4.5%)	7 (15.9%)	1 (2.1%)
(v) others	2 (2.4%)	1 (2.0%)	0 (2.0%)	7 (10.4%)	3 (6.8%)	4 (8.3%)
TOTAL	84	50	38	67	44	48
TOTAL				239		92

Table 4.6: The transition of the distribution of (49a) [CL1 *kara* CL2] in *kara*-clauses

Kara-clause (CL1)	–1800	–1850	–1900	–1950	–2000 (wr)	–2000 (sp)
(i-1) with EM	2	0	2	1	1	1
(i-2) with EV	0	3	1	0	0	2
(i-3) with A	9	1	2	7	8	8
(i-4) with N	11	11	13	11	6	9
TOTAL of (i)	22 (26.2%)	15 (30.0%)	18 (47.4%)	19 (28.4%)	15 (34.1%)	20 (41.7%)
(ii) with SA	3 (3.6%)	2 (4.0%)	0 (0%)	5 (7.5%)	0 (0%)	1 (2.1%)
(iii) with V	53 (63.1%)	31 (62.0%)	12 (31.6%)	23 (34.3%)	18 (40.9%)	27 (56.3%)
(iv) with *n(o) da*	0 (0%)	0 (0%)	4 (8.0%)	14 (20.9%)	8 (18.2%)	0 (0%)
(v) others	6 (7.1%)	2 (4.0%)	4 (10.5%)	6 (9.0%)	3 (6.8%)	0 (0%)
TOTAL	84	50	38	67	44	48
TOTAL				239		92

The first point to notice in Table 4.5 is that the ratio of type (iii), i.e., what Yoshii (1977) calls "description of facts" (see (43) in 4.3.2.3 above), gradually decreases in "main" clauses in the diachronic data as he points out. The decrease in type (iii) after the 1850s is in agreement with his survey. We do not find any convincing reasons why it increases in PDJ in the spoken data. Second, Table 4.5 shows that type (i), i.e., overt expressions of epistemic conjunction interpretation, gradually increases proportionately up to 1900 and levels off at about 30% in the twentieth century. It occupies about half the instances of the spoken data. Third, we can see that type (ii), i.e., overt expressions of speech-act conjunction interpretation, decreases proportionately up to the 1850s, but afterward it increases. On these grounds, we can recognize that the overt expressions of epistemic and speech-act conjunction interpretations remain in more than half of all the instances of *kara*-clauses from LModJ onward. In other words, the interpretation of *kara*-clauses tends to be epistemic or speech-act conjunction from LModJ onward.

Table 4.6 shows that the ratio of type (iii) rapidly decreases in *kara*-clauses after the 1850s, but it increases in the synchronic data. The percentage of type (i) remains approximately between 30% and 50% from the 1800s onward. Type (ii) scarcely appears in *kara*-clauses. The type (iv), i.e., the expression *n(o) da kara*, increases in the twentieth century (Noda 1997). Roughly speaking, Table 4.6 shows that a greater variety of expressions begin to appear in *kara*-clauses in the twentieth century.

Next, we examine instances of (49b) [CL1, CL2 *kara*], i.e., the inversion of a *kara*-clause and its "main" clause, in the same way as above. There are a total of 42 examples in the diachronic data and a total of 46 examples in the synchronic data. We focus on the distributions after the 1850s in both tables since it turns out that the instances of (49b) are sporadic before the 1850s in our data (see Table 4.1 above). Thus, we analyze a total of 35 examples after the 1850s in the diachronic data. The distribution of overt expressions in (58) in the "main" clause (CL1) is given in Table 4.7 and that in the *kara*-clause (CL2) is given in Table 4.8.

(59) [Examples of (49b) in the twentieth century]

(i-1) epistemic conjunction: with an epistemic modality [with EM]

"zya,   yatu   wa   konya   kore   kara
so   he   TOP   this.evening now   from

koko   ni   kuru   kamosirenai   naa.   zekkoo   no
here   to   come   may   FP   big   of

tyansu da   kara   naa ..."
chance COP   KARA   FP

'so, he may be coming over here this evening, because this is a big chance.'

(1978 *Shimbashi*, Ch. 2)

(i-2) epistemic conjunction: with an epistemic verb [with EV]

"haa,	Taroo	toiu	no	wa,	ii	namae	da
well	Taroo	called	NOMI	TOP	good	name	COP
to	omoimasu.		daiiti,	donna	syokugyoo	ni	
QUO	think		first	whatever	occupation	for	
demo	mukimasu		kara	ne. ..."			
INT	suitable		KARA	FP			

'well, I think Taroo is a good name. First, because it is a suitable (name) for any occupation. ...'

(1985 *Taroo*, Ch. 1-1)

(i-3) epistemic conjunction: with an adjective [with A]

| "waruku-naidesu. | gogatu | kara | toreenin'gu-sitemasu | kara. ..." |
| bad-not | May | from | training-do | KARA |

'(my physical condition is) not bad. Because I am in training (for the match) from May.'

(1982 *Issyun no natu*, Ch.1–3)

(i-4) epistemic conjunction: with a noun [with N]

komaru	no	wa	yappari	byooki	de	yo,
trouble	NOMI	TOP	you.know	illness	COP	SF
kusuri	ga	moo	nakunatteiru	kara	yoo.	
medicine	NOM	already	run.out.of	KARA	FP	

'(what) troubles (me) is the illness, you know, because (I've) already run out of medicine.'

(1978 *Shimbashi*, Ch. 2)

(ii) speech-act conjunction: with a speech–act expression [with SA]

| Q:a | P-tyan | zyuku-koo | da | yo ne |
| ah | P | after-school.lessons-instructor | COP | FP FP |

'ah, P, (you) are an instructor of after-school lessons, aren't you?'

P: soosoosoosoo
   yes.yes.yes.yes
   'yes. yes. yes. yes.'

Q: tyuukan   to   ka   itteta   *kara*
   midterm   QUO   Q   said   KARA
   'because you said something about the midterm (examination)'

P: uun
   yes
   'yes.'

(1995 Conversation, Z9507)

(iii) with V

P: uun   de   X-san   daizyoobuna   no   ka   na
   well   then   X   all.rught   COMP Q   FP
   tteiu kai   ga   hossoku-sareta (laugh) uun honto
   called society NOM   was.organized   well really
   ninki   atta   *kara*   X-tyan
   popular   had   KARA   X

'well, then, the society called "is X all right?" was organized, (laugh), well, because X was really popular (at school).'

(1995 Conversation, Z9513)

(iv) with *n(o) da*

N: ... sutoraiku   toka   toru   n   desu   yo.
      strike   so.on   score   NOMI   COP   FP
      iryoku   wa   aru   *kara*.
      power   INT   have   KARA

'I score strikes (in tenpins). Because I have power.'

(1999 Conversation, NJ9910)

Table 4.7: The transition of the distribution of (49b) [CL1, CL2 *kara*] in "main" clauses

Main clause (CL1)	–1900	–1950	–2000 (wr)	–2000 (sp)
(i-1) with EM	1	4	3	0
(i-2) with EV	0	0	2	1
(i-3) with A	1	4	1	0
(i-4) with N	0	2	2	0
TOTAL of (i)	2 (25.0%)	10 (37.1%)	8 (22.9%)	1 (9.1%)
(ii) with SA	4 (50.0%)	8 (29.6%)	13 (37.1%)	4 (36.4%)
(iii) with V	1 (12.5%)	3 (11.1%)	5 (14.3%)	3 (27.3%)
(iv) with *n(o) da*	1 (12.5%)	3 (11.1%)	4 (11.4%)	1 (9.1%)
(v) others	0 (0%)	3 (11.1%)	5 (14.3%)	2 (18.2%)
TOTAL	8	27	35	11
TOTAL		35		46

There is not much difference in distribution between Tables 4.7 and 4.8, i.e., the case of inverted clause order, and Tables 4.5 and 4.6, i.e., the case of canonical clause order. However, it is debatable how the former differs from the latter in terms of discourse role (Thompson, 1985; Schiffrin, 1987; Ford, 1993; etc.). It calls for further investigation based on a broader database in PDJ. I leave the matter open.

Lastly, we examine instances of (49c) [CL *kara*], i.e., the independent use of a *kara*-clause. There are totals of 20 examples in the diachronic data and 55 examples in the synchronic data. Since the instances of (49c) scarcely appear before 1900s in the diachronic data (see Table 4.1 above), we focus on their distribution after 1900. We thus examine a total of 17 examples in the diachronic data. Table 4.9 gives the distribution of overt expressions listed in (58).

Table 4.8: The transition of the distribution of (49b) [CL1, CL2 *kara*] in *kara*-clauses

Kara-clause (CL2)	–1900	–1950	–2000 (wr)	–2000 (sp)
(i-1) with EM	0	2	1	0
(i-2) with EV	0	0	0	1
(i-3) with A	1	3	3	1
(i-4) with N	1	4	5	2
TOTAL of (i)	2 (25.0%)	9 (33.3%)	9 (25.7%)	4 (36.4%)
(ii) with SA	1 (12.5%)	1 (3.7%)	1 (2.9%)	0 (0%)
(iii) with V	2 (25.0%)	4 (14.8%)	10 (28.6%)	7 (63.6%)
(iv) with *n(o) da*	2 (25.0%)	11 (40.7%)	10 (28.6%)	0 (0%)
(v) others	1 (12.5%)	2 (7.4%)	5 (14.3%)	0 (0%)
TOTAL	8	27	35	11
TOTAL		35		46

(60) [Examples of (49c) in the twentieth century][48]

(i-1) epistemic conjunction: with an epistemic modality [with EM]

S: maa,   dakedo hutuuni,   mawari   kara   mireba,
   well   but   generally   other.people   from   see.if
   sooiuhuuni   kaisya   ni   zutto   ite,
   this.way   company   in   all.the.time   exist
   tatoeba,   yasumi mo dete,   "kaisya   sukina
   for.example   day.off too go   company   fond
   n   da   ne"   tte   iuhuuni,   hokano hito
   NOMI   COP   FP   QUO   as   other   person
   wa   miru   daroo   kara   ne.
   TOP   see   guess   KARA   FP

'well, but, generally, if other people see (me), (I am) at (my) office all the time this way, for example, (I) go (to work) on days off, because (I) guess other people see me as (a person to whom they say) "(you are) fond of (your) company".'

I: un.

   yes

   'yes'

S: zibun   de   wa   soo   de   wa   nakutemo.
   myself   for   TOP   so   COP   TOP   not.though

   'for myself, I am not (fond of my company so much), though.'

(2000 Conversation, JN0002)

(i-3) epistemic conjunction: with an adjective [with A]

   "Tokyo   wa   doko   da   ka   sireru[49]   kai"
   Tokyo   TOP   where   COP   Q   know   FP

    'where in Tokyo (do you) know?'

   "soo   sa   ne.   Tokyo   wa   bakani   hiroi
   well   FP   FP   Tokyo   TOP   extremely   broad

   kara   ne"
   KARA   FP

    'well. because Tokyo is extremely spread out'

(1906 *Kusamakura*, Ch. 5)

(i-4) epistemic conjunction: with a noun [with N]

   "yoku   sitteiru   na"
   well   know   FP

    'you know well'

   "koo   miete,   watasi   mo   Edo-kko   da   *kara*   ne"
   this   look   I   too   Edo-born   COP   KARA   FP

    'believe it or not, because I was born in Edo, too'

(1906 *Kusamakura*, Ch. 5)

(ii) speech-act conjunction: with an expression of speech-act [with SA]

K: yappari,   nani,   kaisya   no   zyookyoo
   of.course   well   company   of   situation
   toka   kangaete   sa,   zibun   no
   so.on   consider   FP   my   of
   sekinin   toka   kangaete,   yappa,
   responsibility   so.on   consider   of.course
   yatte-<u>ikanaitoikenai</u>   *kara*   ne.
   do-must   KARA   FP

'of course, well, (I) consider the situation in the company and so on, (I) consider my responsibility and so on, of course, because (I) must (consider these points).'

I: soo   na   no   yo   ne.
   so   COP   NOMI   FP   FP
   'you are right.'

(1995 Conversation, Z9507)

(iii) with V

G: maneezyaa   yobe   tte   iwareteru   *kara*.
   manager   call   QUO   say.to.me   KARA
   'because (the supervisor) instructs me to call the manager (when I have any troubles).'

(2000 Conversation, NJ0001)

(iv) with *n(o) da*

S: nee,   yappari,   tetudatte-morawanaito   ne.
   yes   of.course   help-receive   FP
   'yes, of course, I (need my husband's) help.'

Chapter 4 Development of Japanese *kara*-clauses 175

H: sore   o   taberu   no   wa   hutari   na
   that   ACC   eat   NOMI   TOP   two.of.you COP
   n   desu   kara.
   NOMI   COP   KARA

'it is two of you who eat them.'

S: soosoosoosoo!
   yes.yes.yes.yes
   'that's right!'

(1999 Conversation, NJ9904)

Table 4.9: The transition of the distribution of (49c) [CL *kara*]

Kara-clause	−1950	−2000 (wr)	−2000 (sp)
(i-1) with EM	0	0	1
(i-2) with EV	0	0	0
(i-3) with A	2	1	3
(i-4) with N	3	2	4
TOTAL of (i)	5 (18.5%)	3 (33.3%)	8 (17.8%)
(ii) with SA	0 (0%)	1 (11.1%)	9 (20.0%)
(iii) with V	3 (17.6%)	2 (22.2%)	21 (46.7%)
(iv) with *n(o) da*	6 (35.3%)	2 (22.2%)	2 (4.4%)
(v) others	3 (17.6%)	1 (11.1%)	5 (11.1%)
TOTAL	17	9	45
TOTAL	17		54

First, Table 4.9 shows that the overt expressions of epistemic conjunction interpretations increase proportionately in written colloquial data. In spoken data, they occupy about 20%. Second, as far as the data for the present study are concerned, there are no data of independent *kara*-clauses with overt expressions of speech-act conjunction interpretations before the 1950s. We find such *kara*-clauses in PDJ spoken data. In sum, independent *kara*-clauses with both types of expressions occupy about 20% of all the instances before the 1950s while they hold about 40% in PDJ. Roughly speaking, we recognize that both types of expression are beginning to appear overtly in independent *kara*-clauses in PDJ. Again, there is room for further investigation on the independent use of *kara*-clauses based on a broader database of PDJ.

In this subsection, we have observed the transition of the correlation between syntactic and semantic/pragmatic functions of *kara*-clauses. We have found that the correlation between them becomes overtly expressed from LModJ onward. Seen from the viewpoint of semantic/pragmatic functions, *kara*-clauses tend to be used to express epistemic/speech-act conjunction interpretations in PDJ.

4.4.4 Summary

Section 4.4 examined the developmental process of *kara*-clauses from LModJ to PDJ. Section 4.4.1 noted the detail of the data used for this section. In the light of clause-combining constructions, 4.4.2 traced in detail the developmental process of *kara*-clauses and demonstrated the trend toward more independent clause-combining constructions. We also noticed the frequent use of the inversion of *kara*-clauses and their "main" clauses and that of *kara*-clauses followed by a final particle. It appears that they have some influence on the use of *kara*-clauses independently. In light of the correlation between syntactic and semantic/pragmatic functions, 4.4.3 investigated the transition of the correlation. We recognized that the correlation becomes marked overtly with some types of expressions and the interpretation of *kara*-clause constructions tends toward epistemic/speech-act conjunction in PDJ.

Given the observations in this section and what was pointed out in 4.2 and 4.3 above, we can summarize the developmental process of *kara*-clauses from EModJ to PDJ in the following way:

(61) The developmental path of *kara*-clauses from EModJ to PDJ[50]

EModJ: CL1 *kara* CL2

[[CL1*kara*] CL2]

CL1+CL2: hypotaxis

CL1: hypotactic

CM: SCM

LModJ: to PDJ	CL1 *kara* CL2 [[CL1*kara*] CL2]	a. CL1 *kara* CL2 [CL1 *kara*] [CL2] b. CL1 CL2 *kara* [CL1][CL2 *kara*]	a. CL *kara* ø [CL *kara*] ø b. ø CL *kara* ø [CL *kara*]
	CL1+CL2: hypotaxis	CL1+CL2: parataxis	CL+ø: parataxis ø+CL: parataxis
	CL1: hypotactic	CL1 in (a): paratactic CL2 in (b): paratactic	CL: independent
	CM: SCM	CM: paratactic CM	CM: final-particle-like PM
		Interpretation: content conjunction	Interpretation: epistemic conjunction/ speech-act conjunction

In order to examine the developmental path of *kara*-clauses from the perspective of grammaticalization in the following section, we take up the following two points.

First, let us observe the development of *kara*-clauses in view of their structural function. [CL1+CL2] shows a distinction in clause-combining constructions posited by Hopper and Traugott (2003:176–184) (see 2.2.5 above). It indicates that the relationship between *kara*-clauses and their "main" clauses has become more paratactic. As "CL1" (and "CL2 in (b)" in the case of parataxis) represents, *kara*-clauses have extended from hypotactic to paratactic clauses. Furthermore, they are becoming more paratactic, i.e., independent, in PDJ. "CM" shows that the so-called subordinate clause marker *kara* can be viewed as a clause-final pragmatic marker in the construction [CL *kara*] (see 2.3.2.2 above). The developmental paths under discussion can be summarized in the following way:

(62) The development of *kara*-clauses in structural function
    a. clause-combining constructions:
      hypotaxis > parataxis
    b. *kara*-clauses:
      hypotactic > paratactic > independent
    c. *kara*:
      subordinate clause marker > paratactic clause marker >
      final-particle-like pragmatic marker

Second, we consider the development of *kara*-clauses in view of their semantic/pragmatic function. "Interpretation" indicates an interpretation of *kara*-clauses that is correlated with each construction (see 2.3.1.2). The semantic/pragmatic function of *kara*-clauses has tended toward an epistemic/speech-act conjunction interpretation. The trend can be summarized in the following way:

(63) The development of *kara*-clauses in semantic/pragmatic function:
    content conjunction > epistemic/speech-act conjunction

In the following section, we will discuss the development of *kara*-clauses in the light of grammaticalization.

4.5 Discussion

The aim of this section is to examine the structural and semantic/pragmatic extension of *kara*-clauses from the perspective of grammaticalization. Section 4.5.1 addresses the issue of multiple functions of *kara*-clauses in PDJ. Section 4.5.2 illustrates that the diachronic process and synchronic diversity of *kara*-clauses can be counted as a case of grammaticalization. Section 4.5.3 considers the hypothesis of structural and semantic/pragmatic unidirectionality. Section 4.5.4 takes up some other analogous cases in the history of Japanese and shows that the case of *kara*-clauses is not an exceptional one in Japanese.

4.5.1 Multiple functions of *kara*-clauses in present-day Japanese

In 4.4, we observed that it is in the twentieth century that independent *kara*-clauses become frequent (see Table 4.1 (c)) and those with an overt expression of epistemic/ speech-act conjunction interpretation proportionately increase (see Table 4.9). It follows from these observations that *kara*-clauses become independent of their syntactically associated "main" clauses and have come to be used with more subjective meanings in the last 100 years. Besides, we noticed that the inversion of the *kara*-clause and its "main" clause increased from the 1850s (see Table 4.1 (b)).[51] Together with independent *kara*-clauses, we recognized that the so-called subordinate clause marker *kara* tends to appear "in the sentence-final position" in the twentieth century (see (50) in 4.4.2). "*Kara* in the sentence-final position" can be seen as a final particle in the sense that it occurs in the same position as a final particle and it has its own discourse-pragmatic functions (Alfonso, 1980; Shirakawa, 1991; Ohori, 1995a, 1997a; Iguchi, 1998; Honda, 2001, 2005). Viewed in this light, *kara*-clauses in PDJ can be regarded as being reanalyzed as single independent clauses with a clause-final pragmatic marker (see 2.3.2.2 and 4.2.3). The reanalysis of *kara*-clauses as independent can be represented in the following way.

(64) Reanalysis of *kara*-clauses as independent in PDJ

Canonical			**Independent**		
CL1	*kara*	CL2	CL	*kara*	ø
[[CL1 + SCM] + CL2]			[CL + PM]		ø

Inversion			**Independent**		
CL1	CL2	*kara*	ø	CL	*kara*
[CL1 + [CL2 + SCM]]			ø	[CL + PM]	

We found in the preceding section that the "main" clause of a *kara*-clause constantly has an overt expression of epistemic/speech-act conjunction interpretation from LModJ onward (see Tables 4.5 and 4.7). As pointed out in 4.2.2, *kara*-clause constructions with epistemic/speech-act conjunction interpretation are more paratactic than those with content conjunction interpretation in the sense that *kara*-clauses can be viewed as not being associated with the main verb but with the speech-act performed in their "main" clauses.[52] Therefore, we can postulate that *kara*-clauses have started to acquire multiple functions during the last 100 years as follows:

(65) Structural and semantic/pragmatic extension of *kara*-clause constructions in the twentieth century

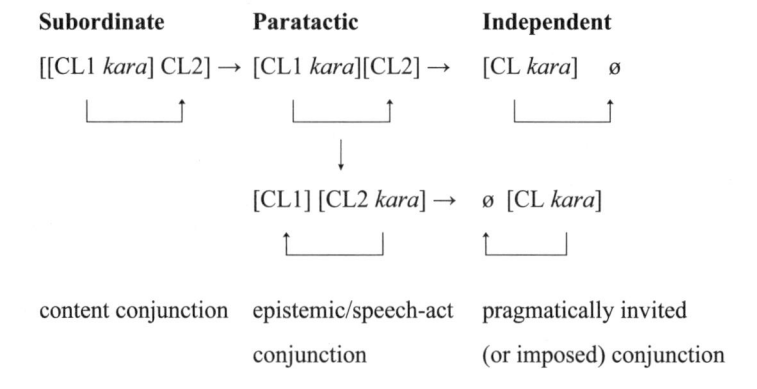

Subordinate	**Paratactic**	**Independent**
[[CL1 *kara*] CL2] →	[CL1 *kara*][CL2] →	[CL *kara*] ø
	↓	
	[CL1] [CL2 *kara*] →	ø [CL *kara*]
content conjunction	epistemic/speech-act conjunction	pragmatically invited (or imposed) conjunction

We now consider the motivations behind this extension. It was claimed in 3.5

above that the development of *because*-clauses is motivated by conventionalization of pragmatic meanings. It also plays a leading role in the development of *kara*-clauses. In the LModJ period, *kara*-clause constructions associated with epistemic/speech-act conjunction interpretation frequently appear (see Tables 4.5 and 4.6). As the association between *kara*-clause constructions and such interpretation becomes reinforced by the frequent use of such constructions, the association is conventionalized as part of *kara*-clause constructions. Once it is conventionalized, the speaker assumes that the hearer would interpret a paratactic *kara*-clause as being pragmatically linked to the following clause.

At the same time, the inversion of a *kara*-clause and its "main" clause becomes frequent after 1850 (see Table 4.1 (b)). This phenomenon can be understood as an indication that a *kara*-clause becomes less integrated into its "main" clause structurally. The inverted *kara*-clause constructions seem to take over their association with epistemic/speech-act conjunction interpretation from the constructions with canonical word order (see Tables 4.7 and 4.8). Thus, the speaker may expect the hearer to understand an inverted construction as being pragmatically linked to the preceding clause.

Furthermore, independent *kara*-clauses are becoming frequently used in the twentieth century (see Table 4.1 (c)). This phenomenon can be viewed as suggesting that *kara*-clauses are becoming more and more paratactic. Independent *kara*-clauses seem to inherit their pragmatic characteristics from those of paratactic *kara*-clauses. They tend to be used with epistemic/speech-act conjunction interpretation (see Table 4.9). As they become frequent in such contexts, their association with such an interpretation becomes stronger. Once it is conventionalized, the speaker may invite the hearer to interpret an independent *kara*-clause as being pragmatically linked to the following or preceding context. As a result, it can be reanalyzed (or grammaticalized) as a single independent clause with a clause-final pragmatic marker in the twentieth century. In fact, *kara* gives rise to a pragmatic effect that is similar to a final particle in Japanese (Alfonso, 1980; Shirakawa, 1991; Ohori, 1995a, 1997a; Iguchi, 1998; Honda, 2001, 2005). The pragmatic effects of *kara* become stronger as the stages in

(65) progress. Hence, it seems reasonable to suppose that *kara* is in the process of developing into a clause-final pragmatic marker in PDJ. On these grounds, we come to the conclusion that the development of *kara*-clauses from subordinate to independent clauses is motivated by conventionalization of pragmatic meanings in the same way as in the case of English *because*-clauses.[53]

It is necessary to mention in passing that final particles may play an important role in the development of *kara* from the causal clause marker to the clause-final pragmatic marker. It was observed in 4.4.2 that some kinds of final particles are becoming frequently used with *kara*, namely [CL1, CL2 *kara* FP] and [CL *kara* FP], in PDJ (see (54) in 4.4.2). It can be postulated that the pragmatic characteristics of inverted paratactic *kara*-clause constructions and independent *kara*-clauses are reinforced by their frequent use with these final particles. It can also be assumed that these *kara*-clauses inherit the characteristics of finality from final particles and the independence of these *kara*-clauses from their "main" clauses may be influenced by the frequent use of final particles.[54]

4.5.2 Development of *kara*-clauses as an instance of grammaticalization

We examine here the developmental paths of *kara*-clauses from the perspective of grammaticalization. Reference to the five principles of grammaticalization proposed by Hopper (1991) (see 2.2.3 above) is made in the same way as for English *because*-clauses.[55] The development of *kara*-clauses is not necessarily a textbook example of grammaticalization, i.e., the change from a lexical to a grammatical item. It does, however, share characteristics associated with grammaticalization (Brinton, 2001).

First, the coexistence of subordinate, paratactic, and independent *kara*-clauses in PDJ can be viewed as an instance of "layering", i.e., the coexistence of older and new layers.[56] With regard to the diachronic and synchronic phenomena of *kara*, the following cases can be counted as instances of "layering" as well; the coexistence of the functions of *kara* as a formal noun and a case particle in LOJ, as a bound morpheme and a case particle in MJ, as a case particle and a clause marker in EModJ to PDJ (see (38) in 4.3.2.2), and as a case particle, a clause marker, and a final particle, i.e., pragmatic marker, in PDJ (see 4.2.1 and 4.4.4).

Second, the development of *kara*-clauses illustrates "divergence". It refers to "a natural outcome of the process of grammaticalization, which begins as a fixing of a lexical form in a specific potentially grammatical environment, where the form takes on a new meaning" (Hopper and Traugott, 2003:118)". As we reviewed in 4.3.2 above, the causal clause marker *kara* in PDJ diverged from the case particle in EModJ. Further, the latter is said to diverge from a formal noun, which may have come from a lexical noun (S. Ono, 1953, 1966). Turning to *kara* in PDJ, we recognize that it is in the process of diverging from a subordinate clause marker to a final particle, i.e., a clause-final pragmatic marker (see 4.2.3 and 4.4.4).

From the viewpoint of interpretation, *kara*-clauses seem to be in the process of diverging from content to epistemic/speech-act conjunction interpretation in PDJ. In 4.2.2, we noted that an interpretation of *kara*-clauses as content conjunctions typically associates with a subordinate *kara*-clause whereas that as epistemic/speech-act conjunctions associates with a paratactic *kara*-clause in PDJ (Takubo, 1987; Uno, 1997). We then showed that *kara*-clauses are developing from less to more independent clauses in 4.4.2 and that the trend of the interpretation of *kara*-clauses is from content to epistemic/speech-act conjunctions in 4.4.3. From these observations, we can say that *kara*-clauses are in the process of taking on new meanings when they are paratactic or independent clauses in PDJ. In this sense, they can be counted as an instance of "divergence" although we do not necessarily speak of lexical items.

Third, the development of *kara* from an ablative case marker to a causal clause marker represents "persistence", i.e., the retention of the original meanings in its grammaticalized form. The meaning "from" in the ablative case marker is retained in the causal meaning, i.e., "logical 'fromness'" (Ohori, 1998a:3) in the clause marker (see 4.2.1).[57] In addition, we noticed that the "causal" meaning of *kara* is extended to some other semantic/pragmatic meanings (see 2.3.1.2 and 4.2.2) and to the function as a clause-final pragmatic marker (see 2.3.2.2 and 4.2.3). Such extensions can be understood as an instance of "persistence" in the sense that the original "causal" meaning is retained in newer semantic/pragmatic functions of paratactic and independent *kara*-clauses.

Lastly, the development of *kara* from a formal noun via a case marker to a clause marker and a pragmatic marker can be viewed as "de-categorialization". It is the tendency of a major grammatical category such as noun and verb, i.e., a relatively "open" lexical category, to develop into a minor grammatical category, i.e., a relatively "closed" category (Hopper and Traugott, 2003:107). Although the OJ *kara* as a formal noun is not a full member of the noun category, it loses its properties as a noun later in history (see 4.3.2).

So far, we have shown that the diachronic process and synchronic functional diversity of *kara*-clauses share some characteristics associated with grammaticalization based on Hopper's (1991) principles of grammaticalization. We can say that the case of *kara*-clauses can be counted as a case of grammaticalization.

4.5.3 Development of *kara*-clauses and the hypothesis of unidirectionality

Having noted that the developmental process of *kara*-clauses can be viewed as an instance of grammaticalization, we then go on to consider the hypothesis of unidirectionality in grammaticalization (see 2.2.4). We here focus on two kinds of unidirectionality, namely a cline of clause-combining constructions (see 2.2.5) and subjectification (see 2.2.6). In 3.5.2 above, it was pointed out that the developmental process of English *because*-clauses poses a counter-example to the former, whereas it provides a good example of the latter. In this subsection, we will show that the same is true of *kara*-clauses in Japanese.

First, we consider the cline of clause-combining constructions. It predicts that the direction is toward less paratactic clause-combining constructions, i.e., parataxis > hypotaxis > subordination, along with grammaticalization. Contrary to the cline, it was shown in the preceding sections (see 4.3.2.3 and 4.4.2) that *kara*-clauses are developing toward more paratactic clause-combining constructions. In addition, on the assumption that an independent *kara*-clause is paratactic to the preceding or following discourse, the increase in independent *kara*-clauses in PDJ is understood to show that *kara*-clauses are becoming more and more paratactic. Their developmental process can be summarized as follows:[58]

(66) The development of *kara*-clauses in terms of clause-combining constructions

   hypotaxis   >   parataxis   >   paratactic to discourse

In conclusion, the diachronic process and synchronic diversity of *kara*-clauses are counted as another counter-example to the cline of clause-combining constructions in grammaticalization.

Next, we examine the hypothesis of semantic/pragmatic unidirectionality toward more subjective meanings, i.e., subjectification, in the process of grammaticalization.[59] As we discussed in 3.5.2, causality in the epistemic/speech-act domain is more subjective than that in the content domain. Viewed in this light, we see that the gradual increase in *kara*-clauses associated with epistemic/speech-act conjunction interpretation in their developmental process (see 4.4.3) exemplifies subjectification in grammaticalization.

Furthermore, the function of *kara* as a pragmatic marker in the case of independent *kara*-clauses (see 2.3.2.2 and 4.2.3) presents another example of subjectification. It is more subjective than that of a subordinate or paratactic clause marker in the sense that the speaker may expect the hearer to interpret an independent *kara*-clause as being related to the preceding or following discourse (Ohori, 1995a, 1997a; R. Suzuki, 1998a, 1999a, 1999b, among others).[60] Thus, the increase in independent *kara*-clauses in PDJ (see 4.4.2) can be counted as another instance of subjectification in the process of grammaticalization.

On these grounds, the direction of the semantic/pragmatic development of *kara*-clauses is toward an increase in subjective meanings along with grammaticalization. We can summarize the development in the following way:

(67) The development of *kara*-clauses in terms of semantic/pragmatic functions

        content conjunction   less subjective

    > epistemic/speech-act conjunction   ↓

    > pragmatically invited (or imposed) conjunction   more subjective

       to discourse

We conclude that the semantic/pragmatic aspect of the development of *kara*-clauses supports the hypothesis of semantic/pragmatic unidirectionality in the process of grammaticalization.

We demonstrated in this subsection that the development of *kara*-clauses from subordinate to independent clauses is not in accord with the unidirectional cline of clause-combining constructions whereas it is in accord with the hypothesis of semantic/pragmatic unidirectionality in grammaticalization.

4.5.4 Other analogous cases in Japanese

This section briefly touches upon some other analogous cases in Japanese. We can observe similar patterns of structural and semantic/pragmatic extensions to *kara*-clauses in Japanese.

First, the development of a *node*-clause, i.e., another causal clause in Japanese, seems to attest to the semantic/pragmatic extension toward an increase in subjective meanings and to the structural extension toward a more paratactic relation to their "main" clauses. Haraguchi (1971) studies how *node*-clauses come to share many syntactic and semantic characteristics with *kara*-clauses in LModJ.[61] He points out that *node*-clauses, which mainly express an objective causal relation in LModJ, show a tendency to express a subjective causal relation. In Sweetser's (1990) definition, the interpretation of *node*-clauses is developing from content to epistemic/speech-act conjunction interpretation. Furthermore, *node*-clauses appear independently in PDE colloquial discourse in the same way as *kara*-clauses do.[62]

(68) sumimasen   ga,   moo   owari   desu   *kara/node*.
    excuse.me   but   now   end   COP   because
    ' (Lit.) Excuse me, but *because* we close now.' =
    ' Excuse me, but we are closing now, you know.'

We can predict that the semantic/pragmatic and structural extension of *node*-clauses is developing in the same direction as *kara*-clauses. It would be interesting to trace the developmental process of *node*-clauses toward independent clauses and to study their synchronic state in more detail. Our future tasks include investigating developmental paths undergone by some other causal clauses in Japanese from the perspective of grammaticalization.

Second, the reanalysis of a subordinate clause as an independent clause with a clause-final pragmatic marker in Japanese has been the focus of considerable study in the literature. Here, it is useful to introduce R. Suzuki's (1998b) list of such examples. She introduces some recent studies on such phenomena from the perspective of grammaticalization and discusses motivations for grammaticalization and pragmatic development. The clause-final elements in the following list are reported as being in the process of developing into clause-final pragmatic markers, i.e., final particles, in PDJ.[63]

(69) Clause-final morphemes as clause-final pragmatic markers
    (adapted from R. Suzuki, 1998b:129)
    Subordinate clause-final morphemes:
        Ohori (1995a, 1997a) on subordinate clause markers in general
        Nakayama et al. (1997) on *kedo* 'but'
        Iguchi (1998) on *kara* 'because'
    Embedded clause-final morphemes:
    - Complement clause-final morphemes:
        Okamoto (1995) on complementizers
        Horie (1998) on the polyfunctionality of *no*

Mayes (1991) on the quotative *to* and *tte*

R. Suzuki (1999a, 1999b) on the quotative *tte*

- Other clause-final morphemes:

R. Suzuki (1998a, 1999a) on *wake* 'reason'

The development of *kara*-clauses is included in the phenomena that are frequently observed in Japanese.[64] As R. Suzuki (1998b:130) points out "grammaticization of clause-final elements is the result of conventionalization of pragmatic inferences due to their frequent use in interactional contexts". These phenomena are also regarded as instances of subjectification (Traugott, 1990, 1995a, 1997, 1999a, etc.; and Traugott and Dasher, 2002). It would be interesting to explore some other clause-final elements in Japanese in the light of grammaticalization.

We have so far presented some analogous cases to the development of *kara*-clauses in Japanese. They suggest that the structural and semantic/pragmatic extensions of *kara*-clauses occur recurrently in Japanese.

In this chapter, we have looked closely at the developmental process of *kara*-clauses. We introduced earlier studies on *kara*-clauses in 4.2 and 4.3. We focused on the structural and semantic/pragmatic development of *kara*-clauses from EModJ onward in 4.4. Lastly, we examined their development from the perspective of grammaticalization in 4.5. It was pointed out that *kara*-clauses are in the process of being reanalyzed as a single independent clause with a clause-final pragmatic marker in PDJ. Moreover, it was shown that the case of *kara*-clauses is treated as an instance of grammaticalization although this is not a textbook case. We then examined the hypothesis of unidirectionality in grammaticalization. It was demonstrated that the case of *kara*-clauses does not conform to the unidirectional cline of clause-combining constructions while it is a case in support of the hypothesis of semantic/pragmatic unidirectionality in the course of grammaticalization. We noticed that the development of *kara*-clauses toward greater independence from their "main" clauses is motivated by conventionalization of pragmatic meanings. I hope to have illustrated that *kara*-clauses, which are generally labeled as subordinate clauses, have multiple functions in PDJ and that such diversity of functions is motivated. The developmental path of *kara*-clauses appears quite similar to that of *because*-clauses. A comparison between them will be made in the following chapter.

Notes

1. I am indebted to John Roberts for the following comment. Reason and purpose clauses are closely linked both semantically and, in some languages, syntactically. For example, Thompson and Longacre (1985) say that many languages use the same morphology for purpose and reason clauses (see also Quirk et al., 1985:564). Amele (Pupan) also uses the same morpheme =*nu* to express purpose or reason. "The semantic explanation for the fact that one morpheme can serve these functions is that both purpose and reason clauses can be seen as providing *explanations* for the occurrence of a given state or action. ... They differ in that purpose clauses express a motivating event which must be *unrealized* at the time of the main event, while reason clauses express a motivating event which may be *realized* at the time of the main event (Thompson and Longacre 1985:185)."

    Japanese also uses the same morpheme *tame* to express purpose or reason. See also Heine et al. (1991) and Heine and Kuteva (2002:246–247).

2. One of the topics that have attracted much attention for a long time is the difference between *kara*-clauses and *node*-clauses, both of which share many syntactic and semantic characteristics in PDJ. Nagano (1979 [1952]) is known as one of the earliest studies discussing the difference between these clauses in detail. Mikami (1972 [1953]) notes that *kara*-clauses are syntactically more independent of their associated "main" clauses than *node*-clauses in PDJ. See also Shigemi (1996) for a discussion of the differences between these clauses. For further details of the studies concerning these clauses, see Iwasaki (1995), H. Tanaka (2004:282–339), Ito (2005:10–57), etc. See Yabe (1997, 2002) for the sociolinguistic studies of these clauses based on the conversational data.

3. For more recent discussion on the classification of subordinate clauses proposed by Minami, see Minami (1999), Ohori (1999), and Onoe (2001:333–353). Kuno (1973) presents some syntactic tests to examine the relationship between subordinate clauses and their associated main clauses in Japanese. Ohori (1992, 2000) discusses syntax and semantics of dependent clauses in Japanese in the framework of Role and Reference Grammar (Foley and Van Valin 1984, Van Valin 1993, 2005, and Van Valin and LaPolla 1997). Hasagawa (1996) studies *te*-forms of verbals in the framework of Role and

Reference Grammar and Construction Grammar (Fillmore, 1988; Fillmore et al., 1988; etc.).

For further details of complex sentences in PDJ, see, for example, Masuoka (1997), Maeda (2002), Noda et al. (2002), Minami (2004), H. Tanaka (2004), Tsunoda (2004), and Ito (2005).

4. Takubo's (1987) study is intended as a proposal for modifying Minami's (1974) classification of subordinate clauses in Japanese. Minami (1974, 1993) categorizes subordinate clauses in Japanese into three groups based on the examination of the degree of syntactic dependency of a preceding clause (a subordinate clause) on a consequent clause (a main clause). He classifies *kara*-clauses into a single group called "Group C" where the degree of syntactic dependency of *kara*-clauses on their associated main clause is the least of all his groups, i.e., a group of more paratactic clause-combining constructions in our terms.

5. In the case of English *because*-clauses with an epistemic conjunction interpretation, as mentioned in 3.2.2, *because*-clauses are related to the speaker's belief or conclusion that is expressed in the "main" clause whether it is overtly indicated or not. In the case of Japanese *kara*-clauses, the speaker's belief or conclusion is usually indicated by epistemic expressions attached to the "main" verb in the "main" clause.

6. For example, see Kokuritsu Kokugo Kenkyujo (1951), Matsumura (1969), Kitajo (1989), Mizutani (1985, 1989, 2001), Shirakawa (1991), Itani (1992), Ohori (1992, 1995a, 1997a), Higashiizumi (1993), Takahashi (1993), Y. Kato (1992, 1994), Kuroda (1994), Okamoto (1995), Nakayama and Ichihashi-Nakayama (1997), Iguchi (1998), R. Suzuki (1998a, 1999a, 1999b), Fujii (2000), Honda (2001, 2005), and Shirakawa (2001). See also Shimokawa (1989) for a discussion of how an "incomplete" sentence is interpreted in discourse.

7. There is a difference in nuance or pragmatic effect between *kara* such as in (11') and *n(o) da kara* such as in (12), both of which function as a clause-final pragmatic particle. We may say that the former sounds more neutral than the latter. The latter sounds pushy or reproaching the addressee. I thank Kinsuke Hasagawa for bringing this point to my attention. See Noda (1995) and Kuwahara (2003) for further details of the nuance of reproach in the *n(o) da kara* construction. On this subject, see also Ohori (1995a, 1997a) and Iguchi (1998:118–119). The pragmatic effects of *kara* call for further systematic investigation based on broader base of data.

See Lamarre (2002b) for a discussion of a similar functional extension from a clause-linking particle to an utterance-final pragmatic particle in Hakka.

8. See Page xi for approximate stages of Japanese used in the present study. The present

section uses an approximate literal representation of *rekisiteki kanazukai* 'traditional orthography' for Old and Middle Japanese examples. I thank Eric Long for his advice and comments on romanization of historical texts in Japanese.

9. The history of causal expressions in Japanese introduced here is mainly based on K. Kobayashi (1996), Y. Kobayashi (1982), Konoshima (1966, 1983), Sakakura (1993), Y. Yamada (1954), Yamaguchi (1980, 1996), Yuzawa (1958, 1970), unless otherwise specified. I am indebted to Eric Long for checking the examples from the secondary source against the original as far as possible.

    Note that causal expressions introduced here are defined as such by different scholars. It is beyond the scope of the present study to go into details about each causal expression here.

10. Verbals include verbs, adjectives, and some auxiliaries in Japanese.
11. The example here is from EMJ.
12. The name *izenkei* 'perfective form' is replaced by the new name *kateikei* 'hypothetical/ conditional form' from EModJ in the literature of Japanese linguistics (e.g., K. Kobayashi 1996:27). See Ohori (1998b) for an investigation of the development of *ba* from the perspective of grammaticalization.
13. For more details about causal expressions in MJ and EModJ, see C. Kobayashi (1973, 1977). Matsumoto (1997) discusses the development of *ni-yotte* from the perspective of grammaticalization.
14. See Haraguchi (1970) for further details of the development of *node*-clauses. Mikami (1972 [1953]) notes that *node* is on its way to becoming a *setuzoku-zyosi* 'conjunctive particle'. The fact that *node*-clauses express a smaller range of meanings than do *kara*-clauses in PDJ, and that there is considerable variation in the acceptability of many *node*-clauses, seem to be due to the relatively later development of *node*-clauses.
15. The inventory shows approximate time when each item comes to appear. It is mainly based on the previous studies taken up in this section and *NKD*. The symbol for (23) is as follows.

    --- [ ]: used with another function indicated in [ ]
16. The discussion of historical change in the use of *kara* in 4.3.2 is mainly based on Ishigaki (1955), Konoshima (1966, 1983), Matsumura (1969), and Yamaguchi (1980, 1996).

    Note that the following development is broadly observed in Japanese (Fujiwara 1990, 1993, 1998, 2004, etc., T. Kobayashi 2003).

    Noun/Case particle   >   Conjunctive particle   >   Final particle
17. Another type of *kara* [*kaku* (adverb) + *nomi* (focus particle) + *kara*] is not considered

here since there is only one example of that in *Man'yoosyuu* (Ishigaki 1955:112–113).
18. According to Ishigaki (1955:84), *kara* cannot be regarded as an independent lexical item since *kara* never serves as a subject. However, it is said to have a noun-like character in that it appears in the initial position of a phrase.

    M. Yamada (1936) considers [noun denoting place + *kara*] in OJ as a case particle. Konoshima (1966:103) reports that there are only few examples of such *kara* in OJ. He finds only nine examples of *kara* preceded by a place noun in *Man'yoosyuu*. For a detailed observation on *kara ni* in *Man'yoosyuu*, see Chiba (1997).

    S. Ono (1953, 1966) suggests that *kara* is related to the bound morpheme *-kara* which appears in *ya-kara* 'tribe', *hara-kara* 'siblings' and the bound morpheme *-gara* which appears in *tomo-gara* 'group of fellows', *kuni-gara* 'national character' and *hito-gara* 'personal character'. In my opinion, however, speakers of PDJ are hardly aware of the boundary in these words. He concludes that *kara* would have been a lexical noun meaning 'self', 'character', or 'nature' formerly (Ishigaki, 1955:83–129). It is reported that the conjunctive expression *nagara*, which can be analyzed as [*na* (genitive particle) + *kara*], is also related to *kara* (Ishigaki, 1955:84–92; Yamaguchi, 1980:215–220).
19. Ishigaki's (1955) proposal that the shared meaning of *kara* is *manima (ni)* 'following' or 'with' seems generally accepted by Japanese historical grammarians. However, Konoshima (1966:104) points out a case where it is hard to interpret *kara* as *manima (ni)*.
20. The symbol for (29) is as follows.
    ---: obsolete
21. For more details about the change of *kara* from a formal noun to a case particle, see Ishigaki (1955). Ishigaki (1955:100–101) explains that the meaning 'by way of' or 'via' is extended from the meaning 'following' or 'with'.

    One kind of *kara* directly following a noun in OJ becomes obsolete by MJ and the other becomes a bound morpheme. See Ishigaki (1955) for detail.
22. In OJ, *yori* covers a wider range of meaning than *kara*, such as 'from' (source, i.e., starting point of time/space), 'than' (comparative), 'by way of' (path), 'by' (ways or means), and 'because' (reason/cause) (Konoshima, 1966:101–103; 1983:117–119; H. Suzuki, 1952). *Kara* gradually takes over the function of *yori* throughout the history of the written language of Japanese.
23. A descendant of *kara-ni* 'as soon as' is used in the fixed expression *miru karani* 'at first glance' in PDJ.

    (i) miru   *karani*   ayasigena   otoko
        look   KARANI   dangerous.looking   man

'dangerous-looking man (whom you can see) at first glance'

(*Gakken Kokugo Daiziten*)

24. See Yamaguchi (1996:180) for another phrasal expression *mono-yuwe* 'because'.
25. Konoshima (1966:114–115) notes that EMJ texts are rather nostalgic and do not reflect the spoken language of that time. See Yamaguchi (1996:204) for an example of *kara* used as a causal clause marker in EMJ. It can probably be analyzed as *kara-ni* without *ni* or *kara* functioning as a case particle.
26. In PDJ, *yori* is mainly used in a comparative sentence such as:

    (i) Taro   wa   Hanako   yori   se   ga   takai.
        Taro   TOP   Hanako   YORI   height   NOM   tall
        'Taro is taller than Hanako.'

    The use of *yori* as a ablative case particle appears in formal or written language in PDJ.

    (ii) tadaima   yori   kaigi   o   kaisai-itasimasu.
         Now   YORI   conference   ACC   open
         '(I) now (declare) the conference open.'

27. Another example of *kara* in LMJ is *kara-ha*, which can be interpreted as expressing a causal relation. Konoshima (1966:120–121) regards it as being essentially the same as *kara* with emphasis. Yamaguchi (1996:207) notes that this expression might have facilitated the extension of *kara* as a case particle to *kara* as a subordinator.
28. See C. Kobayashi (1973, 1977) for details of causal clause subordinate markers in MJ.
29. See Note 18 in Chapter 4.
30. Yoshii (1977) shows that *node* starts to appear, albeit sporadically, around 1800 and becomes used regularly around 1850. It continues to be in constant use around 1890. He explains that it comes to extend the range of meanings that *kara* covers with a gradual change in verbal conjugation, i.e., from the adnominal to dictionary form. As a result, it coexists with *kara* in PDJ. For further details of the development *node*-clauses, see Haraguchi (1981). He points out a trend of *node* toward expressing a subjective causal relation (i.e., epistemic and speech-act conjunction in our terms). See also Mio (1995 [1942]:284) for a survey of [*desu* (copula) + *kara/node*].
31. Nagano (1979 [1952]) discusses various differences between *kara*-clauses and *node*-clauses in PDJ. From his observation that the expressions (43a)–(43f), i.e., the expressions based on speaker's subjectivity, appear in the "main" clause of *kara*-clauses whereas they do not in the "main" clause of *node*-clauses, he concludes that *kara* marks a subjective causal relation while *node* expresses an objective causal relation. His conclusion, however, aroused a great deal of controversy especially over the acceptability of some of the examples that he presents. See Iwasaki (1995) for further

details of the controversy.
32. It seems better to count the example of "question" given by Nagano (1979 [1952]) as "conjecture" on the grounds that it is usually interpreted as seeking confirmation of what is said in the utterance and *desyoo* with a falling intonation usually expresses "conjecture". We will count examples such as (43'f) as epistemic conjunctions in 4.4.
33. Yoshii (1977:31–32) states that the decrease of (43g) in ratio is due to the emergence of some other causal clause markers such as *node*-clauses and *mon-da-/desu-kara*-clauses. Roughly speaking, Nagano's (1979 [1952]) argument that *kara* marks a subjective causal relation whereas *node* expresses an objective causal relation can be interpreted as the view that in the ModJ period *kara*-clauses mainly express an epistemic and speech-act conjunction while *node*-clauses usually express content conjunction in the sense of Sweetser (1991). *Node*-clauses mainly express (43g) at the beginning, but the ratio of (43g) gradually decreases in the course of time in the same way as *kara*-clauses. With the decrease of (43g), *node*-clauses gradually come to express (43a)–(43f) from LModJ onward (Yoshii, 1977; Haraguchi, 1981). Thus, the difference between *kara*-clauses and *node*-clauses is vague in some environments in PDJ. The important point to note is that Yoshii's survey supports Nagano's claim diachronically and it would be the key to the controversy over the acceptability of some of Nagano's examples. I would like to discuss this matter in a separate paper.
34. We find no instances of "CL1 CL2 *kara*" in the data for the present study.
35. A repetition of utterances made by a different speaker and an echo question is not included in (c) but in (d), if any.
36. We are not concerned here with the spoken data for the following reasons. First, they are different from the written colloquial data in terms of punctuation. Second, the original transcriptions of the spoken data adopt different conventions of punctuation.
37. We notice that the ratio of *kara*-clauses marked by a final particle in the spoken data is smaller than that in the written colloquial data in PDJ. One of the reasons for this is presumably a richer source of information on clause boundary available in spoken discourse with the help of intonation and prosody. On the contrary, a writer is likely to overuse a final particle without realizing it in an attempt to adopt characteristics of spoken discourse in the written colloquial discourse. It is beyond the scope of the present study to take the matter further.
38. There are no instances of (a') in the diachronic data. We find only one instance of such in the synchronic written colloquial data.

"konomama	mesi	kutte	kaisya	e	iku	tte
leave.it.as.it.is	meal	eat	company	to	go	QUO

Chapter 4 Development of Japanese *kara*-clauses   195

iu	no	mo	sukosi	nan	da	*kara*	yoo,
say	NOMI	INT	just	what	COP	KARA	FP
moosukosi		syoobu	sinai	ka?"			
more game		do.not		Q			

'Because it's just boring that we have a meal and go to work, would you like another game?'

(1978 *Shimbashi*, Ch. 2)

39. See also (49c) above.
40. The punctuation is not taken into consideration in (55).
41. We classify an adjective and a noun as (i-3) and (i-4) respectively only when they are non-past tense form and are clearly interpreted as expressing "speakers' (subjective) attitudes and opinions" (Bybee et al. 1994:176) in order to compare the developmental process of *kara*-clauses in Japanese with that of *because*-clauses in English. They are not main subjects of Yoshii's (1977) study.
42. Here, we limit ourselves to presenting examples of overt expressions of epistemic and speech-act conjunctions that appear in "main" clauses. These expressions also appear in *kara*-clauses as shown in Table 4.6, Table 4.8, and Table 4.9.
43. Numerous attempts have been made by scholars to examine *n(o) da* in the literature of Japanese linguistics. However, it remains an unsettled question how it functions in discourse and what brings various semantic/pragmatic effects. For recent comprehensive studies on *n(o) da*, See Noda (1995, 1997), for instance.
44. We find no instances of (i-2) with an epistemic verb such as *sitteiru* 'know' in the whole database of Japanese for the present study. Most of instances of (i-2) in Japanese are with *omou* 'think' and its variant forms.
45. See also (49a-1).
46. (iv) includes variant forms of *n(o) da*, such as *n(o) desu, no* followed by a final particle such as *yo, ne, sa,* etc. The present study separately counts the number of expressions of epistemic/speech-act conjunctions that overtly appear in the "main" clause and the *kara*-clause. Thus, two *no da*'s in one sentence, e.g., (i) below, are counted as (iv) in (58) respectively.

(i)
modotte-kita	n	da	*kara*,			
came.back	NOMI	COP	KARA			
Taro	wa	Hanako	o	aiste-iru	n	daroo.
Taro	TOP	Hanako	ACC	love	NOMI	guess

'Because Taro came back, I guess he loves her.'

47. We are not concerned here with comparing the written colloquial data and the spoken

data in the synchronic data. A closer study of PDJ *kara*-clauses, based on a broader base of data in different genres (e.g., written/spoken language, written colloquial language/ natural conversation, formal/informal conversation, etc.), will be necessary for understanding PDJ *kara*-clauses in detail.

48. In the same way as the case of independent *because*-clause, we give some instances of independent *kara*-clauses that appear with the overt expressions listed in (49) above although we admit that the labels epistemic or speech-act "conjunction" may not be appropriate. See Note 43 in Chapter 3.
49. This could be non-standard in PDJ.
50. We have so far used the term "subordinate" in the traditional sense in this chapter. In (61), we use a set of terms defined for the cline of clause-combining constructions in grammaticalization (see 2.2.5). Thus, the subordinate *because*-clause in PDE is labeled as "hypotactic" here.
51. As for the inversion of *kara*-clause and its "main" clause, the ratio of clauses with overt expressions of epistemic/speech-act conjunction interpretation remains almost steady from 1850s onward (see Table 4.7 and Table 4.8). The ratio does not differ much from that of canonical clause order (see Table 4.5 and Table 4.6).
52. The constructions with two clauses connected by *kara* in either canonical or inverted clausal order, i.e., [CL1 *kara* CL2] or [CL1 CL2 *kara*], are called *kara*-clause constructions henceforth.
53. For further arguments for conventionalization of pragmatic meanings in the course of grammaticalization, see Onodera (1993, 1995, 1996, 2000, 2004), Ohori (1995a, 1997a), and R. Suzuki (1998a, 1998b, 1999a, 1999b) in particular.
54. For a discussion of motivations for the reanalysis of clause-final morpheme as clause pragmatic particles, see R. Suzuki (1999a:182-186).
55. Strictly speaking, some of the principles may not be applicable to the developmental processes of *kara*-clauses. Our concern here is to identify characteristics of grammaticalization that are shared by the developmental processes of *kara*-clauses.
56. See Note 49 in Chapter 3 for the definition of "layers" in the principle of "layering". In a strict sense, it is more suitable to count the coexistence of a *kara*-clause, a *node*-clause, a *tame*-clause, etc., in a functional domain called "causal clauses" in PDJ as an example of "layering". The fuller study of causal clauses in Japanese lies outside the scope of the present study. We will touch upon the development of *node*-clauses in 4.5.4 below.
57. The semantic change from a formal noun to an ablative case marker and that from an ablative case marker to a causal clause marker exemplifies the trend from more to less concrete meanings in the process of grammaticalization (Sweetser, 1990; Heine et al.,

1991; Bybee et al., 1994, etc.) On this subject, see 2.2.4 above.
58. Note that the causal subordinate *kara*-clauses in PDJ correspond to "hypotactic" in the cline of clause-combining constructions (see 2.2.5).
59. See Note 53 in Chapter 3 above on the subject of semantic change in general.
60. For further details of speaker-hearer roles in language use in the light of grammaticalization, see Hopper and Traugott (2003:Ch.4), Levinson (2000), and Traugott and Dasher (2002:Ch. 2).
61. For some other studies on *node*-clauses in comparison with *kara*-clauses, see Note 2 in Chapter 4. Yoshii (1977) studies the distribution of several causal clauses in transition from 1680s to 1950s. Matsumoto (1997) discusses another causal marker *tame* 'for/because' from the perspective of grammaticalization.
62. The example with *kara* is taken from Alfonso (1980:1203). Some may find it more preferable to say "... owari-*na node*" in which the plain form of *na* (i.e., the adnominal form of the copula *da*) precedes *node* in place of the polite form *desu*.
63. The list is elaborated upon R. Suzuki (1998b:129). Here, the year of publication is renewed, and the gloss and some explanations for words are added. For arguments for clause-initial items developing into clause-initial pragmatic markers in Japanese, see Matsumoto (1988), Mori (1996, 1999), and Onodera (1993, 1995, 1996, 2000, 2004), among others.
64. Fujiwara (1990, 1993, 1998, 2004, etc.) points out the phenomena under discussion are widely observed in many dialects in PDJ.

Chapter 5

Comparison of English *because*-clauses and Japanese *kara*-clauses

5.1 Introduction

Chapters 3 and 4 explored the developmental path of English *because*-clauses and that of Japanese *kara*-clauses respectively. This chapter makes a comparison between them and summarizes the findings. Section 5.2 compares their developmental processes and enumerates their similarities and differences. Section 5.3 discusses some implications of the findings for both the study of grammaticalization and other areas of linguistics.

5.2 Comparison

The developmental processes of *because*-clauses and *kara*-clauses have some characteristics in common. It will be useful to make an approximate distinction between synchronic and diachronic points of view. From the synchronic point of view, they are similarly in the process of being reanalyzed as an independent main clause with a pragmatic marker at the clause edge. To be precise, *because*-clauses are in the process of being reanalyzed as an independent clause with a clause-initial pragmatic marker in PDE (discussed in 3.2–3.4) and *kara*-clauses as an independent clause with a clause-final pragmatic marker in PDJ (discussed in 4.2–4.4). They can be summarized in the following way.[1]

(1) Reanalysis of subordinate *because*-clauses/*kara*-clauses as independent

		English			Japanese	
Subordinate:	CL1	*because*	CL2	CL1	*kara*	CL2
	[CL1	[SCM	CL2]]	[[CL1	SCM]	CL2]
Independent:	ø	*because*	CL	CL	*kara*	ø
		[PM	CL]	[CL	PM]	

The ongoing processes under discussion can be viewed as instances of reanalysis of subordinate clauses as independent and of reanalysis of clause-initial and clause-final elements as pragmatic marker, i.e., pragmaticalization (see 2.3.2 above).

From the diachronic point of view, the whole developmental processes of *because*-clauses and *kara*-clauses and their synchronic functional diversity can be counted as cases of grammaticalization although neither of them are necessarily textbook cases (discussed in 3.5.1 and 4.5.1). From the perspective of grammaticalization, the development of *because*-clauses and *kara*-clauses from subordinate to independent clauses can be summarized in the following way (discussed in 3.5.2 and 4.5.2).[2]

(2) The development of *because*-clauses and *kara*-clauses in terms of clause-combining constructions

    (subordination >) hypotaxis > parataxis > paratactic to discourse

               less paratactic   →   more paratactic

(3) The development of *because*-clauses and *kara*-clauses in terms of semantic/pragmatic function

        content conjunction interpretation   less subjective

    > epistemic/speech-act conjunction interpretation   ↓

    > pragmatically invited (or imposed) conjunction   more subjective
       to discourse

In view of clause-combining constructions, the relationship between *because*-clauses/ *kara*-clauses and their "main" clauses has been developing from less to more paratactic in the course of grammaticalization. Furthermore, they are becoming more paratactic in PDE and PDJ in that they are not syntactically associated with clauses but pragmatically associated with the preceding or following discourse. Thus, the structural aspect of their developmental processes provides a counter-example to the cline of clause-combining construction in grammaticalization, which hypothesizes a unidirectional continuum of the development toward more dependent clause-combining constructions (see 2.2.5). In view of semantic/pragmatic functions, both *because*-clauses and *kara*-clauses have been extending from less to more subjective meanings along with grammaticalization. Therefore, the semantic/pragmatic aspect of their developmental processes is illustrative of subjectification (see 2.2.6). Moreover, from several observations in the preceding chapters, we can recognize that the development of *because*-clauses and *kara*-clauses is motivated by conventionalization of pragmatic meanings and some discourse factors (discussed in 3.5.2 and 4.5.2).

To sum up, there are striking similarities in the developmental processes of *because*-clauses and *kara*-clauses despite their typological distinctions. Both of them tend to develop in the same direction in terms of structure, i.e., toward more independent structure, and in terms of semantic/pragmatic meanings, i.e., toward more subjective meanings. From the perspective of grammaticalization, their developmental processes are characterized as subjectification along with grammaticalization. In addition, reflection on their developmental processes shows that conventionalization of pragmatic meanings and discourse factors similarly play an important role in the course of grammaticalization. Viewed in this light, the framework of grammaticalization is one of the best methods of comparing and explaining the process of functional extension undergone by causal clause constructions in linguistically unrelated languages.

Let us now focus on the differences between English *because*-clauses and Japanese *kara*-clauses in their developmental processes. We here take up the following three points. First, as has been noticed in (1) above, they differ in the position of pragmaticalization. The reanalysis and pragmaticalization of *because* as a pragmatic marker occur clause-initially in PDE whereas those of *kara* as a pragmatic marker take place clause-finally in PDJ. Such difference appears to be based on the typological characteristics of English and Japanese, i.e., prepositional versus postpositional. Indeed, there are ample examples of clause-initial pragmatic markers in PDE and some examples of clause-initial items that are newly assuming pragmatic functions in spoken discourse (see 3.5.4). They are in favor of the clause-initial position as a place for pragmaticalization at least in earlier stages of English.[3] It is probable that English has a preference for the clause-initial position as a place of pragmaticalization.[4] On the other hand, recent studies on Japanese conjunctives have pointed toward the plausibility that both clause-initial and clause-final positions are places of pragmaticalization in Japanese.[5] For example, *kara* is pragmaticalized in both positions in spoken or written colloquial PDJ. The so-called conjunction *dakara* 'therefore', which is said to develop from the combination of the copula *da* and *kara*, is developing the function of clause-initial pragmatic marker (Maynard, 1989b; 2004:197–217; K. Kato, 1995).[6] The so-called subordinate clause marker *kara*, as shown in this study, is developing the function of clause-final pragmatic marker in PDJ. Japanese chooses both positions as a place of pragmaticalization. Thus far, we have recognized that English prefers the clause-initial position as a place of pragmaticalization whereas Japanese makes use of both positions.[7] The position of pragmaticalization appears to be affected by the typological characteristics of languages. However, both positions seem to be potential places for pragmaticalization. It appears that some languages tend to prefer one position to another as a place of pragmaticalization and other languages tend to make use of both. There remains a question as to whether or not there are any other motivations than typological characteristics of languages for the tendency. This question can be developed by studying pragmatic-discourse functions of clause-combining constructions in discourse.

Second, the paths of structural development of *because*-clause and *kara*-clause constructions are not necessarily identical, even though they are developing in the same direction. We found only a few examples of the inversion of a *because*-clause and its "main" clause in Table 3.1 in 3.4.2. On the other hand, there are many examples of *kara*-clauses with inverted clause order in Table 4.1 in 4.4.2. From these observations, their processes of structural development are summarized as follows:

(4) Comparison of the structural development of *because*-clause and *kara*-clause constructions

Structural development of *because*-clauses

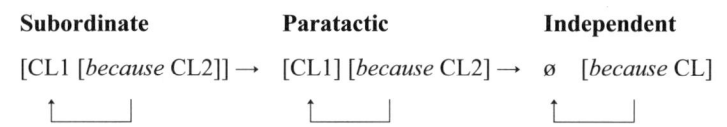

Subordinate	**Paratactic**	**Independent**
[CL1 [*because* CL2]] →	[CL1] [*because* CL2] →	ø [*because* CL]

Structural development of *kara*-clauses

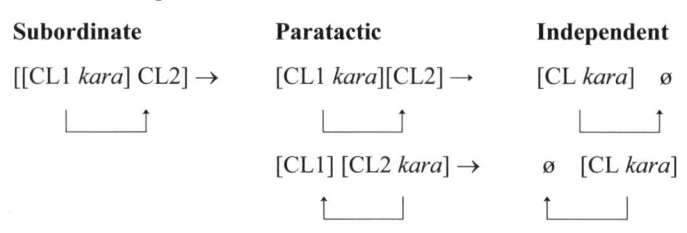

Subordinate	**Paratactic**	**Independent**
[[CL1 *kara*] CL2] →	[CL1 *kara*][CL2] →	[CL *kara*] ø
	[CL1] [CL2 *kara*] →	ø [CL *kara*]

We proposed that *because*-clauses have developed along one path (discussed in 3.4.2 and 3.5.2) whereas *kara*-clauses have developed along both types of paths (discussed in 4.4.2 and 4.5.2). Added to this, we can see that *because*-clauses and *kara*-clauses differ in the length of time that they have taken to become independent. Admittedly, when they are recognized as being independent ones is open to debate. As far as the data for the present study is concerned, subordinate *because*-clauses appear around 1600 and independent uses start to occur from the 1950s onward (see Table 3.1 in 3.4.2), while subordinate *kara*-clauses occur around 1700 and independent uses become frequent from the 1900s onward (see Table 4.1 in 4.4.2). It follows from these observations that *because*-clauses take longer to become independent than *kara*-clauses do. This leads us to ask what causes the difference in the length of time they take to develop. It is broadly observed that several items with similar meanings and functions, such as *for/because, kara/node,* etc., compete with each other in the course of development (Du Boir, 1985). A comparison of the development of other causal clauses with *because*-clauses/*kara*-clauses may help to answer this question,[8] which awaits further study.

Lastly, we point out some differences in usage between *because*-clause constructions and *kara*-clause constructions in PDE and PDJ. In the case of epistemic conjunction interpretation, it can be assumed that a *because*-clause is associated with the speaker's belief or conclusion that is expressed in its "main" clause, whether it is overtly expressed, as in (5a), or not, as in (5b) (see 3.2.2). Example (5) can be represented as (5').

(5) [Epistemic conjunction in English]
    a. He must be here *because* his bicycle is outside.   (*CHEL*, vol.1: 252)
    b. John loved her, *because* he came back.   (Sweetser, 1990:77)

(5')
    a. [(I believe/conclude/etc.) he is here][*because* (I know/see/etc.) his bicycle is outside]

    b. [(I believe/conclude/etc.) John loved her][*because* (I know/see/etc.) he came back]

An epistemic expression such as *must be* in (5a) is generally optional in the "main" clause in English. On the other hand, such an expression is usually required in the "main" clause of *kara*-clause in Japanese, as in (6a) and (6b'), in order to have epistemic conjunction interpretation. The examples without such an expression, such as (6a') and (6b), mostly tend to be interpreted as a positive assertion, a simple description of the situation in a novel or narrative, or a stage direction in play scripts.[9]

(6) [Japanese equivalents of (5)]

    a. zitensya   ga   soto   ni   aru   *kara*   kare   wa

        bicycle   NOM outside ay   be   KARA   he   TOP

        koko ni   iru   <u>hazu-da.</u>

        here   at   be   I.believe

        'He must be here *because* his bicycle is outside.'

    a'. zitensya   ga   soto   ni   ar   *kara*   kare   wa

        bicycle   NOM outside at   be   KARA   he   TOP

        koko ni   iru.

        here   at   be

        '(I say for sure/I'm sure) he is here *because* his bicycle is outside.'

    b. John   wa   modotte-kita   *kara*,   kanozyo   o   aisiteita.

               TOP   came.back   KARA   she   ACC   loved.

        'John loved her, *because* he came back.'

    b'. John   wa   modotte-kita   *kara*,   kanozyo   o   aisiteita

               TOP   came.back   KARA she   ACC   loved

       n   <u>daroo.</u>

       NOMI   guess

        '(I) guess John loved her, *because* (I know/see/etc.) he came back.'

These examples suggest that epistemic expressions usually appear in the "main" clause of *kara*-clause construction in the case of epistemic conjunction interpretation.

    Incidentally, as far as the data for the present study is concerned, we can see that epistemic expressions in the "main" clause are more frequent in *kara*-clause construction than *because*-clause construction.

(7) The percentage of epistemic expressions in the "main" clause in all instances in PDE and PDJ[10]

	because-clauses	*kara*-clauses
Written data	15.2% (7/46)	27.3% (12/44)
Spoken data	27.8% (43/159)	47.9% (23/48)

Likewise, in the case of speech-act conjunction interpretation, it can be assumed that a *because*-clause is associated with the speech-act performed in its "main" clause, as in (8), which can be represented as in (8').

(8) [Speech-act conjunction in English]
What are you doing tonight, *because* there's a good movie on.
(Sweetser, 1990:77)

(8') [(I ask) what you are doing tonight][*because* (my motive for asking is that) there's a good movie on]

A speech-act verb is not necessarily required in English as long as some other devices (i.e., the interrogative construction in the case of (8) above) expresses the speech-act performed in the "main" clause. On the other hand, such a verb is usually required in Japanese, at least in its equivalents of (8). (9a) and (9b), both of which are without a speech-act verb, are not felicitous in the same context as (8). To the contrary, (9a') and (9b'), both of which are with the speech-act verb *kiku* 'ask', are felicitous.

(9) [Japanese equivalents of (8)][11]
    a. ?? kon'ya nani   suru   no,   ii   eiga   ga   aru   *kara*.
        tonight what   do   Q   good   movie NOM exist   KARA
      '(Lit.) What (are you) doing tonight, *because* a good movie is.
       = What are you doing tonight, *because* there's a good movie on.'

a'.	kon'ya	nani	suru	no,	ii	eiga	ga	aru	*kara*
tonight	what	do	Q	good	movie	NOM	exist	KARA
kiku	kedo.						
ask	but						

'(Lit.) (I) ask what (you are) doing tonight, but *because* a good movie is. = What are you doing tonight, *because* there's a good movie on.'

b. ??	ii	eiga	ga	aru	*kara*,	kon'ya	nani	suru	no
good	movie	NOM	exist	KARA	tonight	what	do	Q

'(Lit.) *Because* a good movie is, what (are you) doing tonight.
= *Because* there's a good movie on, what are you doing tonight.'

b'.	ii	eiga	ga	aru	*kara*	kiku	kedo,
good	movie	NOM	exist	KARA	ask	but
kon'ya	nani	suru	no			
tonight	what	do	Q			

'(Lit.) (I) ask (you) *because* a good movie is, but what (are you) doing tonight. = *Because* there's a good movie on, what are you doing tonight.'

These examples show that the speech-act verb (of asking in this case) usually needs to be overtly expressed, at least in this context, in Japanese.[12]

The last difference of PDE *because*-clauses and PDJ *kara*-clauses to be noted here is their difference in conventionalized meanings. It was suggested that a similar way of conventionalization of pragmatic meanings is involved in the developmental processes of these clauses (see 3.5.2 and 4.5.2). However, they differ in usage of independent clauses in communication. In other words, what is conventionalized in them is not always identical. There are some cases where independent *kara*-clauses can be interpreted as the causal explanation of an act that the speaker has performed or is about to perform in the given context.[13]

(10) a. (Having opened the door)　　atui　kara.

　　　　　　　　　　　　　　　　　hot　　KARA

　　'Because it is hot.'

　b. atui　kara.　(then open the door)

　　hot　　KARA

　　'Because it is hot.'

It appears that reference is made to the act in the given context in order to interpret what is conveyed by the independent *kara*-clause. To put it differently, an independent *kara*-clause can function as being pragmatically linked to the act in the preceding or following context. On the other hand, it seems infelicitous that an independent *because*-clause appears in the same context as (10) above.[14]

(11) a. ?? (Having opened the door) *Because* it is hot.

　b. ?? *Because* it is hot. (then open the door)

We have so far demonstrated three types of differences in usage between PDE *because*-clauses and PDJ *kara*-clauses from the discourse-pragmatic point of view. A comparison of these clauses from this point of view will clarify how syntactically and/or semantically similar items differ in discourse-pragmatic function. Such differences will be useful resources for applied linguistics.

We have thus far pointed out some differences between *because*-clauses and *kara*-clauses in their developmental processes. We should not overlook that discourse-pragmatic functions of these clauses underlie these differences.

In this section, we summarized some similarities and differences in the developmental processes of *because*-clauses and *kara*-clauses. In the following section, we will discuss some implications for the study of grammaticalization as well as languages in general.

5.3 Implications

There are several points to make in relation to the findings of the present study. First, the cline of clause-combining constructions in grammaticalization calls for further investigation. It posits a unidirectional development from less to more dependent clause-combining constructions. On the contrary, *because*-clauses and *kara*-clauses are developing from less to more independent clause-combining constructions. Moreover, some other causal clauses such as English *for*-clauses and Japanese *node*-clauses are developing in the same direction as *because*-clauses and *kara*-clauses (see 3.5.4 and 4.5.4). Likewise, studies of other languages report the ongoing development of independent clauses from causal subordinate clauses. In present-day spoken German, for instance, the causal subordinate *weil*-clauses tend to use main clause constructions (Keller, 1995, 1998:221–237; Günthner, 1996). They resemble the case of English *because*-clauses developing toward independent main clauses. Günthner (1996) illustrates that the *weil*-clause is reinterpreted as a coordinate conjunction for particular discourse-pragmatic functions in colloquial spoken German, and points out that this construction contradicts the unidirectionality in clause combining. Again, the phenomenon of causal subordinate *nikka*-clauses appearing independently in present-day spoken Korean resembles the case of the Japanese *kara*-clause being reanalyzed as an independent clause with a clause-final pragmatic marker (Sohn, 1993, 1996, 2003).[15] Taking these examples into consideration, it seems reasonable to assume that causal clauses tend to develop in a direction away from that which the cline of clause-combining constructions in grammaticalization postulates.[16] Further study on the cline, based on more examples of causal clauses not only in English and Japanese but also in other languages, will clarify this assumption. Also, an inquiry into which types of clause-combining constructions conform to the cline will be one of our future tasks.

Second, the hypothesis of unidirectionality awaits further study. On the one hand, the cases of *because*-clauses and *kara*-clauses pose counter-examples to the hypothesis of structural unidirectionality toward increasing bondedness, which underlies the cline of clause-combining constructions in grammaticalization. Recently, many counter-examples to the hypothesis of structural unidirectionality have been reported.[17] On the other hand, the cases of *because*-clauses and *kara*-clauses are in agreement with the hypothesis of semantic/pragmatic unidirectionality toward increasing subjective meanings in the process of grammaticalization. Recent studies on historical semantics and pragmatics argue for the tendency toward greater subjectivity in semantic change (Traugott, 1990, 1995a, 1999a; and Traugott and Dasher, 2002, in particular). The question then arises as to which cases of grammaticalization illustrate which kinds of unidirectionality or tendency, which unidirectionality or tendency is stronger than others, and what motivates such phenomena. The unidirectional hypothesis awaits further systematic exploration.

Third, the diachronic process and synchronic diversity of *because*-clauses and *kara*-clauses casts doubt on the dichotomy between coordination and subordination. Recent studies on complex clause constructions from functional and typological perspectives demonstrate that the dichotomy is disputable (Haiman and Thompson, 1984; Thompson, 1987; etc.).[18] The present study provided diachronic and synchronic examples of *because*-clauses and *kara*-clauses that cannot be considered coordinate nor subordinate in the strict sense. These clauses are regarded as pieces of evidence against the sharp distinction between coordination and subordination.[19] Moreover, the present study illustrated that the three-way distinction in complex clause constructions proposed in Hopper and Traugott (2003) is more useful in describing the diachronic process and synchronic diversity of *because*-clauses and *kara*-clauses. In their distinction, adverbial clauses, e.g., *because*-clauses and *kara*-clauses, are categorized as hypotactic, and noun clauses, e.g., restrictive relative clauses, as subordinate (see 2.2.5). In the LME phrasal construction *by (the) cause (that)*, the clause introduced by *that* is a subordinate clause since it functions as a modifier of the noun *cause*. However, a PDE hypotactic *because*-clause in content conjunction interpretation functions as a modifier of the main verb in the "main" clause. Moreover, a paratactic *because*-clause in epistemic/speech-act conjunction interpretation functions as a modifier of the speech-act performed in the "main" clause (see 3.2.2). We confront difficulties in grouping these clauses together with noun clauses in PDE. Similarly, a PDJ *kara*-clause in content conjunction interpretation functions as a modifier of the main verb in the "main" clause, whereas a paratactic *kara*-clause in epistemic/speech-act conjunction interpretation functions as a modifier of the speech-act performed in the "main" clause (see 4.2.2). In sum, these clauses point to the difficulty in grouping adverbial clauses and noun clauses together as subordinates (Thompson and Longacre, 1985). We can say that the distinction given by Hopper and Traugott (2003) describes the difference between adverbial and noun clauses more appropriately.

In addition, the reanalysis of *because*-clauses and *kara*-clauses as independent main clauses is illustrative of insubordination, i.e., "the use of a formally subordinate clause type as a main clause" (Evance, 1988:255) which is reported in Australian languages (Evance, 1988). The cases of *because*-clauses and *kara*-clauses can be viewed as illustrating insubordination in English and Japanese (see also Thompson and Mulac, 1991; Ohori, 1995a, 1997a). The classification of complex sentence constructions leaves room for reexamination using a broader base of examples across languages and time.

Fourth, the ongoing process of reanalysis of *because* and *kara* as a pragmatic marker is in line with recent studies on the emergence of pragmatic markers at the clause edge.[20] In particular, it supports Ohori's (1997a) speculation that "clause edges tend to be loci of pragmaticization" (Ohori, 1997a:479 Note 5). Additionally, the ongoing process of reanalysis of causal subordinate *because*-clauses and *kara*-clauses as independent clauses with a pragmatic marker can be viewed as the emergence of grammatical constructions in their own right (Fillmore, 1988; Fillmore et al., 1988; Goldberg, 1995; Ohori, 2001; etc.) in the sense that they have their own discourse-pragmatic functions that are different from subordinate counterparts (Ohori, 1995a, 1997b).[21] A further direction of our future study will be toward examining pragmatic markers as well as discourse-pragmatic functions of grammatical constructions from the diachronic and synchronic perspectives.

Fifth, the present study demonstrated that the diachronic process and synchronic diversity of *because*-clauses and *kara*-clauses are motivated by conventionalization of pragmatic meanings and their discourse functions. In relation to semantic/pragmatic unidirectionality, it argues that similarities in semantic/pragmatic extension of these clauses are based on their similarities in pragmatic meanings that come to be conventionalized along with grammaticalization and on their similarities in function that they are assigned in discourse. It appears that conventionalization of pragmatic meanings and discourse-pragmatic functions offer the key to an understanding of mechanisms and motivations of language change and synchronic functional diversity. In line with recent research on pragmatic markers (see 2.3.2), the present study adds new evidence for "emergent" pragmatic markers in English and Japanese (Hopper, 1987). Further, the developmental processes of *because*-clauses and *kara*-clauses reported in the present study are cases in support of recent theories of semantics/ pragmatics such as Levinson (2000) on generalized conversational implicature, and Traugott and Dasher (2002) on subjectification and intersubjectification.

Lastly, the whole process of *because*-clauses and *kara*-clauses provides a good illustration of grammaticalization as "continual movement towards structure (Hopper, 1987:142)". In addition, the present study is in line with his view that grammar is "always emergent but never present" (Hopper, 1987:148).[22] Here is another example of the emergence of new construction in PDE spoken discourse. Example (12a) is a so-called canonical causal *because*-clause whereas (12b) is a non-canonical one. However, the latter is often used in spoken PDE.

(12) a. *Just because* you have a big car, it *doesn't mean* you can drive carelessly.
  b. *Just because* you have a big car *doesn't mean* you can drive carelessly.

Hopper (p.c.) points out that an example such as (12b), i.e., what he calls the *just because* construction, differs from canonical causal *because*-clauses in that the *just because* always precedes a main clause, and the main clause usually contains an admonition or a negative. In practice, *just because* is often followed by *doesn't mean*. We should notice that often *doesn't* lacks a subject and it sometimes seems as if the *just because* clause acts as a subject. The following example, which we may call an

Chapter 5   Comparison of English *because*-clauses and Japanese *kara*-clauses   213

ancestor of the *just because* construction, is found in the database for the present study.

(13) *Because* he was unfaithful to his wife, it *doesn't follow* in every way he's absolutely vile.   (1905 *Where angels fear to tread*)

In comparison with (12b) above, (13) is canonical or "grammatical" in that *doesn't* has the subject *it*, which refers to what is expressed in the preceding *because*-clause. (13) is similar to (12b) in that the *because*-clause precedes a main clause, and *doesn't follow* in the main clause has a similar meaning as *doesn't mean*. It appears that the *just because* construction has developed in PDE on the basis of these similarities in structure and semantics/pragmatics. Next, observe the following example that is found in our database.[23]

(14) The reason they sacked me was *because* I joined the union and I was the shopsteward.   (1993 *Liverpool Echo & Daily Post* [BNC])

In (14), it seems as if the *because*-clause functions as a complement clause, i.e., the one that is usually introduced by *that*. From the examples (12b) and (14), we can see that *because*-clauses sometimes assume a noun-clause-like function in PDE spoken discourse. The use of *because*-clauses such as (14) seems to have something to do with the *just because* construction in (12b). We have already shown that *because* introduces a noun clause in spoken PDE (Hirose, 1991, 1998).

(15) *Because* he seldom wrote you doesn't necessarily mean he loves you no longer.
                              (*Shogakukan Random House English-Japanese Dictionary*)

It will be interesting to examine the developmental process of these constructions over a span of 100 years or so to observe how a new construction emerges and how it interacts with semantic/pragmatic factors in discourse over the course of time. An observation of discourse data is important for our understanding of grammaticalization as well as the real state of languages in flux.

In this section, we compared the diachronic and synchronic phenomena of English *because*-clauses and Japanese *kara*-clauses, and discussed some implications of the findings for the study of grammaticalization and that of languages in general. A large number of questions remain unanswered, but I hope to have shown that a contrastive study of grammaticalization from both diachronic and synchronic perspectives, which constitutes the focus of the present study, is necessary for expanding our understanding of diachronic and synchronic phenomena in different languages. Our future tasks will be a cross-linguistic comparison of structurally and/ or semantically similar constructions (Bybee et al., 1994; Yap et al., 2004) and a comparison of grammaticalization episodes in different languages that were reported individually. Lastly, it is important to bear in mind that we can make a contribution to the study of grammaticalization with numerous diachronic and synchronic studies on Japanese that have been made in the literature of Japanese linguistics. Not only is an approach to the study of language from the perspective of grammaticalization "the happy reunion of English philology and historical linguistics" (Rissanen, 1990), but it will also happily (re)unite English linguistics (*Eigogaku*) and Japanese linguistics (*Kokugogaku* and *Nihongogaku*) in Japan.

Notes

1. (42) in Chapter 2 is repeated here as (1). We are not concerned here with paratactic *because*-clauses/*kara*-clauses and the inversion of a *kara*-clause and its "main" clause, both of which can be regarded as intermediary stages in the process of grammaticalization. For the discourse factors in their developmental processes, see 3.4.2 and 3.5.2 for *because*-clauses and 4.4.2 and 4.5.2 for *kara*-clauses.
2. Note that the definition of the terms in (2) is based on Hopper and Traugott (2003:176–184) (see 2.2.5 above). "Subordination" in (2) is not meant for an adverbial clause construction but for an embedded clause construction. Thus, it is put into parentheses here. With regard to the cline of clause-combining constructions in grammaticalization such as (2) and others mentioned elsewhere in the present study, what are called subordinate *because*-clauses or *kara*-clauses in the present study are labeled as

"hypotaxis".
3. It may be speculated that many pragmatic markers in English aquire the ability to appear clause-finally once clause-initial items have assumed pragmatic meanings. Further inquiry into this point is beyond the scope of the present study.
4. Some conjunctions occasionally appear clause-finally in spoken PDE. They can be viewed as examples of clause-final pragmatic markers in English. For example, Romaine and Lange (1991) regard *but* in (i) below as a pragmatic marker:

   (i) I really don't want it *but* (Romaine and Lange, 1991:272)

   (ii) We're now leaving, *so* (I owe this example to Wesley M. Jacobsen)

   (iii) His food is rather a problem. He looks fit, *though*. (Quirk et al., 1985:641)

   In (i) and (ii), the speaker may invite (or force) the hearer to understand the clause as being pragmatically linked to the following unsaid clause and to infer what is implicitly meant. In (iii), the speaker may invite (or force) the hearer to interpret the clause followed by *though* as being pragmatically related to the preceding clause.
5. The pragmaticalization in clause-initial position also appears to be based on typological characteristics of Japanese. For a further discussion of how typological characteristics affect the development of pragmatic markers in Japanese, see Onodera (1993:335–346, 2004:205–211). See, in particular, Ohori (1997a) and R.Suzuki (1998b) for arguments for both positions as a place of pragmaticalization in Japanese. See 4.5.4 for further details.
6. The following is a simple example of *dakara* functioning as a clause-initial pragmatic marker.

   (i) Child: gyuunyuu kobosi-tyatta.
          milk   split-have
   'I have my milk spilt (over the table).'
   Mother: *dakara*   itta   desyo.
           DAKARA   told   guess
   '(Lit.) therefore (I) told (you) = you see, I told you.'
7. Ford and Mori (1994) compare causal markers in managing disagreement in English and Japanese from the viewpoint of conversation analysis.
8. Traugott (1992:252) mentions a set of distinctions among causal clauses in terms of a known or "given" in PDE (see Note 27 in Chapter 2). *Since* and *as* are used when it is assumed that the information in these clauses is known or "given". On the other hand, *because* is usually used for new information. For a further discussion of the distribution of causal clauses in conversation, see Ford (1993).

   For a discussion of several competing causal expressions in MJ and EModJ, see C.

Kobayashi (1973, 1977).

9. See Kamio (1990, 1994, 1995, 1997, 2002, etc.) for a discussion of sentences without epistemic expressions and some other types of modality, i.e., "direct forms" (his term), and those sentences with such expressions, i.e., "indirect forms", according to his theory of territory of information.

10. The number in parentheses indicates (the number of epistemic expressions/the number of all instances).

11. Examples (9a') and (9b') with the auxiliary-like expression *n(o) da* sound more felicitous. It is beyond the scope of this section to go into details of *n(o) da*.

    (i) [(9a') with *n(o) da*]

kon'ya	nani	suru	no,	ii	eiga	ga	aru	*kara*
tonight	what	do	Q	good	movie	NOM	exist	KARA

kiku/kite(i)ru	n	da	kedo.
ask/be.asking	NOMI	COP	but

    '(Lit.) (I) ask what (you are) doing tonight, but *because* a good movie is.
    = What are you doing tonight, *because* there's a good movie on.'

    (ii) [(9b') with *n(o) da*]

ii	eiga	ga	aru	*kara*	kiku/kite(i)ru
good	movie	NOM	exist	KARA	ask/be.asking

n	da	kedo,	kon'ya	nani	suru	no
NOMI	COP	but	tonight	what	do	Q

    '(Lit.) (I) ask (you) *because* a good movie is, but what (are you) doing tonight. = *Because* there's a good movie on, what are you doing tonight.'

12. To distinguish examples of speech-act of asking from the rest of the speech-act conjunction interpretations data in PDE and PDJ and to compare their difference in distribution lies outside the scope of this paper.

13. See Iguchi (1998:3.2) for examples of such cases that are observed in the conversational part of novels.

14. I thank Mary Kitagawa for her comment that independent *because*-clauses such as (11) may be used only in a very clear context in English.

15. Günthner (1996) and Sohn (1993, 1996, 2003) point out a close relationship between the reanalysis of subordinate causal clauses as independent and discourse-pragmatic functions of these clauses in present-day spoken languages from grammaticalization viewpoint. The present study is in line with them. However, it has concentrated on giving an overview of the developmental process of *because*-clauses and *kara*-clauses up to the present and has not paid much attention to their discourse-pragmatic functions

Chapter 5   Comparison of English *because*-clauses and Japanese *kara*-clauses   217

in spoken PDE and PDJ. For further details of discourse-pragmatic functions of *because*-clauses in spoken PDE, see Schleppegrell (1991), Stenström and Andersen (1996), and Stenström (1998), for example. A fuller study of discourse-pragmatic functions of *kara*-clauses in spoken PDJ will be necessary to understand the process of reanalysis of these clauses in the course of grammaticalization.

Incidentally, Hopper and Traugott (2003:209–211) discuss some counter-examples to unidirectionality in clause-combining constructions. They take Günthner (1996) on the development of the *weil*-clause in spoken German as one of them.

16. It is broadly admitted in the literature of grammaticalization that there are problematic cases not only for the cline of clause-combining constructions but also for some other generalizations in grammaticalization, as can be seen in the following quotation (Hopper and Traugott, 2003:211): "The presence of counter-examples once more shows that the continua of grammaticalization are not exceptionless. Nevertheless, there is overwhelming evidence of the preponderance of changes from more to less paratactic modes of clause combining."

17. See Note 17 and Note 21 in Chapter 2 above for further details of counter-examples to structural unidirectionality.

18. See Note 18 in Chapter 2 above for some other recent studies on complex clause constructions.

19. See Ohori (1997a) and R. Suzuki (1998a, 1998b, 1999a, 1999b) for detailed arguments against the dichotomy based on so-called subordinate and embedded clauses in Japanese.

20. For studies on the emergence of pragmatic markers in English, see Note 62 in Chapter 3. For those in Japanese, see (69) in 4.4.5. See Lamarre (2002b) for a similar case in Hakka.

21. Useful information on Construction Grammar is given in Ohori (2001, 2002a: Chs. 7–8).

22. For further details of Hopper's more recent view of grammar, see Hopper (2001a, 2001b). For a discussion of the emergence of linguistic structure, see, for example, Du Boir (1985, 1987) and Bybee and Hopper (2001). For a discussion of the *just because* construction, see S. Tanaka (2002:183–184).

23. Examples (13) and (14) above are classified as "others" in the basic classification of *because*-clauses in the present study.

Chapter 6

Conclusion

The present study investigated the diachronic process and synchronic functional diversity of English *because*-clauses and Japanese *kara*-clauses from the perspective of grammaticalization. It demonstrated that they are developing in the same direction in terms of clause-combining construction and semantic/pragmatic function, and that their developmental processes are illustrative of subjectification along with grammaticalization.

In more empirical terms, while both *because*-clauses and *kara*-clauses are generally characterized as causal subordinate clauses, it has been pointed out that they have various functions that cannot be so-called in PDE and PDJ. The present study examined both clauses on the basis of the framework of grammaticalization that can comprehensively account for their synchronic and diachronic phenomena. From the diachronic point of view, it showed that both become more paratactic clause-combining constructions and come to be used to express more subjective meanings. From the synchronic point of view, it proposed that both are in the process of being reanalyzed as an independent clause with a pragmatic marker at the clause edge in PDE and PDJ.

In more theoretical terms, the present study considered the hypothesis of unidirectionality that has been broadly discussed in the literature of grammaticalization. It claimed that the developmental processes of *because*-clauses and *kara*-clauses pose counter-examples to the unidirectional cline of clause-combining constructions in grammaticalization, whereas they support the semantic/pragmatic unidirectionality toward increasingly subjective meanings. It also pointed out that these processes are motivated by conventionalization of pragmatic meanings.

Chapter 2 presented the study of grammaticalization and some other studies that are relevant to the examination of causal clauses in English and Japanese. Section 2.2 introduced the definition of grammaticalization (2.2.1), the research history (2.2.2), some characteristics of grammaticalization (2.2.3), the hypothesis of unidirectionality in grammaticalization (2.2.4), the cline of clause-combining constructions (2.2.5), and subjectification (2.2.6). Section 2.3 considered that *because*-clauses and *kara*-clauses can be divided into three based on Sweetser's (1990) distinction of meanings (2.3.1) and that *because* and *kara*, so-called subordinate clause markers, can be analyzed as pragmatic markers in the sense of Brinton (1996) when a *because*-clause and a *kara*-clause appear without an accompanying "main" clause (2.3.2). Lastly, Section 2.4 noted the method and data used in the present study.

The examination of *because*-clauses (Chapter 3) and *kara*-clauses (Chapter 4) from the perspective of grammaticalization showed that there are striking similarities in their developmental processes although English and Japanese are typologically distinct. From the structural point of view, both clauses are extending toward more paratactic clause-combining constructions. They do not conform to the unidirectional cline of clause-combining constructions in grammaticalization, i.e., parataxis > hypotaxis > subordination (Hopper and Traugott, 2003). From the semantic/pragmatic point of view, they tend to express epistemic/speech-act conjunction interpretation. They conform to the semantic/pragmatic unidirectionality toward more subjective meanings, i.e., subjectification (Traugott, 1989, 1995a, 1997, etc.; and Traugott and Dasher, 2002).

Chapter 3 examined the developmental process of *because*-clauses from the perspective of grammaticalization. Section 3.2 introduced previous studies on their synchronic phenomena. Structurally, they can be distinguished into subordinate, non-subordinate, and independent clauses in PDE (3.2.1). In light of the correlation between the structure and semantics/pragmatics, they are subordinate in the case of content conjunction interpretation while they are non-subordinate, i.e., paratactic, in the case of epistemic/speech-act conjunction interpretation (3.2.2). Considering intonation, the structural independence of *because*-clauses is reflected in the intonational pattern (3.2.3). To summarize, the previous studies reviewed in 3.2 pointed toward a potential functional extension of *because*-clauses in PDE from less to more paratactic clause-combining constructions with an increase in subjective meanings. Section 3.3 introduced earlier studies on the history of English causal clauses and that of *because*. We saw how the LME phrasal construction *by (the) cause (that)* in various forms gradually develops into a single grammatical marker *because* (3.3.2) and begins to take over *for*, the causal subordinate clause marker that survives from OE, during the LModE period (3.3.1).

Section 3.4 looked in detail at the developmental process of *because*-clauses from EModE to PDE. In light of structural functions, we showed that *because*-clauses have become more paratactic clause-combining constructions (3.4.2). In light of semantic/pragmatic functions, we found that the expressions that lead to epistemic/ speech-act conjunction interpretation are starting to become frequent in *because*-clause constructions (3.4.3). Section 3.5 examined the developmental process of *because*-clauses from the perspective of grammaticalization. We proposed that *because*-clauses in PDE are in the process of being reanalyzed as independent clauses with a clause-initial pragmatic marker and that the structural and semantic/pragmatic extension is motivated by conventionalization of pragmatic meanings (3.5.1). Next, we demonstrated that the diachronic process and synchronic diversity of *because*-clauses are properly treated as a case of grammaticalization, if not a textbook case (3.5.2). We further raised the issue of the unidirectional hypothesis in terms of structure and semantics/pragmatics (3.5.3). The development of *because*-clauses from subordinate to independent clauses does not conform to the unidirectional cline of clause-combining constructions, whereas it conforms to the hypothesis of unidirectionality toward an increase in subjective meanings, i.e., subjectification, in the process of grammaticalization. Lastly, we took up some other similar cases of structural and semantic/pragmatic extensions to *because*-clauses in English (3.5.4). They suggest that some types of structural and semantic/pragmatic process undergone by *because*-clauses are recurrently found in the history of English.

Similarly, Chapter 4 explored the developmental process of *kara*-clauses from the perspective of grammaticalization. Section 4.2 introduced previous studies on how they are used in PDJ. We saw that the parallel between the ablative case marker *kara* and the causal clause marker *kara* is counted as one of the instances of the extension of case markers to clause-linkage markers (4.2.1). In the same way as *because*-clauses, it was pointed out that *kara*-clauses are subordinate in the case of content conjunction interpretation while they are paratactic in the case of epistemic/speech-act conjunction interpretation (4.2.2). In addition, they frequently appear without an accompanying grammatically associated "main" clause in PDJ and *kara* in such cases takes on some characteristics of a pragmatic marker (4.2.3). They can be analyzed as single independent clauses with a clause-final pragmatic marker when they appear independently. In sum, the earlier studies reviewed in 4.2 suggested that *kara*-clauses extend from subordinate to paratactic to independent clauses with an increase in subjective meanings in PDJ. Section 4.3 gave an overview of the history of Japanese causal clauses and that of *kara*. We saw that the causal clause marker *kara* becomes widely used in eastern Japan from the LMJ to EModJ period (4.3.1) and that it develops from its function as an ablative case marker, which is traced back to that of a formal noun (4.3.2). Moreover, we noted that the meaning expressed by *kara*-clauses is shifting from content to epistemic/speech-act conjunction and so-called subordinate causal clause marker *kara* begins to appear in sentence-final position from LModJ onward.

Section 4.4 detailed the developmental process of *kara*-clauses from LModJ to PDJ. Considering clause-combining constructions, we recognized their tendency toward greater independence from their "main" clauses (4.4.2). Further, we pointed out that the frequent use of inverted *kara*-clause constructions and that of *kara*-clauses followed by a final particle appear to have some influence on the use of independent *kara*-clauses. Considering semantic/pragmatic functions, we observed that the interpretation of *kara*-clauses tends to be an epistemic/speech-act conjunction in PDJ (4.4.3). In the same way as *because*-clauses, Section 4.5 examined the structural and semantic/pragmatic extension of *kara*-clauses from the perspective of grammaticalization. We proposed that *kara*-clauses in PDJ are in the process of being reanalyzed as independent clauses with a clause-final pragmatic marker and that the structural and semantic/pragmatic extension in PDJ is motivated by conventionalization of pragmatic meanings (4.5.1). We then showed that the diachronic process and synchronic diversity of *kara*-clauses is counted as a case of grammaticalization, if not a textbook example (4.5.2). Moreover, we examined the unidirectional hypothesis in terms of structure and semantics/pragmatics (4.5.3). The development of *kara*-clauses from subordinate to independent clauses is not accord with the unidirectional cline of clause-combining constructions whereas it is accord with the hypothesis of unidirectionality toward an increase in subjective meanings in the process of grammaticalization. Finally, we introduced some other instances of structural and semantic/pragmatic developments that appear to be parallel to that of *kara*-clauses in Japanese (4.5.4). These instances suggest that some types of structural and semantic/pragmatic processes undergone by *because*-clauses are occurring elsewhere in Japanese.

Chapter 5 compared the developmental processes of English *because*-clauses and Japanese *kara*-clauses and discussed some implications of the findings for the study of grammaticalization and some other areas of linguistics. We found significant similarities in their developmental processes (5.2). From the synchronic point of view, both clauses are similarly in the process of being reanalyzed as independent main clauses with a pragmatic marker at the clause edge. From the diachronic point of view, the whole process of *because*-clauses and *kara*-clauses can be viewed as cases of grammaticalization, if not textbook cases. We saw that both are developing in the same direction. Structururally, they are extending toward more paratactic clause-combining constructions. Considering semantic/pragmatic meanings, they are extending toward more subjective meanings. From the perspective of grammaticalization, we concluded that the whole developmental processes of *because*-clauses and *kara*-clauses are characterized as subjectification along with grammaticalization and that conventionalization of pragmatic meanings is crucial to the processes. We then pointed out differences in these clauses in positions of pragmaticalization, in paths of structural extension, and in usage in PDE and PDJ.

Furthermore, we discussed six points to which the present study is relevant, including the study of grammaticalization and languages (5.3). First, we proposed that the unidirectional cline from less to more dependent clause-combining constructions calls for further investigation. It seems reasonable to assume that causal clauses tend to develop in a direction away from that which the cline of clause-combining constructions in grammaticalization postulates. Second, we claimed that the unidirectional hypothesis awaits further systematic exploration because the cases of *because*-clauses and *kara*-clauses posit counter-examples to the structural hypothesis of unidirectionality whereas they are in agreement with the semantic/pragmatic unidirectionality, i.e., subjectification (Traugott, 1989, 1995a, 1997, etc.; and Traugott and Dasher, 2002). Third, we pointed out that the diachronic process and synchronic diversity of *because*-clauses and *kara*-clauses support a recent argument that the distinction between coordination and subordination is elusive (Haiman and Thompson, 1984; Thompson, 1987; etc.). Additionally, the cases of *because*-clauses and *kara*-clauses provided another instance of "insubordination" (Evance, 1988) and the reanalysis of subordinate clauses as independent (Thompson and Mulac, 1991; Ohori, 1995a, 1997a, among others). Fourth, the ongoing process of reanalysis of *because* and *kara* as a pragmatic marker in PDE and PDJ is in line with a view of clause edges as loci of pragmaticization (Ohori, 1997a). Fifth, we considered conventionalization of pragmatic meanings as the key to an understanding of mechanisms and motivations of language change and synchronic functional diversity (Levinson, 2000; and Traugott and Dasher, 2002). Lastly, we discussed Hopper's (1987) view of emergent grammar and maintained that discourse data extends our understanding of the real state of languages in flux as well as grammaticalization.

Over the past few decades, a considerable number of studies have been made of grammaticalization, and numerous examples of grammaticalization from various languages have been reported. The present study carried out a contrastive study of grammaticalization and further provided troublesome but informative cases in English and Japanese. Furthermore, it illustrated that the framework of grammaticalization is a significant approach to structurally and/or semantically similar constructions across language and time. I hope to have shed light on the study of grammaticalization from a new dimension.

References

Aijmer, Karin. 1997   *I think*: an English modal particle. In Swan and Westvik, (eds.), pp. 1–47.

Aijmer, Karin. 2002   *English discourse particles: Evidence from a corpus*. Amsterdam: John Benjamins.

Akimoto, Minoji. 2001   *Bunpooka to wa* [What is grammaticalization?]. In Akimoto, (ed.), pp. 1–25.

Akimoto, Minoji, (ed.), 2001   *Bunpooka: Kenkyuu to kadai* [Grammaticalization: research and issues]. Tokyo: Eichosha.

Akimoto, Minoji. 2002   *Bunpooka to idiomuka* [Grammaticalization and idiomatization]. Tokyo: Hituzi Syobo.

Akimoto, Minoji. 2004   *Bunpooka* [Grammaticalization]. In Akimoto et al., 1–38.

Akimoto, Minoji, Kozue Ogata, Mitsuaki Endo, Yasuhiro Kondo, and Elizabeth Closs Traugott. 2004   *Koopasu ni motoduku gengo kenkyuu* [Linguistic studies based on corpora]. Tokyo: Hituzi Syobo.

Alfonso, Anthony. 1980   *Japanese language patterns: A structural approach*. Tokyo: Sophia University L. L. Center of Applied Linguistics.

Altenberg, Bengt. 1984   Causal linking in spoken and written English. *Studia Linguistica* 38 (1), 20–69.

Arnovick, Leslie K. 1999   *Diachronic pragmatics: Seven case studies in English illocutionary development*. Amsterdam: John Benjamins.

Axmaker, Shelley, Annie Jaisser, and Helen Singmaster, (eds.), 1988   *Proceedings of the fourteenth annual meeting of the Berkeley Linguistics Society (Berkeley Linguistics Society 14)*. Berkeley, Calif.: Berkeley Linguistics Society.

Beths, Frank. 1999   The history of *dare* and the status of unidirectionality. *Linguistics* 37 (6), 1069–1110.

Blakemore, Diane. 1987   *Semantic constraints on relevance*. Oxford: Blackwell Publishing.

Blakemore, Diane. 1992 *Understanding utterances: An introduction to pragmatics.* Oxford: Blackwell Publishing.

Blakemore, Diane. 2002 *Relevance and linguistic meaning: The semantics and pragmatics of discourse markers.* Cambridge: Cambridge University Press.

Blakemore, Diane. 2004 Discourse markers. In Horn and Ward, (eds.), pp. 221–240.

Bolinger, Dwight. 1977 Another glance at main clause phenomena. *Language* 53 (3), 511–519.

Brinton, Laurel J. 1990 The development of discourse markers in English. In Jacek Fisiak, (ed.), pp. 45–71.

Brinton, Laurel J. 1995 Pragmatic markers in a diachronic perspective. *Berkeley Linguistics Society* 21, 377–388.

Brinton, Laurel J. 1996 *Pragmatic markers in English: Grammaticalization and discourse functions.* Berlin: Mouton de Gruyter.

Brinton, Laurel J. 2001 Historical discourse analysis. In Schiffrin, Tannen, and Hamilton, (eds.), pp. 138–160.

Bybee, Joan L. 1985 *Morphology: A study of the relation between meaning and form.* Amsterdam: John Benjamins.

Bybee, Joan L. 1994 The grammaticalization of zero: asymmetries in tense and aspect systems. In Pagliuca, (ed.), pp. 235–254.

Bybee, Joan L. 2003 Mechanisms of change in grammaticalization: the role of frequency. In Joseph and Janda, (eds.), pp. 602–623.

Bybee, Joan L., and Östen Dahl. 1989 The creation of tense and aspect systems in the languages of the world. *Studies in Language* 13 (1), 51–103.

Bybee, Joan, and Paul Hopper, (eds.), 2001 *Frequency and the emergence of linguistic structure.* Amsterdam: John Benjamins.

Bybee, Joan L., William Pagliuca, and Revere D. Perkins. 1991 Back to the future. In Traugott and Heine, (eds.), vol. II, pp. 17–58.

Bybee, Joan, Revere Perkins, and William Pagliuca. 1994 *The evolution of grammar: Tense, aspect, and modality in the languages of the world.* Chicago: University of Chicago Press.

Cabrera, Juan C. Moreno. 1998 On the relationships between grammaticalization and lexicalization. In Ramat and Hopper, (eds.), pp. 211–227.

Carey, Kathleen. 1995 Subjectification and the development of the English perfect. In Stein and Wright, (eds.), pp. 83–102.

Chiba, Kazuko. 1997 Manyoo waka no *kara ni* ni tuite [On *kara ni* in *Manyoo* poems]. *Kokugo to kokubungaku* 74 (10), 16–30.

Chafe, Wallace. 1984 How people use adverbial clauses. *Berkeley Linguistics Society* 10, 437–449.

Chafe, Wallace. 1988 Linking intonation units in spoken English. In Haiman and Thompson, (eds.), pp. 1–27.

Comrie, Bernard. 1998 Perspectives on grammaticalization. In Ohori, (ed.), pp. 7–24.

Cook, Haruko M. 1990 The sentence-final particles *ne* as a tool for cooperation in Japanese conversation. In Hajime Hoji, (ed.), *Japanese/Korean Linguistics* 1, pp. 29–44. Stanford, Calif.: CSLI Publications.

Couper-Kuhlen, Elizabeth. 1996 Intonation and clause combining in discourse: the case of *because*. *Pragmatics* 6 (3), 389–426.

Couper-Kuhlen, Elizabeth, and Bernd Kortmann, (eds.), 2000 *Cause, condition, concession, contrast: Cognitive and discourse perspectives*. Berlin: Mouton de Gruyter.

Craig, Colette. 1991 Ways to go in Rama: a case study in polygrammaticalization. In Traugott and Heine, (eds.), vol. II, pp. 455–492.

Croft, William. 2000 *Explaining language change: An evolutionary approach*. Essex, England: Pearson Education Limited.

Croft, William. 2001 *Radical construction grammar: Syntactic theory in typological perspective*. New York: Oxford University Press.

Dakin, Julian. 1970 Explanations. *Journal of Linguistics* 6, 199–214.

Dancygier, Barbara. 1992 Two metatextual operators: negation and conditionality in English and Polish. *Berkeley Linguistics Society* 18, 61–75.

Dancygier, Barbara. 1998 *Conditionals and prediction: Time, knowledge, and causation in conditional constructions*. Cambridge: Cambridge University Press.

Dancygier, Barbara, and Eve Sweetser. 1996 Conditionals, distancing, and alternative spaces. In Adele Goloberg, (ed.), *Conceptual structure, discourse and language*, pp. 83–98. Stanford, Calif.: CSLI Publications.

Dancygier, Barbara, and Eve Sweetser. 2000   Constructions with *if, since,* and *because*. In Elizabeth Couper-Kuhlen and Bernd Kortmann, (ed.), *Cause, condition, concession, constrast: Cognitive and discourse perspectives*, pp. 111–142. Berlin: Mouton de Gruyter.

Dasher, Richard. 1983   The semantic development of honorific expressions in Japanese. *Papers in Linguistics* 2, 217–228.

Dasher, Richard. 1995   *Grammaticalization in the system of Japanese predicate honorifics*. Ph.D dissertation, Stanford University, USA.

Diessel, Holger. 2001   The ordering distribution of main and adverbial clauses: a typological study. *Language* 77 (3), 433–455.

Diessel, Holger. 2005   Competing motivations for the ordering of main and adverbial clauses. *Linguistics* 43 (3), 449–470.

Dijk, Teun A. van. 1977   *Text and context: Explorations in the semantics and pragmatics of discourse*. London: Longman.

Du Boir, John W. 1985   Competing motivations. In John Haiman, (ed.), *Iconicity in syntax*, pp. 343–365. Amsterdam: John Benjamins.

Du Boir, John W. 1987   the discourse basis of ergativity. *Language* 63 (4), 805–855.

Erman, Britt, and Ulla-Britt Kotsinas. 1993   Pragmaticalization: the case of *ba'* and *you know*. *Stockholm Studies in Modern Philology*, New Series 10, 76–93.

Evans, Nick. 1988   Odd topic marking in Kayardild. In Peter Austin, (ed.), *Complex sentences in Australian languages*, pp. 219–266. Amsterdam: John Benjamins.

Fillmore, Charles J. 1988   The mechanisms of 'Construction Grammar'. In Axmaker et al., (eds.), pp. 33–55.

Fillmore, Charles J., Paul Kay, and Mary Catherine O'Connor. 1988   Regularity and idiomaticity in grammatical constructions: the case of *let alone*. *Language* 64 (3), 501–538.

Finegan, Edward. 1995   Subjectivity and subjectivisation: an introduction. In Stein and Wright, (eds.), pp. 1–15.

Fischer, Olga, Anette Rosenbach, and Dieter Stein, (eds.), 2000   *Pathways of change: grammaticalization in English*. Amsterdam: John Benjamins.

Fischer, Olga, Muriel Norde, and Harry Perridon, (eds.), 2004   *Up and down the cline - The nature of grammaticalization*. Amsterdam: John Benjamins.

Fisiak, Jacek, (ed.), 1990 *Historical linguistics and philology.* Berlin: Mouton de Gruyter.

Foley, William A., and Rober D. Van Valin, Jr. 1984 *Functional syntax and universal grammar.* Cambridge: Cambridge University Press.

Ford, Cecilia E. 1993 *Grammar in interaction: Adverbial clauses in American English conversations.* Cambridge: Cambridge University Press.

Ford, Cecilia E., and Junko Mori. 1994 Causal markers in Japanese and English conversations: a cross-linguistic study of interactional grammar. *Pragmatics* 4 (1), 31–61.

Ford, Cecilia E., and Sandra A. Thompson. 1986 Conditionals in discourse: a text-based study from English. In Elizabeth Closs Traugott, Alice ter Meulen, Judy Snitzer Reilly, and Charles A. Ferguson, (ed.), *On conditionals*, pp. 353–372. Cambridge: Cambridge University Press.

Frajzyngier, Zygmunt. 1996 *Grammaticalization of the complex sentence: A case study in Chadic.* Amsterdam: John Benjamins.

Fraser, Bruce. 1996 Pragmatic markers. *Pragmatics* 6 (2), 167–190.

Fujii, Seiko. 2000 Incipient decategorization of *mono* and grammaticliazation of speaker attitude in Japanese Discourse. In Gisle Andersen and Thorsetein Fretheim, (ed.), *Pragmatic markers and propositional attitude*, pp. 85–118. Amsterdam: John Benjamins.

Fujiwara, Yoichi. 1990 *Bunmatusi no gengogaku* [Linguistics in sentence-final morphemes]. Tokyo: Miyai Shoten.

Fujiwara, Yoichi. 1993 *Gengoruikeiron to bunmatusi* [Linguistic typology and sentence-final morphemes]. Tokyo: Miyai Shoten.

Fujiwara, Yoichi. 1998 *Nihongo bunmatusi no rekisiteki kenkyuu* [Historical study of Japanese sentence-final morphemes]. Tokyo: Miyai Shoten.

Fujiwara, Yoichi. 2004 *Nihongo ni okeru bunmatusi no sonritu* [Existence of sentence-final morphemes in Japanese]. Tokyo: Miyai Shoten.

Geis, Michael L., and Arnold M. Zwicky. 1971 On invited inferences. *Linguistic Inquiry* 2, 561–566.

Genetti, Carol. 1986 The development of subordinators from postpositions in Bodic languages. *Berkeley Linguistics Society* 12, 387–400.

Genetti, Carol. 1991   From postposition to subordinator in Newari. In Traugott and Heine, (eds.), vol. II, pp. 227–255.

Goldberg, Adele E. 1995   *Constructions: A construction grammar approach to argument structure*. Chicago: Chicago University Press.

Görlach, Manfred. 1990   *Introduction to early modern English*. Cambridge: Cambridge University Press.

Givón, Talmy. 1979   *On understanding grammar*. New York: Academic Press.

Green, Georgia M. 1976   Main clause phenomena in subordinate clauses. *Language* 52 (2), 382–397.

Günthner, Susanne. 1996   From subordination to coordination?: verb-second position in German causal and concessive constructions. *Pragmatics* 6 (3), 323–356.

Haiman, John, and Sandra A. Thompson. 1984   'Subordination' in universal grammar. *Berkeley Linguistics Society* 10, 510–523.

Haiman, John, and Sandra A. Thompson, (eds.), 1988   *Clause combining in grammar and discourse*. Amsterdam: John Benjamins.

Halliday, M. A. K. 1970   Language structure and language function. In John Lyons, (ed.), *New horizons in linguistics*, pp. 140–165. Harmondsworth: Penguin.

Halliday, M. A. K. 1979   Modes of meaning and modes of expression: types of grammatical structure, and their determination by different semantic functions. In D. J. Allerton, Edward Carney and David Holdcroft, (ed.), *Function and context in linguistic analysis: A festschrift for William Haas*, pp. 57–79. Cambridge: Cambridge University Press.

Halliday, M. A. K. 1985   *An introduction to functional grammar*. London: Edward Arnold.

Halliday, M. A. K., and Ruqaiya Hasan. 1976   *Cohesion in English*. London: Longman.

Hanson, Kristin. 1987   On subjectivity and the history of epistemic expressions in English. *Papers from the Chicago Linguistics Society* 15, 23–52

Haraguchi, Yutaka. 1971   *Node* no teityaku [The establishment of *node*]. *Shizuoka Joshidaigaku Kenkyuu Kiyoo* 4, 31–43.

Harris, Alice C., and Lyle Campbell. 1995   *Historical syntax in cross-linguistic perspective*. Cambridge: Cambridge University Press.

Hasagawa, Yoko. 1996   *A study of Japanese clause linkage: The connective* te *in Japanese*. Tokyo: Kurosio Publishers & Stanford, Calif.: CSLI Publications.

Haspelmath, Martin. 1998   Does grammaticalization need reanalysis? *Studies in Language* 22 (2), 315–351.

Haspelmath, Martin. 1999   Why is grammaticalization irreversible? *Linguistics* 37 (6), 1043–1068.

Heine, Bernd 2003   Grammaticalization. In Joseph and Janda, (eds.), pp. 575–601.

Heine, Bernd, and Tania Kuteva. 2002   *World lexicon of grammaticalization*. Cambridge: Cambridge University Press.

Heine, Bernd, and Tania Kuteva. 2005   *Language contact and grammatical change*. Cambridge: Cambridge University Press.

Heine, Bernd, and Mechthild Reh. 1984   *Grammaticalization and reanalysis in African languages*. Hamburg: Helmut Buske.

Heine, Bernd, Ulrike Claudi, and Friederike Hünnemeyer. 1991a   *Grammaticalization: A conceptual framework*. Chicago: The University of Chicago Press.

Heine, Bernd, Ulrike Claudi, and Friederike Hünnemeyer. 1991b   From cognition to grammar: evidence from African languages. In Traugott and Heine, (eds.), vol. I, pp. 149–187.

Herring, Suzan C. 1991   The grammaticalization of rhetorical questions in Tamil. In Traugott and Heine, (eds.), vol. I, pp. 253–284.

Higashiizumi, Yuko. 1993   Sentence-final conjunctive elements and implicatures: a comparison of Japanese and English. Unpublished MA thesis, Dokkyo University, Saitama, Japan.

Hikosaka, Yoshinobu. 1997   Genin riyuu o arawasu zyosi no bunpu to rekisi (nooto): "Hoogen bunpoo zenkoku tizu" no kaisyaku [A note on the distribution and history of reason/cause particles: An interpretation of "the grammar map of dialects in Japan"]. In Masanobu Kato, (ed.), *Nihongo no rekisi tiri koozoo*, pp. 545–562. Tokyo: Meiji Shoin.

Hino, Sukenari. 2001   *Keisikigo no kenkyuu: Bunpooka no riron to ooyoo* [Grammaticalization of Japanese pseudonouns and auxiliary verbs: A morphosyntactic and semantic approach]. Fukuoka: Kyushu University Press.

Hirose, Yukio. 1991   On certain nominal use of *because*-clauses: just because *because*-clauses can substitute for *that*-clauses does not mean that this is always possible. *English Linguistics* 8, 16–33.

Hirose, Yukio. 1998   Koobunkan no keisyoo kankei: *because* setu syugo koobun no koobun bunpoo teki bunseki [Relationships between constructions: Construction Grammar analysis of the nominal use of *because*-clauses]. *The Rising Generation*, December 1, 1998, 7–10, 18.

Hojo, Tadao. 1975   Hokkaidoo to Toohoku-hokubu no hoogen [Dialects in Hokkaido and northern Tohoku]. In Hatsutaro Oishi and Yukio Uemura, (ed.), *Hoogen to hyoozyungo: Nihongo hoogengaku gaisetu*, pp. 157–226. Tokyo: Chikuma Shobo.

Honda, Akira. 2001   Bun kootiku no soogo kooisei to bunpooka: setuzoku hyoogen kara syuuzyosi e no tenka o megutte [Interaction between constructing sentences and grammaticalization: the extension of conjunctive expressions to final particles]. *Nintigengogaku ronkoo* [Studies in cognitive linguistics] 1, 143–183.

Honda, Akira. 2005   *Affordance no ninti imiron: seitai sinrigaku kara mita bunpoo gensyoo* [An affordance-theoretical approach to cognitive semantics: Grammar in an ecological-psychological perspective]. Tokyo: University of Tokyo Press.

Hopper, Paul J. 1987   Emergent grammar. *Berkeley Linguistics Society* 13, 139–157.

Hopper, Paul J. 1991   On some principles of grammaticalization. In Traugott and Heine, (eds.), vol. I, pp. 17–35.

Hopper, Paul J. 1996   Some recent trends in grammaticalization. *Annual Review of Anthropology* 25, 217–236.

Hopper, Paul J. 2001a   Grammatical constructions and their discourse origins: prototype or family resemblance?   In Martin Pütz, Susanne Niemeier, and René Dirven, (ed.), *Applied cognitive linguistics I: Theory and language acquisition*, pp. 109–129. Berlin: Mouton de Gruyter.

Hopper, Paul J. 2001b   Hendiadys and auxiliation in English. In Joan Bybee and Michael Noonan, (ed.), *Complex sentences in grammar and discourse: Essays in honor of Sandra A. Thompson*, pp. 145–173. Amsterdam: John Benjamins.

Hopper, Paul J., and Elizabeth C. Traugott. 2003 [1993]   *Grammaticalization*. Cambridge: Cambridge University Press.

Horie, Kaoru. 1998   On polyfunctionality of the Japanese particle *no*: from the perspectives of ontology and grammaticalization. In Ohori, (ed.), pp. 169–192.

Horie, Kaoru. 2001   Kootyakugo ni okeru bunpooka no tokutyoo ni kansuru nintigengogakuteki koosatu: Nihongo to Kankokugo o taisyoo ni [A cognitive linguistic consideration on characteristics of grammaticalization in agglutinating languages: Japanese and Korean]. *Nintigengogaku ronkoo* [Studies in cognitive linguistics] 1, 185–227.

Horn, Laurence R., and Gregory Ward, (eds.), 2004   *The handbook of pragmatics*. Oxford: Blackwell Publishing.

Iguchi (Higashiizumi), Yuko. 1998   Functional variety in the Japanese conjunctive particle *kara* 'because'. In Ohori, (ed.), pp. 99–128.

Imao, Yukiko. 1991   *Kara, node, tame*: sono sentaku zyooken o megutte [*Kara, node, tame*: on the distribution of these particles]. *Nihongogaku* 10 (12), 78–89.

Ishigaki, Kenji. 1955   *Zyosi no rekisiteki kenkyuu* [Historical study of particles]. Tokyo: Iwanami Shoten.

Itani, Reiko. 1992   Japanese conjunction *kedo* ('but') in utterance-final use: A relevance-based analysis. *English Linguistics* 9, 265–283.

Ito, Isao. 2005   *Zyookenhoo kenkyuu: Iwayuru setuzokuzyosi o megutte* [A study of conditionals: The so-called conjunctive particle]. Tokyo: Kindaibungeisha

Iwasaki, Takashi. 1994   *Node*-setu, *kara*-setu no tensu ni tuite [On tense in *node* and *kara*]. *Kokugogaku* 179, 103–114.

Iwasaki, Takashi. 1995   *Node* to *kara* [*Node* and *kara*]. In Tatsuo Miyajiza and Yoshio Nitta, (ed.), *Nihongo no ruigi hyoogen: Hukubun renbun hen*, pp. 506–513. Tokyo: Kurosio Publishers.

Jacobs, Andreas, and Andreas H. Jucker. 1995   The historical perspective in pragmatics. In Jucker, (ed.), pp. 3–33.

Jespersen, Otto. 1909–1949   *A modern English grammar: on historical principles, Part V (Syntax)*. London: George Allen & Unwin Ltd. and Copenhagen: Ejnar Munksgaard. Reprint edition, 1983, Tokyo: Meicho Fukyu Kai.

Journal of Historical Pragmatics. Amsterdam: John Benjamins.

Joseph, Brian D., and Richard D. Janda, (eds.), 2003   *The handbook of historical linguistics*. Oxford: Blackwell Publishing.

Jucker, Andreas H., (ed.), 1995 *Historical pragmatics: Pragmatic developments in the history of English*. Amsterdam: John Benjamins.

Kac, Michael B. 1972 Clauses of saying and the interpretation of *because*. *Language* 48 (3), 626–632.

Kambayashi, Yoji. 1989 Riyuu o arawasu setuzokusi saikoo [Conjunction of reason reconsidered]. *Bungei Gengo Kenyuu: Gengo-hen*, 45–55. University of Tsukuba, Ibaraki, Japan.

Kambayashi, Yoji. 1991 Riyuu o arawasu setuzokusi hokoo: *kara* to *node* [An additional note on the conjunctions of reason: *kara* and *node*]. *Tokai Daigaku Kiyoo* 12, 23–27. Tokai University, Kanagawa, Japan.

Kamio, Akio. 1990 *Zyoohoo no nawabari riron: Gengo no kinooteki bunseki* [The theory of territory of information: The functional analysis of language]. Tokyo: Taishukan Shoten.

Kamio, Akio. 1994 The theory of territory of information: the case of Japanese. *Journal of Pragmatics* 21, 67–100.

Kamio, Akio. 1995 Territory of information in English and Japanese and psychological utterances. *Journal of Pragmatics* 24, 235–264.

Kamio, Akio. 1997 *Territory of information*. Amsterdam: John Benjamins.

Kamio, Akio. 2002 *Zoku zyoohoo no nawabari riron* [A sequel to the theory of territory of information]. Tokyo: Taishukan Shoten.

Kärkkäinen, Elise. 2003 *Epistemic stance in English conversation: A description of its interactional functions, with a focus on* I think. Amsterdam: John Benjamins.

Kato, Kaoru. 1995 "Genin, riyuu" o ukenai *dakara*: *dakara* no syutaiteki sokumen no tossyutu [Non-causal *dakara*: *dakara* with subjective meanings]. *Waseda Nihongo Kenkyuu* 3, 14–31. Waseda University, Tokyo, Japan.

Kato, Yoko. 1992 Hukubun no zyuuzokudo ni kansuru koosatu: Setuzokusetu, syusetu no modality o tyuusin ni site [A study of the degree of dependency of subordinate and main clauses: with special reference to modality therein]. Unpublished MA thesis, University of Tsukuba, Ibaraki, Japan.

Kato, Yoko. 1994 Zyuuzokudo no hikui setuzokusetu no gaien: setuzokusi to no kankei o tyuusin ni [Dependent clauses with a low degree of dependency: with special reference to their relation to conjunctions]. *Heisei 6 nendo syunki taikai yoosi*, 136–143. Kokugo Gakkai, Tokyo.

Keller, Rudi. 1995   The epistemic *weil*. In Stein and Wright, (eds.), pp. 16–30. Cambridge: Cambridge University Press.

Keller, Rudi. 1998   *A theory of linguistic signs*. Translated by Kimberley Duenwald. New York: Oxford University Press.

Kennedy, Graeme. 1998   *An introduction to corpus linguistics*. London: Longman

Kitajo, Junko. 1989   Hukubun bunkei [Subordination]. In Kokuritsu Kokugo Kenkyujo, (ed.), *Danwa no kenkyuu to kyooiku* II, pp. 7–111. Tokyo: Okurasho Insatsukyoku.

Kobayashi, Chigusa. 1973   Tyuusei koogo ni okeru genin riyuu o arawasu zyookenku [Clauses of cause/reason in colloquial Middle Japanese]. *Kokugogaku* 94, 16–44.

Kobayashi, Chigusa. 1977   Kindai kamigatogo ni okeru *sakai* to sono syuuhen [*Sakai* and other clauses of cause/reason in Kansai Area in Early Modern Japanese]. In Kindaigo Gakkai, (ed.), *Kindaigo kenkyu* 5, pp. 309–353. Tokyo: Musashino Shoin.

Kobayashi, Kenji. 1996   *Nihongo zyooken hyoogensi no kenkyuu* [A historical study of Japanese conditionals]. Tokyo: Hituzi Syobo.

Kobayashi, Takashi. 2003   Tunagu kotoba kara toziru kotoba e [From conjunctive expressions to final expressions]. *Gekkan Gengo* 32 (3), 60–67.

Kobayashi, Yoshinori. 1982   Kodai no bunpoo II [Old Japanese syntax II]. In Hiroshi Tsukishima, (ed.), *Koza kokugosi 4: Bunpoosi*, pp. 149–386. Tokyo: Taishukan Shoten.

Kokuritsu Kokugo Kenkyujo. 1951   *Gendai no zyosi zyodoosi: Yoohoo to ziturei* [Particles and auxiliaries in modern Japanese: usage and examples]. Kokuritsu Kokugo Kenkyujo Hookoku 3. Tokyo: Shuei Shuppan.

Konoshima, Masatoshi. 1966   *Kokugo zyosi no kenkyuu: Zyosi-si sobyoo* [A study of Japanese particles: a historical sketch]. Tokyo: Ofusha.

Konoshima, Masatoshi. 1983   *Zyodoosi zyosi gaisetu* [An outline of the history of auxiliaries and particles]. Tokyo: Ofusha.

König, Ekkeard, and Elizabeth C. Traugott. 1988   Pragmatic strengthening and semantic change: the conventionalizing of conversational implicature. In Werner

Hüllen and Rainer Schulze, (ed.), *Understanding the lexicon: Meaning, sense and world knowledge in lexical semantics*, pp. 110–124. Tübingen: Max Niemeyer Verlag.

Kortmann, Bernd. 1997 *Adverbial subordination: A typology and history of adverbial subordinators based on European languages*. Berlin: Mouton de Gruyter.

Krug, Manfred G. 2000 *Emerging English modals: A corpus-based study of grammaticalization*. Berlin: Mouton de Gruyter.

Kuno, Susumu. 1973 *Nihon bunpoo kenkyuu* [A study of Japanese syntax]. Tokyo: Taishukan Shoten.

Kuroda, Kou. 1995 Nihongo no setuzoku hyoogen to bunpoo no 'sinka': *noni* o tyuusin ni [Conjunctive expressions and the 'evolution' of grammar: with special reference to *noni*]. *Kansai Linguistic Society* 15, 111–121. Kansai Linguistic Society, Osaka.

Kuryłowicz, Jerzy. 1965 The evolution of grammatical categories. *Esquisses linguistiques*, vol. II, 38–54. Munich: Fink.

Kuwahara, Fumiyo. 2003 Settoku no *no da kara*: *kara* to hikakusite [A study of *no da kara*]. *Nihongo Kyoiku* 117, 63-72.

Kytö, Merja, and Matti Rissanen. 1997 Language analysis and diachronic corpora. In Raymond Hickey, Merja Kytö, Ian Lancashire, and Matti Rissanen, (ed.), *Tracing the trail of time*, pp. 9–22. Amsterdam: Rodopi.

Kyratzis, Amy, Jiansheng Guo, and Susan Ervin-Tripp. 1990 Pragmatic conventions influencing children's use of causal constructions in natural discourse. *Berkeley Linguistics Society* 16, 205–214.

Lakoff, George. 1984 Performative subordinate clauses. *Berkeley Linguistics Society* 10, 472–480.

Lamarre, Christine. 2002a Zyosi e no miti: Kango no "了", "得", "倒" no syokinoo o megutte [Path to particle: on various functions of "了", "得", and "倒" in Chinese]. In Toshio Ohori, (ed.), *Nintigengogaku II: kategoriika* [Cognitive Linguistics II: Categorization], pp. 185–215. Tokyo: University of Tokyo Press.

Lamarre, Christine. 2002b Modality keesiki no bunpooka o meguru itikoosatu: Hakkago no "saki ni/ toriaezu ---site okinasai" o imisuru bunmatu keesiki "正"

[A thought on grammaticalization of modality: sentence-final "正" in Hakka meaning "first, do it"]. Ms., University of Tokyo, Tokyo, Japan.

Langacker, Ronald W. 1990   Subjectification. *Cognitive Linguistics* 1, 5–38.

Langacker, Ronald W. 1991   *Foundations of cognitive grammar*, vol. II. Stanford, Calif.: Stanford University Press.

Language Sciences 23 (2–3). 2001.   Oxford: Elsevier Science.

Lass, Roger. 2000   Remarks on (uni)directionality. In Fischer, Rosenbach, and Stein, (eds.), pp. 207–227.

Lehmann, Christian. 1985   Grammaticalization: synchronic variation and diachronic change. *Lingua e Stile* 20 (3), 303–318.

Lehmann, Christian. 1986   Grammaticalization and linguistic typology. *General Linguistics* 26 (1), 3–22.

Lehmann, Christian. 1988   Towards a typology of clause linkage. In Haiman and Thompson, (eds.), pp. 181–225.

Lehmann, Christian. 1989   Latin subordination in typological perspective. In Gualtiero Calboli, (ed.), *Subordination and other topics in Latin: Proceedings of the third colloquium on Latin linguistics*, pp. 153–179. Amsterdam: John Benjamins.

Lehmann, Christian. 1995 [1982]   *Thoughts on grammaticalization*. München: Lincom Europa.

Leuschner, Torsten. 1998   At the boundaries of grammaticalization: what interrogatives are doing in concessive conditionals. In Ramat and Hopper, (eds.), pp. 159–187.

Levinson, Stephen C. 1983   *Pragmatics*. Cambridge: Cambridge University Press.

Levinson, Stephen C. 2000   *Presumptive meanings: The theory of generalized conversational implicature*. Cambridge, Mass.: The MIT Press.

Lindquist, Hans, and Christian Mair, (eds.), 2004   *Corpus approaches to grammaticalization in English*. Amsterdam: John Benjamins.

Lyons, John. 1977   *Semantics*. Cambridge: Cambridge University Press.

Lyons, John. 1993   Subjecthood and subjectivity. In Mrina Yaguello, (ed.), *Subjecthood and subjectivity: the status of the subject in linguistic theory*, pp. 9–17. Paris: Ophrys.

Maeda, Naoko. 2000   Gendai Nihongo ni okeru genin/riyuubun no san-bunrui [A three-way distinction of reason/cause sentences in present-day Japanese]. In Susumu Yamada, Yasuto Kikuchi, and Yosuke Momiyama, (ed.), *Nihongo: Imi to bunpoo no huukei*, pp. 301–315. Tokyo: Hituzi Syobo.

Maeda, Naoko. 2002   Hukubun no ruikei to nihongo kyooiku [The classification of complex sentences and Japanese language teaching]. In Ueda, (ed.), pp. 249–272.

Makino, Seiichi, and Michio Tusutsui. 1986   *A dictionary of basic Japanese grammar*. Tokyo: The Japan Times.

Martin, Samuel. 1975   *A reference grammar of Japanese*. New Haven, Conn.: Yale University Press.

Maruyama, Takehiko. 1996   Setuzoku-zyosi *kara* no "hi-riyuu yoohoo" ni kansuru siron [An essay on the non-reason conjunctive particle *kara*]. *Sawarabi* 5, 34–45.

Maruyama, Takehiko. 1997   "Zyookyoo keikoku gata" no riyuubun ni tuie [On causal sentences intended as warnings]. *Sawarabi* 6, 29–37.

Masuoka, Takashi. 1997   *Hukubun* [Complex sentences]. Tokyo: Kurosio Publishers.

Masuoka, Takashi, and Yukonori Takubo. 1992   *Kiso Nihongo bunpoo: Kaiteiban* [Basic Japanese grammar: a revised edition]. Tokyo: Kurosio Publishers.

Matsumoto, Yo. 1988   From bound grammatical markers to free discourse markers: history of some Japanese connectives. In Axmaker et al., (eds.), pp. 340–351.

Matsumoto, Yo. 1996   Ruikeiron II: bunpooka [Typology II: grammaticalization]. In Masaru Kajita and Yasuhiko Kato, (ed.), *Kaigai gengogaku zyoohoo* 8, pp. 93–101. Tokyo: Taishukan Shoten.

Matsumoto, Yo. 1997   From attribution/purpose to cause: image schema and grammaticalization of some cause markers in Japanese. In Marjolyn Verspoor, Kee Dong Lee, and Eve Sweetser, (ed.), *Lexical and syntactical constructions and the construction of meaning: Proceedings of the bi-annual ICLA meeting in Albuquerque, July 1995*, pp. 287–307. Amsterdam: John Benjamins.

Matsumoto, Yo. 1998   Semantic change in the grammaticalization of verbs into postpositions in Japanese. In Ohori, (ed.), pp. 25–60.

Matsumura, Akira, (ed.), 1969   *Kotengo gendaigo zyosi zyodoosi syoosetu* [A detailed explanation of particles and auxiliaries in classical and modern Japanese]. Tokyo: Gakutosha.

Matthiessen, Christian, and Sandara A. Thompson. 1988   The structure of discourse and 'subordination'. In Haiman and Thompson, (eds.), pp. 275–329.

Maynard, Senko K. 1989a   *Japanese conversation: self-contextualization through structure and interactional management*. Norwood, NJ.: Ablex Publishing.

Maynard, Senko K. 1989b   Functions of the discourse marker *dakara* in Japanese conversation. *Text* 9 (4), 389–414.

Maynard, Senko K. 1990   *An introduction to Japanese grammar and communication strategies*. Tokyo: The Japan Times.

Maynard, Senko K. 1993   *Discourse modality: Subjectivity, emotion and voice in the Japanese language*. Amsterdam: John Benjamins.

Maynard, Senko K. 2004   *Danwa gengogaku* [Discourse linguistics]. Tokyo: Kurosio Publishers.

Mayes, Particia. 1991   Grammaticization of *to* and *tte* in Japanese. Ms., University of California, Santa Barbara, Calif., USA.

McCullough, Helen Craig. 1988   *Bungo manual: Selected reference materials for students of classical Japanese*. Ithaca, NY: East Asia Program, Cornell University.

McTear, M. F. 1980   *The pragmatics of* because. Ulster Polytechnic: Mimeo.

Meillet, Antoine. 1958 [1912]   L'évolution des formes grammaticales. *Scientia Rivista di Scienza*, 12 (26, 6). Reprinted in Antonie Meilet, 1958, *Linguistique historique et linguistique générale*, pp. 130–148. Paris: Champion.

Mikami, Akira. 1972 [1953]   *Gendai gohoo zyosetu: Sintakusu no kokoromi* [An introduction to modern Japanese syntax]. Tokyo: Kurosio Publishers.

Minami, Fujio. 1964   Hukubun [Complex sentences]. In Motoki Tokieda and Yoshimoto Endo (ed.), *Kooza gendaigo 6*, pp. 71–89. Tokyo: Meiji Shoin.

Minami, Fujio. 1974   *Gendai Nihongo no koozoo* [The structure of modern Japanese]. Tokyo: Taishukan Shoten.

Minami, Fujio. 1993   *Gendai Nihongo bunpoo no rinkaku* [The outline of modern Japanese syntax]. Tokyo: Taishukan Shoten.

Minami, Fujio. 1999   Kaisooteki koozookan: sono mondaiten to tenboo [View of layered structure: its problems and prospects]. *Gekkan Gengo* 28 (11), 88–94.

Minami, Fujio. 2004   Hukubun kenkyuu [Study of complex sentences]. *Kokubungaku Kaisyaku to Kansyoo,* January, 2004, 74–83.

Mio, Isago. 1995 [1942]   *Hanasi-kotoba no bunpoo: Kotobazukai hen* [A grammar of spoken Japanese: Ways of using words]. Tokyo: Kurosio Publishers.

Mittwoch, Anita. 1977   How to refer to one's own words: speech-act modifying adverbials and the performative analysis. *Journal of Linguistics* 13, 153–189.

Mizutani, Nobuko. 1985   *Nitiei hikaku hanasi kotoba no bunpoo* [A contrastive analysis of grammar in spoken Japanese and English]. Tokyo: Kurosio Publishers.

Mizutani, Nobuko. 1989   *Nihongo kyooiku no naiyoo to hoohoo: Koobun no nitiei hikaku o tyuusin ni* [How to teach Japanese as a foreign language: A contrastive study of constructions in Japanese and English]. Tokyo: Aruku.

Mizutani, Nobuko. 2001   *Zoku nitiei hikaku hanasi kotoba no bunpoo* [A sequel to a contrastive analysis of grammar in spoken Japanese and English]. Tokyo: Kurosio Publishers.

Mori, Junko. 1996   Historical change of the Japanese connective *datte*: its form and functions. In Noriko Akatsuka, Shoichi Iwasaki, and Susan Strauss, (ed.), *Japanese/Korean Linguistics* 5, pp.201–218. Stanford, Calif.: CSLI Publications.

Mori, Junko. 1999   *Negotiating Agreement and disagreement in Japanese: Connective expressions and turn construction.* Amsterdam: John Benjamins.

Morita, Yoshiyuki. 1989   *Kiso nihongo ziten* [A dictionary of basic Japanese]. 2nd Edition. Tokyo: Kadokawa Shoten.

Morreall, John. 1977   More explanations. *Papers in Linguistics* 10 (1–2), 241–245.

Morreall, John. 1979   The evidential use of *because*. *Papers in Linguistics* 12, 231–238.

Nagano, Masaru. 1979 [1952]   *Kara* to *node* wa doo tigau ka [How are *kara* and *node* different from each other?]. In Shiro Hattori et al., (ed.), *Nihon no gengogaku* 4, pp. 467–488. Tokyo: Taishukan Shoten.

Nagata, Ryota. 2000   Setuzoku-zyosi *kara* no yoohookan no kankei ni tuite: hatuwa kaisyaku no kanten kara [The relationship between uses of the Japanese conjunction *kara*: from the viewpoint of utterance interpretation]. *Nihongo*

Kyoiku 107, 36–44.

Nakayama, Toshihide, and Kumiko Ichihashi-Nakayama. 1997 Japanese *kedo*: discourse genre and grammaticization. In Ho-min Sohn and John Haig, (ed.), *Japanese/Korean Linguistics* 6, pp.607–618. Stanford, Calif.: CLSI Publications.

Nihongo no Kenkyu [Studies in the Japanese Language], 1 (3). 2005. Tokyo: Nihongo Gakkai (The Society for Japanese Linguistics).

Nitta, Yoshio, (ed.), 1995 *Hukubun no kenkyuu* [Studies of complex sentences]. 2 vols. Tokyo: Kurosio Publishers.

Noda, Harumi. 1995 *No da kara* no tokuisei [The peculiarity of *no da kara*]. In Nitta, (ed.), pp. 221–245.

Noda, Harumi. 1997 No (da) *no kinoo* [The function of *no (da)*]. Tokyo: Kurosio Publishers.

Noda, Hisashi, Takashi Masuoka, Mayumi Sakuma, and Yukinori Takubo. 2002 *Hukubun to danwa* [Complex sentences and discourse]. Tokyo: Iwanami Shoten.

Ohori, Toshio. 1992 Diachrony in clause linkage and related issues. Ph.D. dissertation, University of California, Berkeley, USA.

Ohori, Toshio. 1995a Remarks on suspended clauses: a contribution to Japanese phraseology. In Masayoshi Shibatani and Sandra A. Thompson, (ed.), *Essays in semantics and pragmatics: In honor of Charles J. Fillmore*, pp. 201–218. Amsterdam: John Benjamins.

Ohori, Toshio. 1995b Case markers and clause linkage: toward a sematic typology. In Eugene H. Casad, (ed.), *Cognitive linguistics in the Redwoods: The expansion of a new paradigm in linguistics*, pp. 693–712. Berlin: Mouton de Gruyter.

Ohori, Toshio. 1997a Framing effects in Japanese non-final clauses: toward an optimal grammar-pragmatics interface. *Berkeley Linguistics Society* 23, 471–480.

Ohori, Toshio. 1997b Scalar implicature to zyookenbun no seiritu: *unless* to *but* [Scalar implicature and the rise of conditional sentences: *unless* and *but*]. *The Rising Generation*, March, 1997, 16–18.

Ohori, Toshio. 1998a Introduction. In Ohori, (ed.), pp. 1–5.

Ohori, Toshio. 1998b Polysemy and paradigmatic change in the Japanese conditional marker *ba*. In Ohori, (ed.), pp. 135–162.

Ohori, Toshio, (ed.), 1998   *Studies in Japanese grammaticalization: Cognitive and discourse perspectives.* Tokyo: Kurosio Publishers.

Ohori, Toshio. 1999   Ruikeiron kara mita bunkoozoo no kaisoosei: Mimami-model to RRG no setuzoku riron [The layer of sentences from the perspective of linguistic typology: the theory of clause linkage in Minami-model and RRG]. *Gekkan Gengo* 28 (11), 103–109.

Ohori, Toshio. 2000   Gengoteki tisiki to site no koobun: hukubun no ruikeiron ni mukete [Construction as linguistic knowledge: toward a typology of complex sentences]. In Shigeru Sakahara, (ed.), *Nintigengogaku no hatten*, pp. 281–315. Tokyo: Hituzi Syobo.

Ohori, Toshio. 2001   Koobun rion: sono haikei to hirogari [Construction grammar: its background and development]. *The Rising Generation*, December, 2001, 2–6.

Ohori, Toshio. 2002a   *Ninti gengogaku* [Cognitive linguistics]. Tokyo: University of Tokyo Press.

Ohori, Toshio. 2002b   Constructions and contextual information: the pre- vs. postposing of adverbial clauses. A paper presented at the Twentieth National Conference of the English Linguistic Society of Japan at Aoyama Gakuin University on 16 November, 2002

Ohori, Toshio. 2004   Bunpooka no hirogari to mondaiten [Spread and problems in grammaticalization]. *Gekkan Gengo* 33 (4), 26–33.

Ohori, Toshio. 2005   Nihongo no bunpooka kenkyuu ni atatte [Perspectives on grammaticalization in Japanese]. *Nihongo no Kenkyuu* [Studies in Japanese Linguistics] 1 (3), 1–17.

Ohori, Toshio, and Uno Watanabe Ryoko. 2001   Grounding and knowledge structure in conditionals: preliminaries to a semantic typology of clause linkage. *English Linguistics* 18 (1), 224–249.

Okamato, Shigeko. 1995   Pragmaticization of meaning in some sentence-final particles in Japanese. In Masayoshi Shibatani and Sandra A. Thompson, (ed.), *Essays in semantics and pragmatics: In honor of Charles J. Fillmore*, pp. 219–246. Amsterdam: John Benjamins.

Ono, Susumu. 1953   *Kara* to *kara ni* no hurui imi ni tuite. [On the meaning of *kara* and *kara ni* in pre-Old Japanese]. In Kindaichi hakusi koki kinen ronbunsyu ukankokai, (ed.), *Kindaichi hakusi koki kinen: Gengo minzoku ronsoo*, pp. 234–258. Tokyo: Sanseido.

Ono, Susumu. 1966   *Nihongo no nenrin* [History of Japanese]. Tokyo: Shinchosha.

Ono, Tsuyoshi. 1992   The grammaticalization of the Japanese verbs *oku* and *shimau*. *Cognitive Linguistics* 3 (4), 367–390

Onodera, Noriko Okada. 1993   Pragmatic change in Japanese: conjunctions and interjections as discourse markers. Ph.D. dissertation, Georgetown University, USA.

Onodera, Noriko Okada. 1995   Diachronic analysis of Japanese discourse markers. In Jucker, (ed.), pp. 393–437.

Onodera, Noriko. 1996   Doosi kara setuzoku hyoogen e: Nihongo ni okeru grammaticalization to subjectification no iti zirei [From verbs to conjunctions: a case study of grammaticalization and subjectification in Japanese]. In Gengogakurin 1995–1996 hensyuu iinkai, (ed.), *Gengogakurin 1995–1996*, pp. 457–474. Tokyo: Sanseido.

Onodera, Noriko. 2000   Development of *demo* type connectives and *na* elements: two extremes of Japanese discourse markers. *Journal of Historical Pragmatics* 1 (1), 27–55.

Onodera, Noriko Okada. 2004   *Japanese discourse markers: Synchronic and diachronic discourse analysis*. Amsterdam: John Benjamins.

Onoe, Keisuke. 2001   *Bunpoo to imi I* [Grammar and meaning I]. Tokyo: Kurosio Publishers.

Östman, Jan-Ola. 1981   *You know: A discourse-functional approach*. Amsterdam: John Benjamins.

Östman, Jan-Ola. 1982   The symbiotic relationship between pragmatic particles and impromptu speech. In Nils Erik Enkvist, (ed.), *Impromptu speech: A symposium*, pp. 147–177. Åbo: Åbo Akademi.

Pagliuca, William, (ed.), 1994   *Perspectives on grammaticalization*. Amsterdam: John Benjamins.

Powell, Mava Jo. 1992   The systematic development of correlated interpersonal and metalinguistic uses in stance adverbs. *Cognitive Linguistics*, 3 (1), 75–110.

Quirk, Randolph, Sidney Greenbaum, Geoffrey Leech, and Jan Svartvik. 1972   *A grammar of contemporary English*. London: Longman.

Quirk, Randolph, Sidney Greenbaum, Geoffrey Leech, and Jan Svartvik. 1985 *A Comprehensive grammar of the English language*. London: Longman.

Ramat, Anna Giacalone. 1998 Testing the boundaries of grammaticalization. In Ramat and Hopper, (eds.), pp. 107– 127.

Ramat, Anna Giacalone, and Paul Hopper. 1998 Introduction. In Ramat and Hopper, (eds.), pp. 1–11.

Ramat, Anna Giacalone, and Paul J. Hopper, (eds.), 1998 *The limits of grammaticalization*. Amsterdam: John Benjamins.

Ramat, Paolo. 1992 Thoughts on degrammaticalization. *Linguistics* 30 (3), 549–560.

Rissanen, Matti. 1990 On the happy reunion of English philology and historical linguistics. In Jacek Fisiak, (ed.), pp. 353–369.

Rissanen, Matti. 1997a Introduction. In Rissanen, Matti, Merja Kytö, and Kirsi Heikkonen, (ed.), *Grammaticalization at work: Studies of long-term developments in English*, pp. 1–15. Berlin: Mouton de Gruyter.

Rissanen, Matti. 1997b Optional *that* with subordinators in Middle English. In Raymond Hickey and Stanislaw Puppel, (ed.), *Language history and linguistic modeling: A festschrift for Jacek Fisiak on his 60th birthday*, pp. 373–383. Berlin: Mouton de Gruyter.

Rissanen, Matti. 1998 Towards an integrated view of the development of English: notes on causal linking. In Jacek Fisiak and Marcin Krygier, (ed.), *Advances in English Linguistics (1996)*, pp. 389–406. Berlin: Mouton de Gruyter.

Rissanen, Matti. 1999 Syntax. In Roger Lass (ed.), *The Cambridge History of the English Language*, vol. III, pp. 187–331. Cambridge: Cambridge Univercity Press.

Rissanen, Matti. 2002 On the development of English adverbial subordinators. A paper presented at the Twentieth National Conference of the English Linguistic Society of Japan at Aoyama Gakuin University on 17 November, 2002.

Rissanen, Matti. 2003 On the development of English adverbial connectives. In Masatomo Ukaji, Masayuki Ike-Uchi, and Yoshiki Nishimura,(ed.), *Current Issues in English Linguistics: Special publications of the English Society of*

Japan, vol. 2, pp. 229–247. Tokyo: Kaitakusha.

Rissanen, Matti, Merja Kytö, and Minna Palander-Collin, (eds.), 1993 *Early English in the computer Age: Explorations through the Helsinki Corpus.* Berlin: Mouton de Gruyter.

Rissanen, Matti, Merja Kytö, and Kirsi Heikkonen, (ed.), 1997 *Grammaticalization at work: Studies of long-term developments in English.* Berlin: Mouton de Gruyter.

Romaine, Suzanne, and Deborah Lange. 1991 The use of *like* as a marker of reported speech and thought: a case of grammaticalization in progress. *American Speech* 66 (3), 227–279.

Rutherford, William E. 1970 Some observations concerning subordinate clauses in English. *Language* 46 (1), 97–115.

Sakakura, Atssuyoshi. 1993 *Nihongo hyoogen no nagare* [History of Japanese]. Tokyo: Iwanami Shoten.

Schiffrin, Deborah. 1987 *Discourse markers.* Cambridge: Cambridge University Press.

Schiffrin, Deborah. 2001 Discourse markers: language, meaning, and context. In Schiffrin, Tannen, and Heidi E. Hamilton, (eds.), pp. 54–75.

Schiffrin, Deborah, Deborah Tannen, and Heidi E. Hamilton, (eds.), 2001 *The handbook of discourse analysis.* Oxford: Blackwell Publishing.

Schleppegrell, Mary J. 1991 Paratactic *because. Journal of Pragmatics* 16, 323–337.

Schwenter, Scott A., and Elizabeth C. Traugott. 1995 The semantic and pragmatic development of subjective complex prepositions in English. In Andreas H. Jucker, (ed.), *Historical pragmatics: Pragmatic developments in the history of English,* pp. 243–273. Amsterdam: John Benjamins.

Schwenter, Scott A., and Elizabeth C. Traugott. 2000 Invoking scalarity: the development of *in fact. Journal of Historical Pragmatics* 1 (1), 7–25.

Schourup, Lawrence C. 1985 *Common discourse particles in English Conversation: Like, well, y'know.* New York: Garland.

Shibatani, Masayoshi. 1990 *The languages of Japan.* Cambridge: Cambridge University Press.

Shibatani, Masayoshi. 1991   Grammaticization of topic into subject. In Traugott and Heine, (eds.), vol. II, pp. 93–133.

Shigemi, Kazuyuki. 1996   *Kara* to *node* no koobunteki kinoo no sai ni tuite [On the difference in structural function of *kara* and *node*]. *Gobun* 65, 25–36. Osaka University, Osaka, Japan.

Shimokawa, Yutaka. 1978   Bun ketugoo kankei – meidai soogo kankei: zentai tekisuto no kaisooteki koosei [Relationship between sentences – interrelationship between propositions: layered structure of the whole text]. *Energea* 5, 17–34.

Shimokawa, Yutaka. 1989   On so-called zero-pronominal: deletion and host parasite structure. *Text* 9 (3), 339–338.

Shirakawa, Hiroyuki. 1991   *Kara* de iisasu bun [Sentences ending with *kara*]. *Hiroshima Daigaku Kyooiku-gakubu Kiyoo Dai-2-bu* 39, 249–255. Hiroshima University, Hiroshima, Japan.

Shirakawa, Hiroyuki. 1995   Riyuu o arawasanai *kara* [Non-reason *kara*]. In Nitta, (ed.), pp. 189–219. Tokyo: Kurosio Publishers.

Shirakawa, Hiroyuki. 2001   Setuzokuzyosi *si* no kinoo [Function of the conjunctive particle *si*]. In Nakau Minoru Kyoozyu Kanreki Kinen Ronbunsyuu Hensyuuiinkai (ed.), *Imi to katati no interface* 2, pp. 825–836. Tokyo: Kurosio Publishers.

Shopen, Timothy, (ed.), 1985   *Language typology and syntactic description.* 3 vols. Cambridge: Cambridge University Press.

Sohn, Sung-Ock S. 1993   Cognition, affect, and topicality of the causal particle *-nikka* in Korean. In Patricia M. Clancy, (ed.), *Japanese/Korean Linguistics* 2, pp. 82–97. Stanford, Calif.: CSLI Publications.

Sohn, Sung-Ock S. 1996   On the development of sentence-final particles in Korean. In Noriko Akatsuka, Shoichi Iwasaki, and Susan Strauss, (ed.), *Japanese/Korean Linguistics* 5, pp. 219–234. Stanford, Calif.: CSLI Publications.

Sohn, Sung-Ock S. 2003   On the emergence of intersubjectivity: an analysis of the sentence-final *nikka* in Korean. In William McClure, (ed.), *Japanese/Korean Linguistics* 12, pp. 52–63. Stanford, Calif.: CSLI Publications.

Stein, Dieter, and Susan Wright, (eds.), 1995   *Subjectivity and subjectivisation: Linguistic perspectives*. Cambridge: Cambridge University Press.

Stenström, Anna-Brita. 1998   From sentence to discourse: *cos (because)* in teenage talk. In Andreas H. Jucker and Yael Ziv, (ed.), *Discourse markers: Descriptions and theory*, pp. 127–146. Amsterdam: John Benjamins.

Stenström, Anna-Brita, and Gisle Andersen. 1996   More trends in teenage talk: a corpus-based investigation of the discourse items *cos* and *innit*. In Carol E. Percy, Charles F. Meyer, and Ian Lancashire, (ed.), *Synchronic corpus linguistics: Papers from the sixteenth international conference on English language research on computerized corpora (ICAME 16)*, pp. 189–203. Amsterdam-Atlanta: Radopi.

Stubbs, Michael. 1983   *Discourse analysis: The sociolinguistic analysis of natural language*. Oxford: Basil Blackwell.

Suzuki, Hiroshi. 1952   *Syuuekisyo no kokugogakuteki kenkyuu: Kenkyuu hen* [A study in *Syuuekisyo*: Study volume]. Osaka: Seibundo.

Suzuki, Ryoko. 1998a   From a lexical noun to an utterance-final pragmatic particle: *wake*. In Ohori, (ed.), pp. 67–92.

Suzuki, Ryoko. 1998b   Grammaticization of clause-final elements: A commentary on Iguchi's paper. In Ohori, (ed.), pp. 129–134.

Suzuki, Ryoko. 1999a   Grammaticization in Japanese: a study of pragmatic particleization. Ph.D. dissertation, University of California, Santa Barbara, USA.

Suzuki, Ryoko. 1999b   Multifunctionality: the developmental path of the quotative *tte* in Japanese. In Laura Michaels. Boulder, (ed.), *Conceptual structure, discourse and language (CSDL) III*, pp. 50-64. CO: University of Colorado.

Suzuki, Yoshikazu. 2000   Iwayuru "riyuu o arawasanai *kara*" ni tuite [On so-called non-reason *kara*]. *Kobe Daigaku Bungakubu Kiyoo* 27, 311–328. Kobe University, Hyogo, Japan.

Svartvik, Jan, (ed.), 1990   *The London-Lund Corpus of Spoken English: Description and research*. Lund: University Press.

Swan, Toril, and Olaf Jansen Westvik, (eds.), 1997   *Modality in Germanic languages: Historical and comparative perspectives*. Berlin: Mouton de Gruyter.

Sweetser, Eve. 1982   Root and epistemic modals: causality in two worlds. *Berkeley Linguistics Society* 8, 484–507.

Sweetser, Eve. 1988   Grammaticalization and semantic bleaching. In Axmaker et al., (eds.), pp. 389–405.

Sweetser, Eve. 1990 *From etymology to pragmatics: Metaphorical and cultural aspects of semantic structure*. Cambridge: Cambridge University Press.

Tabor, Whitney, and Elizabeth Closs Traugott. 1998 Structural scope expansion and grammaticalization. In Ramat and Hopper, (eds.), pp. 229–272.

Takahashi, Taro. 1993 Syooryaku ni yotte dekita zyutugo keisiki [Predicates made through ellipsis]. *Nihongogaku* 12 (9), 18–26.

Takubo, Yukinori. 1987 Toogo koozoo to bunmyaku zyoohoo [Syntactic structure and contextual information]. *Nihongogaku* 6 (5), 37–48.

Tanaka, Hiroshi. 2004 *Nihongo hukubun hyoogen no kenkyuu: setuzoku to zyozyutu no koozoo* [A study on complex sentences in Japanese: structure of conjunction and predicate]. Tokyo: Hakuteisha.

Tanaka, Shigenori. 2002 Nitizyoo gengo no bunpoosei: *because* no syiyoo o megutte [Grammaticality in daily conversation: the usage of *because*]. In Ueda, (ed.), pp. 173–191.

Thompson, Sandra A. 1985 Grammar and written discourse: initial vs. final purpose clauses in English. *Text* 5 (1–2), 55–84.

Thompson, Sandra A. 1987 "Subordination" and narrative event structure. In Russel S. Tomlin, (ed.), *Coherence and grounding in discourse*, pp. 435–454. Amsterdam: John Benjamins.

Thompson, Sandra A., and Robert E. Longacre. 1985 Adverbial clauses. In Shopen, (ed.), vol. II, pp. 171–234.

Thompson, Sandra A., and Anthony Mulac. 1991 A quantitative perspective on the grammaticization of epistemic parentheticals in English. In Traugott and Heine, (eds.), vol. II, pp. 313–329.

Thorne, James P. 1986 Because. In Eieter Kastovsky and Aleksander Szwedek, (ed.), *Linguistics across historical and geographical bounderies: In hohour of Jack Fisiak on the occasion of his fiftieth birthday*, vol. II, pp. 1063–1066.

Traugott, Elizabeth Closs. 1982 From propositional to textual and expressive meaning: some semantic-pragmatic aspects of grammaticalization. In Winfred P. Lehmann and Yakov Malkiel, (ed.), *Perspectives on historical linguistics*, pp. 245–271. Amsterdam: John Benjamins.

Traugott, Elizabeth Closs. 1986   On the origins of "and" and "but" connectives in English. *Studies in Language* 10 (1), 137–150.

Traugott, Elizabeth Closs. 1988   Pragmatic strengthening and grammaticalization. In Axmaker et al., (eds.), pp. 406–416.

Traugott, Elizabeth Closs. 1989   On the rise of epistemic meanings in English: an example of subjectification in semantic change. *Language* 65 (1), 31–55.

Traugott, Elizabeth Closs. 1990   From less to more situated in language: the unidirectionality of semantic change. In Sylvia Adamson, Vivien Law, Nigel Vincent, and Susan Wright, (ed.), *Papers from the 5th International Conference on English Historical Linguistics*, pp. 497–517. Amsterdam: John Benjamins.

Traugott, Elizabeth Closs. 1992   Syntax. In Hogg, Richard M. Blake, N.F., Burchfield, (ed.), *The Cambridge History of the English Language*. vol. I, pp. 168–289. Cambridge: Cambridge Univercity Press.

Traugott, Elizabeth Closs. 1995a   Subjectification in grammaticalization. In Stein and Wright, (eds.), pp. 31–54.

Traugott, Elizabeth Closs. 1995b   The role of the development of discourse markers in a theory of grammaticalization. Paper presented at ICHL XII, Manchester, 1995, Version of 11/97. (http://www.stanford.edu/ ~traugott/ect-papersonline.html).

Traugott, Elizabeth Closs. 1996   Grammaticalization and Lexicalization. In Keith Brown and Jim Miller, (ed.), *Concise encyclopedia of syntactic theories*, pp. 181–187. Oxford: Elsevier Science.

Traugott, Elizabeth Closs. 1997   Subjectification and the development of epistemic meaning: the case of *promise* and *threaten*. In Swan and Westvik, (eds.), pp. 185–210.

Traugott, Elizabeth Closs. 1999a   The role of pragmatics in semantic change. In Jef Verschueren, (ed.), *Pragmatics in 1998: Selected papers from the 6th international pragmatics conference*, vol. 2, pp. 93–102. Antwerp: International Pragmatics Association (IPrA).

Traugott, Elizabeth Closs. 1999b   The rhetoric of counter-expectation in semantic change: a study in subjectification. In Andreas Blank and Peter Koch, (ed.), *Historical semantics and cognition*, pp. 177–196. Berlin: Mouton de Gruyter.

Traugott, Elizabeth Closs. 2001   Legitimate counterexamples to unidirectionality. Paper presented at Freiburg University, October 17th 2001 (http://www.stanford.edu/ ~traugott/ect-papersonline.html).

Traugott, Elizabeth Closs. 2003a   Constructions in grammaticalization. In Joseph and Janda, (eds.), pp. 624–647.

Traugott, Elizabeth Closs. 2003b   From subjectification to intersubjectification. In Raymond Hickey, (ed.), *Motives for language change*, pp. 124–139. Cambridge: Cambridge University Press.

Traugott, Elizabeth Closs. 2004   Historical pragmatics. In Horn and Ward, (eds.), pp. 538–561.

Traugott, Elizabeth Closs, and Richard B. Dasher. 2002   *Regularity in semantic change*. Cambridge: Cambridge University Press.

Traugott, Elizabeth Closs, and Bernd Heine, (eds.), 1991   *Approaches to grammaticalization*. 2 vols. Amsterdam: John Benjamins.

Traugott, Elizabeth Closs, and Ekkehard König. 1991   The semantics-pragmatics of grammaticalization revisited. In Traugott and Heine, (eds.), vol. I, pp. 189–218.

Tsunoda, Mie. 2004   *Nihongo no setu/bun no rensetu to modality* [Clause/sentence combining and modality in Japanese]. Tokyo: Kurosio Publishers.

Uchida, Mitsumi. 2002   *Causal relations and clause linkage: Consequential particle clauses and their use*. Osaka: Osaka University Press.

Ueda, Hiroto, (ed.) 2002   *Nihongogaku to gengokyooiku* [Japanese linguistics and language teaching]. Tokyo: University of Tokyo Press.

Uno, Ryoko. 1996   *Te, node, kara* setu o hukumu inga no hukubun no bunseki: keitaiteki toogoosei to imiteki toogoosei no sookan [An analysis of complex sentences bearing causal clauses marked by *te, node,* and *kara*: correlation of syntactic and semantic integration]. Ms., University of Tokyo, Tokyo, Japan.

Uno, Ryoko. 1997   A cognitive analysis of Japanese causals with the connective *kara*: content and epistemic readings. Unpublished MA thesis, University of Tokyo, Tokyo, Japan.

Uno, Ryoko Watanabe. 2001   Introducing speaker's construal in semantic relations hierarchy: a case of Japanese causal clauses. Paper presented at RRG Conference in LSA at Santa Barbara.

Van Valin, Robert D., Jr. 1993   A synopsis of role and reference grammar. In Robert D. Van Valin, Jr., (ed.), *Advances in role and reference grammar*, pp. 1–164. Amsterdam: John Benjamins.

Van Valin, Robert D., Jr. 2005   *Exploring the syntax-semantics interface*. Cambridge: Cambridge University Press.

Van Valin, Robert D., Jr., and Randy J. LaPolla. 1997   *Syntax: Structure, meaning and function*. Cambridge: Cambridge University Press.

Whaley, Lindsay J. 1997   *Introduction to typology:The unity and diversity of language*. Thousand Oaks, Calif.: SAGE Publications.

Wiegand, Nancy. 1982   From discourse to syntax: *for* in early English causal clauses. In Anders Ahlqvist, (ed.), *Papers from the 5th international conference on historical linguistics*, pp. 384–393. Amsterdam: John Benjamins.

Wischer, Ilse, and Gabriele Diewald, (eds.), 2002   *New Reflections on grammaticalization*. Amsterdam: John Benjamins.

Yabe, Hiroko. 1997   "Nokketyau kara ne" kara "moositeorimasu node" made [*Kara* and *node* in conversational data among female office workers]. In Gendai Nihongo Kenkyuukai, (ed.), *Zyosei no kotoba: Shokuba-hen*, pp. 139–154. Tokyo: Hituzi Syobo.

Yabe, Hiroko. 2002   *Kara* to *node* no siyoo ni miru syokuba no dansei no gengokoodoo [*Kara* and *node* in conversational data among male office workers]. In Gendai Nihongo Kenkyuukai, (ed.), *Dansei no kotoba: Shokuba-hen*, pp. 133–148. Tokyo: Hituzi Syobo.

Yamada, Masaki. 1936   *Edo kotoba no kenkyuu: Ukiyoburo Ukiyodoko no goho* [A study of Japanese in the Edo period: The usage of words in *Ukiyoburo* and *Ukiyodoko*]. Tokyo: Musashino Shobo.

Yamada, Yoshio. 1954   *Naratyo bunpoosi* [Historical syntax in the Nara period] Tokyo: Hobunkan.

Yamaguchi, Gyoji. 1980   *Kodai setuzokuhoo no kenkyuu* [A study in Old Japanese clause linkage]. Tokyo: Meiji Shoin.

Yamaguchi, Gyoji. 1996   *Nihongo setuzokuhoosiron* [A historical study of Japanese clause linkage]. Osaka: Izumi Shoin.

Yap, Foong Ha, Stephen Matthews, and Kaoru Horie. 2004   From pronominalizer to pragmatic marker: implications for unidirectionality from a crosslinguistic perspective. In Fischer et al., (eds.), pp. 137–168.

Yonekura, Hiroshi. 2001   Setuzokusi *since* no bunpooka: kooki tyuueigo o tyuusin ni [Grammaticalization of the conjunction *since*: with special attention to late Middle English]. In Akimoto, (ed.), pp. 27–58.

Yoshii, Kazuto. 1977   Kindai Tokyoogo ingakankei hyoogen no tuuziteki koosatu: *kara* to *node* o tyuusin to site [A diachronic consideration of the expression of causal relation in the modern Tokyo dialect: with special reference to *kara* and *node*]. *Kokugogaku* 110, 19–36.

Yoshikawa, Yasuo. 1955   Setuzokusi *kara* to kanyoogo *kara-wa* [On the conjunctive particle *kara* and the colloquial expression *kara-wa*]. *Kokugo Kenkyuu* 3.

Yuzawa, Kokichiro. 1958   *Muromati zidai gengo no kenkyuu: Shoomono no gohoo* [A study in Japanese in the Muromati period: the usage of words in *Shomono*]. Tokyo: Kazama Shobo.

Yuzawa, Kokichiro, 1970   *Tokugawa zidai gengo no kenkyuu: Kamigata hen* [A study of Japanese in the Tokugawa period]. Tokyo: Kazama Shobo.

Dictionaries

Gakken Kokugo Daiziten [Gakken dictionary of Japanese], 2nd Edition. 1988   Tokyo: Gakushu Kenkyusha.

Middle English Dictionary (MED). 1956   Ann Arbor: University of Michigan Press.

Nihon Kokugo Daijiten (NKD) [Dictionary of the Japanese language], 2nd Edition. 2000   Tokyo: Shogakukan.

The Oxford English Dictionary (OED), 2nd Edition. 1989   Oxford: Clarendon Press.

Shogakukan Random House English-Japanese Dictionary. 1988   Tokyo: Shogakukan.

Zenyaku Dokkai Kogo Ziten (ZDKZ) [Dictionary of classical Japanese with translation]. 1995   Tokyo: Sanseido.

List of data (English)

Diachronic

*(D): Drama, (N): Novel, [ ]: URL

1387-1400 The Canterbury Tales. by Geoffrey Chaucer, (N). [Librarius].
1590 (prtd.) Tamburlaine the Great, Parts 1 and 2, by Christopher Marlowe, (D). [Perseus Project].
1594-5 Romeo and Juliet, by William Shakespeare, (D). [The plays of William Shakespeare].
1603-4 The Phoenix, by Thomas Middleton, (D). [The Plays of Thomas Middleton].
1606 A Trick to catch the old one, by Thomas Middleton, (D). [The Plays of Thomas Middleton].
1607-8 Coriolanus, by William Shakespeare, (D). [The plays of William Shakespeare].
1612-3 The Duchesse of Malfi, by John Webster, (D). [Project Gutenberg].
1633 The Jew of Malta, by Christopher Marlowe, (D). [Perseus Project].
1676 The man of mode, or, Sir Fopling Flutter, by Sir George Etherege, (D). [Bibliomania].
1677 The Rover, or, the banish'd cavaliers, by Aphra Behn, (D). [English Server].
1682 Venice preserved, by Thomas Otway with conspirators, (D). [Bibliomania].
1697 The provoked wife, Sir John Vanbrugh, (D). [Bibliomania].
1724 Roxana: the fortunate mistress, by Daniel Defoe, (N). [Naked Word].
1728 The beggar's opera, by John Gay, (D). [Bibliomania].
1759 The history of Rasselas, Prince of Abissinia, by Samuel Johnson, (N). [The Internet Public Library].
1759-67 Tristram Shandy, by Laurence Sterne, (N). [Project Gutenberg].

1764	The castle of Otranto, by Horace Walpole, (N). [Project Gutenberg].
1777	The school for scandal, by Richard Brinsley Sheridan, (D). [Project Gutenberg].
1778	Evelina, or, the history of a young lady's entrance into the world, by Fanny Burney, (N). [A Celebration of Women Writers].
1792	The massacre: taken from the French, by Elizabeth Inchbald, (D). [A Celebration of Women Writers].
1813	Pride and prejudice, by Jane Austen, (N). [The works of Jane Austen].
1816	Headlong hall, by Thomas Love Peacock, (N). [The Thomas Love Peacock Society].
1818	Nightmare abbey, by Thomas Love Peacock, (N). [The Thomas Love Peacock Society].
1834	The last days of Pompeii, by Edward George Bulwer-Lytton, (N). [Project Gutenberg].
1843	Windsor castle, by William Harrison Ainsworth, (N). [Project Gutenberg].
1847–8	Vanity fair, by William Makepeace Thackeray, (N). [Bibliomania].
1848	Mary Barton, by Elizabeth Cleghorn Gaskell, (N). [Project Gutenberg].
1861	Great expectations, by Charles Dickens, (N). [Bibliomania].
1863	The water-babies, by Charles Kingsley, (N). [Project Gutenberg]
1872	Erewhon, by Samuel Butler, (N). [Project Gutenberg].
1889	Silvie and Bruno, by Lewis Carroll (Charles Lutwidge Dodgson), (N). [Bibliomania].
1891	News from nowhere, or, an epoch of rest, by William Morris, (N). [Electronic Text Center].
1897	The invisible man (HTML-version), by Herbert George Wells, (N). [Online Literature Library].
1898	The beauty stone, by Sir Arthur Wing Pinero and J. Comyns Carr, (D). [Gilbert and Sullivan Archives].
1902	The grand Babylon hotel, by Arnold Bennett, (N). [Eldrich Press].
1905	Where angels fear to tread, by Edward Morgan Forster, (N). [The Humanities Text Initiative].
1909	The silver box, by John Galsworthy, (D). [Project Gutenberg],

1911   The innocence of Father Brown, by Gilbert Keith Chesteron, (N). [English Server].

1911   Zuleika Dobson, by Sir Henry Maximilian Beerbohm, (N). [Electronic Text Center].

1919   Moon and sixpence, by William Somerset Maugham, (N). [Project Gutenberg].

1919   Night and day, by Adeline Virginia Woolf, (N). [Litrix Reading Room].

1921   Crome yellow, by Aldous Leonard Huxley, (N). [Project Gutenberg].

[URL in 2005]
Librarius (www.librarius.com)

[URLs in 2000-2001]
Bibliomania (http://www.bibliomania.com)

A Celebration of Women Writers (http://digital.library.upenn.edu/women)

Eldrich Press (http://www.eldrichpress.org)

Electronic Text Center, University of Virginia Library (http://etext.lib.virginia.edu)

English Server (http://www.eserver.org)

Gilbert and Sullivan Archives (http://math.idbsu.edu/gas)

The Humanities Text Initiative, Digital Library Production Service, University of Michigan (http://www.hti.umich.edu)

The Internet Public Library (http://www.ipl.org)

Litrix Reading Room (http://www.litrix.com)

Naked Word (hrrp://www.nakedword.org)

Online Literature Library (http://www.literature.org)

Perseus Project, Tufts University (http://www.perseus.tufts.edu)

The Plays of Thomas Middleton (http://www.tech.org/~cleary/homepage/html)

Project Gutenberg (http://www.gutenberg.net)

The Plays of William Shakespeare, The Electronic Literature Foundation (http://www.theplays.org)

The Thomas Love Peacock Society (http://www.thomaslovepeacock.net)

The Works of Jane Austen, The Electronic Literature Foundation (http://elf.chaoscafe.com)

Diachronic (Helsinki Corpus)

*[ ]: Prototypical text category, Text type

ME3

[Imaginative narration, Fiction] The Canterbury tales, by Geoffrey Chaucer.

[Imaginative narration, Fiction] Confessio Amantis, by John Gower.

ME4

[Imaginative narration, Fiction] The History of Reynard the Fox, by William Caxton.

[Imaginative narration, Romance] Le Morte D'Arthur, by Thomas Malory.

[Drama: mystery play] Ludus Coventriae.

[Drama: mystery play] Mankind.

[Drama: mystery play] The Wakefield Pageants in the Towneley Cycle.

[Drama: mystery play] The York Plays.

[Drama: mystery play] Digby Plays.

[Private letter] Letter(s) by John Shillingford, Paston Letters, The Stonor Letters, The Cely Letters.

EMBE1

[Diary] The Diary of Henry Machyn, by Henry Machyn.

[Diary] Journal, by Edward VI.

[Imaginative narration, Fiction] A Caveat or Warening for Commen Cursetors, by Thomas Harman.

[Comedy] Roister Doister, by Nicholas Udall.

[Comedy] Gammer Gvrtons Nedle, by William Stevenson (?).

[Correspondence: Private] Beaumont Papers, Clifford Letters of the Sixteenth Century, The Correspondence of Sir Thomas More, Original Letters (Illustrative of English History), Plumpton Correspondence.

EMBE2

[Diary] The Diary of Richard Madox, by Richard Madox.

[Diary] Dairy of Lady Margaret Hoby, by Margaret Hoby.

[Imaginative narration, Fiction] A Nest of Ninnies, by Robert Armin.
[Imaginative narration, Fiction] The Pleasaunt History of … Iack of Newberie, by Thomas Deloney.
[Comedy] The Merry Wives of Windsor, by William Shakespeare.
[Comedy] A Chaste Maid in Cheapside, by Thomas Middleton.
[Correspondence: Private] Barrington Family Letters, The Correspondence of Lady Katherine Paston, the Ferrar Papers, The Knyvett Letters, Letters of Philip Gawdy, Letters of the Lady Brilliana Harley, The Oxinden Letters.

EMBE3

[Diary] The Diary of Samuel Pepys, by Samuel Pepys.
[Diary] The Diary of John Evelyn, by John Evelyn.
[Imaginative narration, Fiction] Penny Merriments (= Samuel Pepys's Merriments).
[Imaginative narration, Fiction] Oroonoko, by Aphra Behn.
[Comedy] The Relapse or Virtue in Danger, by John Vanbrugh.
[Comedy] The Beaux Stratagem, by George Farquhar.
[Correspondence: Private] Correspondence of the Family of Haddock, Correspondence of the Family of Hatton, Diaries and Letters of Philip Henry, Letters of John Pinney, Original Letters of Eminent Literary Men, The Oxinden and Peyton Letters.

Synchronic (LLC)

*The speakers are British and educated to university level.

Conversations recorded in 1960s

S.1.1   1964   Conversations between equals
                        A   male academic, age c.44
                        B   male academic, age c.60

S.1.2   1963   Conversations between equals
                A   male academic, age c.43
                B   male academic, age c.62

S.2.1   1963   Conversations between equals
                a   male academic, age c.43
                B   male academic, age c.34

S.2.2a 1969   Conversations between equals
                a   male academic, age c.48
                A   male stockbroker, age c.35

S.4.1   1969   Conversations between intimates and equals
                a   male undergraduate, age 25
                b   female housewife and teacher, age 24 (married to a)

Conversations recorded in 1970s

S.1.7   1972   Conversations between equals
                a   male academic, age 30–40
                A   male primary school teacher, age c.30
                B   male secondary school teacher, age c.30

S.1.10 1975   Conversations between equals
                A   female lecturer, age c.52
                b   female academic, age c.40
                c   male businessman, age c.52

S.2.3   1974   Conversations between equals
                a   female academic, age c.40
                A   male legal civil servant, age 38–40
                B   male architect, age 43–45

S.2.4a   1970   Conversations between equals
                  A   male academic, age c.35
                  B   male academic, age c.30
                  c   female housewife, age c.30
                  d   male academic, age c.35 (husband of c)

S.4.2   1971   Conversations between intimates and equals
                  a   female academic, age c.40
                  b   male solicitor, age c.40

List of data (Japanese)

Diachronic
*[ ]: URL

1592	Amakusaban Heike Monogatari. [NBTF]
1593	Amakusaban Isoho Monogatari. [NBTF]
1703	Sonezaki sinzyuu, by Chikamatsu Monzaemon. Chikamatsu zyoorurisyuu. Tokyo: Yuhodo. 1912–1914. [JTIC].
1713	Sukeroku. Koten nihon bungaku taikei 98. Tokyo: Iwanami Shoten. 1965. [NKB].
1721	Sinzyuu yoigoosin, by Chikamatsu Monzaemon. Koten nihon bungaku taikei 49. Tokyo: Iwanami Shoten. 1958. [NKB].
1736	Sibaraku. Koten nihon bungaku taikei 98. Tokyo: Iwanami Shoten. 1965. [NKB].
1742	Kenuki. Koten nihon bungaku taikei 98. Tokyo: Iwanami Shoten. 1965. [NKB].
1748	Kanadehon tyuusingura, by Izumo Takeda, Miyoshi Shoraku, and Namiki Senryu. Tokyo: Iwanami Shoten. 1937. [JTIC].
1770	Tatumi no sono, by Muchusanjin Negoto Sensei. Koten nihon bungaku taikei 59. Tokyo: Iwanami Shoten. 1958. [NKB].

1770	Yuusihoogen, by Inakarojin Tadano Jijii. Koten nihon bungaku taikei 59. Tokyo: Iwanami Shoten. 1958. [NKB].
1772	Kanoko moti, by Kimuro Booun. Koten nihon bungaku taikei 100. Tokyo: Iwanami Shoten. 1966. [NKB].
1773	Kiki zyoozu, by Komatsuya Hyakki. Koten nihon bungaku taikei 100. Tokyo: Iwanami Shoten. 1966. [NKB].
1776	Koomanzai angya nikki, by Koikawa Harumachi. Koten nihon bungaku taikei 59. Tokyo: Iwanami Shoten. 1958. [NKB].
1778 (?)	Dootyuu sugoroku. Koten nihon bungaku taikei 59. Tokyo: Iwanami Shoten. 1958. [NKB].
1779	Tai no misozu, by Shokusanjin. Koten nihon bungaku taikei 100. Tokyo: Iwanami Shoten. 1966. [NKB].
1782	Gozonzi no syoobaimono, by Kitao Masanobu. Koten nihon bungaku taikei 59. Tokyo: Iwanami Shoten. 1958. [NKB].
1783	Uzisyuui, by Shumokuan Aruji. Koten nihon bungaku taikei 59. Tokyo: Iwanami Shoten. 1958. [NKB].
1785	Daihi no senroppon, by Shiba Zenko. Koten nihon bungaku taikei 59. Tokyo: Iwanami Shoten. 1958. [NKB].
1785	Edo umare uwaki no kabayaki, by Santo Kyoden. Koten nihon bungaku taikei 59. Tokyo: Iwanami Shoten. 1958. [NKB].
1785	Kiruna no ne kara kane no naru ki, by Tourai Sanna. Koten nihon bungaku taikei 59. Tokyo: Iwanami Shoten. 1958. [NKB].
1787	Soomagaki, by Santo Kyoden. Koten nihon bungaku taikei 59. Tokyo: Iwanami Shoten. 1958. [NKB].
1788	Bunbu nidoo mangoku toosi, by Houseido Kisanji. Koten nihon bungaku taikei 59. Tokyo: Iwanami Shoten. 1958. [NKB].
1789	Koosizima tokini aizome, by Santo Kyoden. Koten nihon bungaku taikei 59. Tokyo: Iwanami Shoten. 1958. [NKB].
1790	Keiseikai syizyuuhatte, by Santo Kyoden. Koten nihon bungaku taikei 59. Tokyo: Iwanami Shoten. 1958. [NKB].
1790	Shingaku hayasomekusa, by Santo Kyoden. Koten nihon bungaku taikei 59. Tokyo: Iwanami Shoten. 1958. [NKB].

List of data   261

1791	Nisiki no ura, by Santo Kyoden. Koten nihon bungaku taikei 59. Tokyo: Iwanami Shoten. 1958. [NKB].
1795	Katakiuti gizyo no hanabusa, by Nansensho Somahito. Koten nihon bungaku taikei 59. Tokyo: Iwanami Shoten. 1958. [NKB].
1798	Keiseikai futasuzimiti, by Umebori Kokuga. Koten nihon bungaku taikei 59. Tokyo: Iwanami Shoten. 1958. [NKB].
1801	Meika no tokuu mimasu no tamagaki, by Sakurada Jisuke. Koten nihon bungaku taikei 54. Tokyo: Iwanami Shoten. 1961. [NKB].
1802–22	Tokaidootyuu hizakurige, by Jippensha Ikku. Koten nihon bungaku taikei 62. Tokyo: Iwanami Shoten. 1958. [NKB].
1809	Ukiyoburo, by Shikitei Sanba. Koten nihon bungaku taikei 63. Tokyo: Iwanami Shoten. 1957. [NKB].
1813	Osome Hisamatu ukina no yomiuri, by Tsuruya Namboku. Koten nihon bungaku taikei 54. Tokyo: Iwanami Shoten. 1961. [NKB].
1832–33	Syunsyoku umegoyomi, by TamenagaShunsui. Koten nihon bungaku taikei 64. Tokyo: Iwanami Shoten. 1962. [NKB].
1833–35	Syunsyoku tatumi no sono, by TamenagaShunsui. Koten nihon bungaku taikei 64. Tokyo: Iwanami Shoten. 1962. [NKB].
1842 (?)	Kagekiyo. Koten nihon bungaku taikei 98. Tokyo: Iwanami Shoten. 1965. [NKB].
1843	Narukami. Koten nihon bungaku taikei 98. Tokyo: Iwanami Shoten. 1965. [NKB].
1859	Kosode soga azami no iruonui, by Kawatake Mokuami. Koten nihon bungaku taikei 54. Tokyo: Iwanami Shoten. 1961. [NKB].
1887	Ukigumo, by Futabatei Shimei. Tokyo: Shun'yodo. 1947. [JTIC].
1895	Takekurabe, by Higuchi, Ichiyo. Shinchoo-bunko no 100-satsu. Tokyo: Shinchosha.
1896	Wakaremiti, by Higuchi, Ichiyo. Shinchoo-bunko no 100-satsu. Tokyo: Shinchosha.
1897	Konszyikiyasya, by Ozaki, Koyo. Shinchoo-bunko no 100-satsu. Tokyo: Shinchosha.
1902	Zyunsa, by Kunikida, Doppo. Shinchoo-bunko no 100-satsu. Tokyo:

Shinchosha.

1906 Kusamakura, by Natsume, Soseki. Shinchoo-bunko no 100-satsu. Tokyo: Shinchosha.

1907 Heibon, by Futabatei, Shimei. Shinchoo-bunko no 100-satsu. Tokyo: Shinchosha.

1912–13 Gan, by Mori Ogai. Tokyo: Shoten. 1948. [JTIC].

1914 Kokoro, by Natsume, Soseki. Shinchoo-bunko no 100-satsu. Tokyo: Shinchosha.

1918 Umareizuru nayami, by Arishima, Takeo. Shinchoo-bunko no 100-satsu. Tokyo: Shinchosha.

1918 Zigokuhen, by Akutagawa Ryunosuke. Tokyo: Hosokawa Shoten. 1947. [JTIC].

1920 Yuuzyoo, by Mushanokoji, Saneatsu. Shinchoo-bunko no 100-satsu. Tokyo: Shinchosha.

1924 Tizin no ai, by Tanizaki, Jun'ichiro. Shinchoo-bunko no 100-satsu. Tokyo: Shinchosha.

1927 Kappa. by Akutagawa Ryunosuke. Tokyo: Hosokawa Shoten. 1946. [JTIC].

1935 Aside, by Ishikawa, Jun. Shinchoo-bunko no 100-satsu. Tokyo: Shinchosha.

1936 Kaze tatinu, by Hori, Tatsuo. Shinchoo-bunko no 100-satsu. Tokyo: Shinchosha.

1941 Roboo no isi, by Yamamoto, Yuzo. Shinchoo-bunko no 100-satsu. Tokyo: Shinchosha.

1947 Syozyo kaitai, by Ishikawa, Jun. Shinchoo-bunko no 100-satsu. Tokyo: Shinchosha.

[URL in 2005]
NBTF: Nihon Bungaku-too Text File (www.let.osaka-u.ac.jp/~okajima/bungaku.htm)
[URLs in 2000-2001]
JTIC: Japanese Text Initiative Collection, University of Virginia
(http://etext.virginia.edu/japanese/texts.html)

NKB: Nihon Koten Bungaku Sakuhin Database (http://www.nijl.ac.jp)

Synchronic (written colloquial)

1952 Nobi, by Oka, Shohei. Shincho-bunko no 100-satsu. Tokyo: Shinchosha.
1956 Kinkakuzi, by Mishima, Yukio. Shincho-bunko no 100-satsu. Tokyo: Shinchosha.
1964 Nireke no hitobito, by Kita, Morio. Shincho-bunko no 100-satsu. Tokyo: Shinchosha.
1967 Amerika hiziki, by Nosaka, Akiyuki. Shincho-bunko no 100-satsu. Tokyo: Shinchosha.
1970 Kokoo no hito, by Nitta, Jiro. Shincho-bunko no 100-satsu. Tokyo: Shinchosha.
1978 Shimbashi karasumoriguti seisyun-hen, by Shina, Makoto. Shincho-bunko no 100-satsu. Tokyo: Shinchosha.
1982 Issyun no natu, by Sawaki, Kotaro. Shincho-bunko no 100-satsu. Tokyo: Shinchosha.
1985 Taroo monogatari, kooko hen, by Sono, Ayako. Shincho-bunko no 100-satsu. Tokyo: Shinchosha.

Synchronic (spoken)

I. Osyaberi namatyuukei in *Nihongo Journal*, 1999.4–2000.3. Tokyo: Aruku.
   Conversations between intimates, recorded presumably in 1999–2000
   Speakers of Tokyo dialects only

NJ9904, NJ9910
(N and S: married couple, H and S: co-workers)
   H: female worker, age late 20s
   N: male worker, age late 20s
   S: female worker, age late 20s

NJ9908, NJ0002 (coworkers)

I: female editor, age 30s

　　　K: male worker, age 30s

　　　S: male worker, age 30s

NJ9909

　　　H: female pharmacist, age late 20s to 30s

　　　K: female writer, age late 20s to 30s

　　　Y: female editor, age late 20s to 30s

NJ9911, NJ0003

(H and M: friends, H and S: friends, M and S meet for the first time)

　　　H: female worker, age 20s

　　　M: male worker, age 20s

　　　S: female worker, age 20s

NJ0001 (friends)

　　　G: female undergraduate, age late teenage to early 20s

　　　N: female undergraduate, age late teenage to early 20s

　　　O: male undergraduate, age late teenage to early 20s

II. *Zatudan siryoo, Nihongo bogo wasya no zatudan ni okeru "monogatari" no kenkyuu* [A study of spoken narratives by native speakers of Japanese], by Lee, Reien, 2000. Tokyo: Kurosio Publishers.

　　　Conversations between friends, recorded in 1995

　　　Speakers of the Tokyo dialect only

　　　( ): the place where they have lived longest in their life

Z95–6

　　　P: female postgraduate, age 23, (Tokyo)

　　　Q: female postgraduate, age 24, (Tokyo)

Z95–7

　　　P: female undergraduate, age 21, (Tokyo)

　　　Q: female undergraduate, age 21, (Kanagawa)

Z95–8
 P: female undergraduate, age 20, (Tokyo)
 Q: female undergraduate, age 21, (Chiba)

Z95–11
 P: female undergraduate, age 20, (Tokyo)
 Q: female undergraduate, age 19, (Chiba)

Z95–12
 P: female undergraduate, age 19, (Tokyo)
 Q: female undergraduate, age 19, (Tokyo)

Z95–13
 P: female undergraduate, age 19, (Tokyo)
 Q: female undergraduate, age 20, (Tokyo)

Z95–15
 P: female undergraduate, age 20, (Tokyo)
 Q: female undergraduate, age 20, (Kanagawa)

Author index

a
Aijmer   38, 44, 48, 114
Akimoto   42, 113
Akimoto et al.   42
Alfonso   3, 30, 32, 36, 47-48, 117-118, 122, 179, 181, 197
Altenberg   46, 51, 56, 108-109
Andersen   51, 54, 58-59, 100, 108, 217
Arnovick   49
Axmaker et al.   42

b
Beths   43
Blakemore   48, 114
Bolinger   54, 108-109
Brinton   34, 36, 38, 48-49, 114, 182, 220
Bybee   9, 217
Bybee et al.   1, 9, 42-43, 111, 113, 195, 197, 214

c
Cabrera   16
Campbell   42, 44
Carey   45
Chafe   51, 56, 66, 108-109
Chiba   192
Comrie   42
Cook   48
Couper-Kuhlen   46, 51, 54, 60-61, 64, 67, 83, 99-100, 108-109
Craig   44
Croft   42, 44

d
Dahl   9
Dakin   24
Dancygier   46-47
Dasher   1, 10, 22, 42, 45, 51, 106, 108, 113-114, 117, 188, 197, 210, 212, 220, 224
Diessel   114
Diewald   42
Du Boir   204, 217

e
Erman   38
Evance   38, 44, 211, 224

f
Fillmore   125, 190, 211
Fillmore et al.   125, 190, 211
Finegan   45
Fischer et al.   42, 44
Foley   44, 189
Ford   51, 66-67, 108, 111, 114, 171, 215
Frajzyngier   44
Fraser   48
Fujii   43, 190
Fujiwara   191, 197

g
Geise   69
Genetti   120
Givón   9, 15, 19
Goldberg   125, 211

Green   54, 108
Greenberg   9
Günthner   44, 209, 216-217

h
Haiman   9, 16, 44, 108, 210, 224
Halliday   20-21, 23, 34, 36, 46, 48, 56, 108
Hanson   114
Haraguchi   186, 191, 193-194
Harris   42, 44
Hasagawa   189
Haspelmath   43
Hassan   20-21, 23, 46
Heine   9, 20, 41, 43-44, 110, 189
Heine et al.   1, 9-11, 20, 41-42, 113, 189, 196
Herring   45
Higashiizumi   190
Hikosaka   137
Hino   42
Hirose   213
Hojo   137
Honda   118, 126, 179, 181, 190
Hopper   1, 8, 10-20, 41-45, 52, 69, 74, 95, 99-101, 105, 113-115, 177, 182-184, 197, 210, 212, 214, 217, 220, 224
Horie   43, 187
Humboldt   9

i
Ichihashi-Nakayama   43, 187, 190
Iguchi   118, 126, 179, 181, 187, 190, 216

Imao 121
Ishigaki 132-135, 137-141, 191-192
Itani 190
Ito 189-190
Iwasaki 30, 47, 121, 189, 193

j

Jacobs 49
Jacobsen 46, 215
Janda 42
Jespersen 23, 108-109, 111, 114
Joseph 42
Jucker 49

k

Kac 108
Kambayashi 47
Kamio 48, 216
Kärkkäinen 114
Kato, K. 202
Kato, Y. 121, 190
Keller 209
Kennedy 49
Kitajo 190
Kobayashi, C. 131, 140, 191, 193, 215
Kobayashi, K. 191
Kobayashi, T. 191
Kobayashi, Y. 191
König 10, 20-21, 69, 110, 113-114
Konoshima 120, 128, 131, 133-136, 139-140, 191-193
Kortmann 46, 72, 104, 110-111
Kotsinas 38
Krug 8, 41-42, 49
Kuno 189

Kuroda 190
Kuryłowicz 8
Kuteva 42, 110, 189
Kuwahara 190
Kyratzis et al. 47

l

Lakoff 54, 108
Lamarre 44, 190, 217
Langacker 16, 45
Lange 43, 115, 215
LaPolla 44, 189
Lass 43
Lehmann 8-9, 11, 15-16, 19, 42-43, 53
Leuschner 44
Levinson 108, 113, 197, 212, 224
Lindquist 42
Longacre 108, 189, 211
Lyons 45

m

Maeda 48, 190
Mair 42
Makino 36, 48
Martin 36, 120, 132
Maruyama 48
Masuoka 48, 121, 190
Matsumoto 42-44, 191, 197
Matsumura 190-191
Matthiessen 16-17, 108
Mayes 188
Maynard 48, 202
McCullough 128-129
McTear 108
Meillet 7, 9
Mikami 121, 189, 191
Minami 121, 189-190
Mio 193
Mittwoch 108

Mizutani 190
Mori 197, 215
Morita 121
Morreal 24
Mulac 43, 106, 211, 224

n

Nagano 121, 143, 189, 193-194
Nagata 48
Nakayama 43, 187, 190
Noda 190, 195

o

Ohori 1, 37-38, 42, 44, 46, 110, 112, 114, 118, 120, 125-126, 179, 181, 183, 185, 187, 189-191, 196, 211, 215, 217, 224
Okamoto 187, 190
Onodera 38-39, 42, 196-197, 215
Onoe 189
Ono, S. 183, 192
Ono, T. 43
Östman 33, 48

p

Pagliuca 42
Powell 44

q

Quirk et al. 53-55, 65, 108-109, 189, 215

r

Ramat, A. 10, 16, 42, 44
Ramat, P. 44
Reh 9, 20, 42-43
Rissanen 42, 45, 49, 73, 105, 110, 114, 214
Rissanen et al. 42, 49

Roberts 44, 189
Romaine 43, 115, 215
Rutherford 108-109, 114

S

Sakakura 120, 128, 191
Schiffrin 3, 25-26, 29, 33-35, 45-46, 48, 51-52, 64, 108, 171
Schleppegrell 48, 51, 57-58, 64, 99, 108-109, 217
Schourup 33
Schwenter 22, 44, 114
Shibatani 36, 42
Shigemi 189
Shimokawa 46, 190
Shirakawa 31-32, 47-48, 117-118, 124,-125, 179, 181, 190
Shopen 44
Sohn 216
Stenström 51, 53-54, 58-59, 65, 99-100, 108-109, 217
Stubbs 54, 108,-109
Suzuki, H. 129, 192
Suzuki, R. 39, 42, 102, 185, 187-188, 190, 196-197, 215, 217
Suzuki, Y. 48
Svartvik 49
Sweetser 2, 20, 26-27, 29, 32-33, 44, 46-47, 51-52, 61, 104, 108-109, 111, 113, 196, 204, 206, 220

t

Tanaka, H. 189-190
Tanaka, S. 108, 217
Tabor 15-16, 19, 43-44, 114
Takahashi 190
Takubo 29-30, 47-48, 117, 121-122, 159, 183, 190
Thompson 16-17, 43-44, 106, 108, 114, 171, 189, 210-211, 224
Thorne 108-109
Traugott 1, 8, 10, 14-22, 28-29, 41-45, 47-49, 51-52, 63, 69, 74, 95, 101-102, 104, 106, 108, 110, 113-115, 117, 177, 183-184, 188, 197, 210, 212, 214-215, 217, 220, 224
Tsunoda 190
Tsutsui 36, 48

u

Uchida 45
Uno 32-33, 46-48, 117, 121, 123, 159, 183

v

van Dijk 24, 29, 47
Van Valin 44, 189

w

Whaley 44
Wiegand 114
Wischer 42

y

Yabe 189
Yamada, M. 192
Yamada, Y. 191
Yamaguchi 120, 130, 136-137, 139, 141-142, 191-193
Yap et al. 214
Yonekura 110
Yoshii 83, 131, 141-143, 145-146, 148, 152, 160, 193-195, 197
Yoshikawa 141
Yuzawa 139, 191

z

Zwicky 69

Subject index

a

ablative case marker 119-120, 221
ablative case particle 134-135, 137, 139
action-based causal relation 25-26, 29
actually 106
adjunct 53-55, 65
adverbial clauses 17, 19, 66, 210
adverbial phrases 34
adverbial subordinators 104
ahida 130
analogy 14
appositional relative 18
as 72, 105, 114, 215
attrition 11

b

ba 128-131
be going to/be gonna 12
because 37, 71, 73, 123, 199-201, 204, 209
because (that) 73, 111
because of 111
because-clause 1-3, 14, 20, 22, 26, 35, 38
Bergen Corpus of London Teenage Language (COLT) 58-59
bleaching 20
British National Corpus (BNC) 41, 77
but 215
by (the) cause (that) 71-72, 111, 113, 210

c

case marker 120, 184
case particle 135-136, 140-141, 183, 191-192
causal clause marker 76, 143, 221
causal clause 23, 142
causal meaning 2
causality 24, 29
'cause, 'cos 54, 58, 108, 111
clause chaining 18
clause (-linkage) marker 20, 120, 140, 184
cline of clause-combining constructions 4, 16-17, 19-20, 101-102, 184-186, 197, 201, 209-210, 214, 217, 219-221, 223-224
coalescence 11, 43
cohesion-marking 21
common discourse particles 33
complementizers 187
condensation 11, 43
conjecture 143
conjunctive particle 37, 191
Construction Grammar 190, 217
content conjunction 26-27, 29-30, 32, 60, 62-63, 83, 95-96, 98, 103, 122-123, 127, 141, 145-146, 159, 177-178, 180, 183, 186, 200, 211, 220, 222
conventionalization of pragmatic inferences 188
conventionalization of pragmatic meanings 4, 99, 112, 181-182, 201, 207, 211, 219, 221-224
conventionalized 98
coordination 18, 123, 210, 224
coordinator 56
cosubordination 44

d

dakara 202, 215
de-categorialization 12-13, 101, 184
declination reset 67
degrammaticalization 44
description of facts 143, 145, 167
despite 109
desyoo 122
dictionary form 141
direct form 216
discourse marker 33-34, 58, 114,
disjunct 53-55, 66
divergence 11-12, 100, 113, 183

e

Edo/Tokyo dialect 41
embedded clauses 17, 217
emergence 217

Subject index

emergent 212
epistemic conjunction
    26-27, 29-30, 32, 48,
    61-62, 64, 68, 83-84,
    87-88, 90, 93, 95-96,
    98, 103, 122-124, 127,
    141, 145-146, 159-164,
    167-168, 172-173, 175,
    177-181, 183, 185-186,
    200, 204, 210-211,
    220-222
explanation 25, 29
expressive 21, 45-46
external 23, 28-29

f

fact-based causal relation
    25-26, 29
fading 20
final particle 48, 148,
    154-155, 179, 182-183,
    187, 191, 222
fixation 11, 43
for 71, 73, 105, 110-111,
    113-114, 204, 209
for (that) 70-71, 105
for ... for-thi/therfore 70
for py/pi (pe) 69
formal noun 135-136,
    141, 183-184

g

ga 132-133, 136
generalized
    conversational
    implicature 212
given 45, 104
grammaticalization 1,
    4, 7-14, 19-20, 22, 41-43,
    49, 99, 101, 108, 112-113,
    182, 184-188, 201, 209,
    212, 214, 216, 219-224

h

hara-kara 192
Helsinki Corpus (HC)
    40, 49, 77, 80, 82
hito-gara 192
hodo-ni 130-131
hypotaxis 4, 17-19,
    44, 52, 59, 62, 68, 76,
    95-96, 101-102, 177-178,
    184-185, 197, 200, 210,
    215
hypothetical/conditional
    191

i

I think 106, 114
ideational 21
implication 25, 29
in fact 106
indeed 106
independent 14, 35,
    52, 68, 76, 91, 93, 96-99,
    102, 127, 147-148, 153,
    171, 176-178, 180-181,
    184-185, 199-200, 203,
    216, 220-222
independent clause 1,
    38, 52, 124
indirect forms 216
insubordination 211,
    224
interactional 108
interactional particle
    48
interjection 34
internal 23, 28-29
interpersonal 34, 37, 48
intersubjectification 45,
    212
intonation 65-67
intonation unit 109

inversion 168, 180-181
izenkei 128, 191

j

just because 212, 217
juxtapositon 18

k

kaku-nomi-kara 191
kakutei-zyooken
    'confirmed conditional'
    128
kara 37, 132-142, 187,
    189, 199-201, 204, 209
kara ni 134, 136, 192-193
kara-clause 1-3, 14, 20,
    22, 29-33, 36-38
kara-ha 193
kara-ni-wa 120
kateikei 191
katei-zyooken
    'hypothetical
    conditional' 130
kedo 187
keisiki-meisi 'formal
    noun' 132
knowledge-based causal
    relation 25-26, 29
known 45, 104
kuni-gara 192

l

layering 11-12, 99, 113,
    182, 196
let alone 115
let's 106, 115
London-Lund Corpus
    (LLC) 41, 49, 58, 77

m

manima (ni) 192
metalinguistic meanings

44
metatextual   46
mild reason   30
mon-da-/desu-kara   194
mono   137
mono-kara   136-137
mono-yuwe   193
morphologization   15

n

n(o) da   195, 216
n(o) da kara   168, 190
nagara   192
ne   154, 195
ne + verb + *pas*   12
necessary cause   23
necessary motive   23
ni   132-133, 136
nikka   209
ni-yotte   130-131
no   117, 122, 132-133, 187
node   121, 131, 142, 186, 189, 191, 193-194, 197, 204, 209
non-causal meaning   3
non-referential   23
non-restrictive   109
non-subordination   14, 52, 56-57, 59, 62, 68, 76, 83, 109, 118, 123, 127, 147-148, 159, 220
now (that)   70
nu (þæt)   69, 110

o

objective   47
obligatorification   11, 43
opinion   143-144
order   143-144

p

par cause de   72

paradigmatization   11, 43
parataxis   4, 17-18, 52, 56-57, 59, 62, 68, 76, 83, 95-96, 98, 101-102, 159, 177-178, 180-181, 184-185, 200, 203, 219-220, 222
perfective form   128
persistence   11-12, 100, 183
polygrammaticalization   44
pragmatic enrichment   20
pragmatic marker   1, 3, 33-37, 59-60, 64, 68, 76, 96-97, 99, 102-103, 112, 114-115, 124, 126-127, 146, 178, 181, 183-184, 187, 199-200, 202, 211-212, 219-222, 224
pragmatic particle   33, 125
pragmatic strengthening   20
pragmatic(al)ization   38, 108, 200, 202, 211
pragmatics   9
presuppositional   21
propositional   21, 48, 108
punctuation unit   109

q

question   143-144

r

reanalysis   1, 14, 38, 97, 200, 202, 211, 216, 219, 221, 223
referential   23, 46
relative clauses   17

request   143, 144
restrictive   19, 109
rhetorical   28-29
Role and Reference Grammar   44, 189
routinalization   45

s

sa   154, 195
sakai(-ni/de)   140
semantic-pragmatic tendencies   21
sentence-final position   145-147, 152-153, 179, 222
setuzoku-zyosi 'conjunctive particle'   118-119, 128, 148
since   104-105, 110-111, 113-114, 215
sith(en)/sin (that)   70
sith(ence)/since   71
sippan   70
so   56, 215
social   46
specialization   11, 13
speech-act conjunction   26-27, 29-30, 32, 61, 63-64, 68, 83-85, 87-88, 90, 93, 95-96, 98, 103, 122-124, 127, 141-142, 145-146, 159-160, 162, 165, 167, 169, 174, 176-181, 183, 185-186, 200, 206, 210-211, 220-222
subjectification   1, 4, 22, 45, 101-103, 108, 185, 201, 212, 219-221, 223-224
subjective   47
subjective meanings   97
subjectivity   45

subordinate clause
 marker   59, 68, 96, 119,
 127, 139, 141, 178, 183
subordinate conjunctive
 particle   34
subordination   1-2, 4, 14,
 17-19, 35, 37-38, 51-53,
 59, 62, 68, 75-76, 83,
 94-98, 101-102, 109, 117,
 123, 127, 147-148, 159,
 180, 184, 200, 203, 210,
 219-220, 222, 224
subordinator   56, 108
suspended clauses   125
(swa) þæt(te)   69
swelc/seice(e)   69
syn   70
syntacticization   15
syuusi-kei   141
syuuzyosi 'final particle'
 3, 36, 118, 148, 154

t

tame   121, 189
te-form   121, 139-140,
 189
text-structuring
 functions   34, 37, 48
textual   21
þa   70
þæm/þam/þan/þon (þe)
 69
þær (þær)   69
þæs (þe)   69
that   70
that-deletion   106, 114
þe   110
þonne   70
þonne (þonne, þe)   69
though   215
þy/þe   69
to, tte   188

tomo-gara   192
typology   9

u

unidirectional hypothesis
 4, 43, 224
unidirectionality   13,
 15-16, 19-20, 44, 101-103,
 113, 184-185, 209, 219,
 223
unless   110

v

volition   143-144

w

wake   102, 188
weil   209, 217
well   106

y

ya-kara   192
yo   154, 195
yori   135-137, 140, 192-193
yuwe-ni   130
*zyuui-setuzoku-
 zyosi* 'subordinate
 conjunctive particle'
 34

【著者紹介】

東泉　裕子（ひがしいずみ　ゆうこ）

北海道函館市出身.
1996年獨協大学大学院外国語学研究科博士後期課程単位取得満期退学．博士（英語学）（獨協大学，2004年）．
現在，東京海洋大学日本語補講講師，東京学芸大学留学生センター非常勤講師．

【主な著書・論文】
Keisuke Maruyama, Mami Doi, Yuko Iguchi, Kazuko Kuwabara, Masahiro Onuma, Tatsuya Yasui, and Ryuko Yokosuka. 1999. *Writing Business Letters in Japanese*. Tokyo: The Japan Times.
井口厚夫・井口裕子．1994.『日本語文法整理読本：解説と演習』東京：バベル・プレス．
Iguchi, Yuko. 1998. "Functional variety in the Japanese conjunctive particle *kara* 'because'." In Ohori, Toshio. (ed.), *Studies in Japanese Grammaticalization: Cognitive and Discourse Perspectives*. Tokyo: Kurosio Publishers.
（それぞれ，井口裕子として刊行）

Hituzi Linguistics in English No. 2

From a Subordinate Clause to an Independent Clause
A History of English *because*-clause and Japanese *kara*-clause

発行	2006年2月28日　初版1刷
定価	12800円＋税
著者	© 東泉裕子
発行者	松本　功
装丁	向井裕一（glyph）
印刷所	三美印刷株式会社
製本所	田中製本印刷株式会社
発行所	株式会社 ひつじ書房

〒112-0002 東京都文京区小石川 5-21-5
Tel.03-5684-6871　Fax.03-5684-6872
郵便振替 00120-8-142852
toiawase@hituzi.co.jp　http://www.hituzi.co.jp/

ISBN4-89476-269-2　C3082

造本には充分注意しておりますが，落丁・乱丁などがございましたら，小社かお買上げ書店にておとりかえいたします．ご意見，ご感想など，小社までお寄せ下されば幸いです．

Hituzi Linguistics in English

No. 1 Lexical Borrowing and its Impact on English
Makimi Kimura-Kano   8400YEN

No. 2 From a Subordinate Clause to an Independent Clause
Yuko Higashiizumi   13440YEN

No. 3 ModalP and Subjunctive Present
Tadao Nomura 15750YEN